CHILDREN OF ABRAHAM
AN INTRODUCTION TO JUDAISM FOR MUSLIMS

THE HARRIET AND ROBERT HEILBRUNN INSTITUTE
FOR INTERNATIONAL INTERRELIGIOUS UNDERSTANDING
OF THE AMERICAN JEWISH COMMITTEE

Founded in 1998, the Institute encourages interreligious dialogue throughout the world through exchanges among seminaries, colleges, universities, and learned societies. It has developed strong cooperative ties to the Vatican, the World Council of Churches in Geneva, the Organization for Security and Cooperation in Europe, the Ibn Khaldún Society, and ecumenical organizations in Europe, Africa, Asia, and South America.

PUBLICATIONS

Children of Abraham:
An Introduction to Islam for Jews
by Khalid Durán, with Abdelwahab Hechiche

Children of Abraham:
An Introduction to Judaism for Muslims
by Reuven Firestone

CHILDREN OF ABRAHAM
AN INTRODUCTION TO JUDAISM FOR MUSLIMS

Reuven Firestone

Dr. Stephen Steinlight
Executive Editor

Rabbi A. James Rudin
Senior Adviser on Interreligious Affairs

A publication of
THE HARRIET AND ROBERT HEILBRUNN INSTITUTE
FOR INTERNATIONAL INTERRELIGIOUS UNDERSTANDING
OF THE AMERICAN JEWISH COMMITTEE

In association with
KTAV PUBLISHING HOUSE, INC.

Library of Congress Cataloging-in-Publication Data

Firestone, Reuven, 1952-
    Children of Abraham: an introduction to Judaism for Muslims/ by Reuven Firestone.
    p. cm.
        ISBN 0-88125-721-4 (Muslim hc) -- ISBN 0-88125-720-6 (Muslim pb) -- ISBN
    0-88125-7-23-0 (Israel hc) -- ISBN 0-88125-724-9 (Israel pb)
    1. Judaism. 2. Judaism--Relations--Islam. 3. Islam--Relations--Judaism. I. Title.

Bm565 .F48 2001
296'.024'2971--dc21

                                                                    2001029182

Distributed by
Ktav Publishing House, Inc.
900 Jefferson Street
Hoboken, NJ 07030
201-963-9524 FAX 201-963-0102
Email ktav@compuserve.com

Contents

Foreword

Why publish this book and its companion volume, Khalid Durán's *Children of Abraham: An Introduction to Islam for Jews,* and why publish them now? The appearance of these works by Khalid Durán and Reuven Firestone responds to a significant period in the 1500-year relationship between Islam and Judaism. This period is fraught with danger and laden with opportunity. We at the American Jewish Committee are drawn to this task precisely because of the "civilizational" storm now looming and because of the enormous importance of what is at stake. We cannot and will not stand idle in the face of this great challenge. In a shrinking world with boundaries between the local and the global disappearing, there is an obligation to enhance mutual understanding and reduce mutual ignorance and suspicion.

These first two volumes of a series we have called the *Children of Abraham* will, we earnestly hope, render an important service to Jews and to Muslims by reminding us of uplifting, revivifying, and unifying seminal truths.

First and foremost, they tell us about the striking theological and moral resemblance between Judaism and Islam. Indeed, no two other major religions on earth are closer to each other. Of the three great monotheistic faiths, Judaism and Islam are most akin; both literally descend from

Abraham, our common biological and spiritual father. Knowledge of that connection has been largely lost among most Jews and Muslims, a casualty of the enmity of recent times.

The books also remind us of the long, rich, and often mutually nourishing historical relations between Jews and Muslims in many lands and the extraordinary gifts to humankind that Muslim-Jewish interaction generated in advancing knowledge and culture. True, as these volumes show, that history is complex; it did not always rise to the level of the earthly paradise some imagine to have existed in the Golden Age of Moorish Spain, but, even in its less glorious moments, it was generally far less fraught than Jewish-Christian history.

Finally, given the understandable contemporary preoccupation with the threat of Muslim fundamentalism (generally referred to among experts as Islamism), the *Children of Abraham* underscores the wide gap between the great universal religion of Islam and the totalitarian political ideology of Islamism.

These volumes of the *Children of Abraham* are groundbreaking in a number of ways.

Professor Firestone's work offers a unique encounter with Judaism designed specifically for Muslims. A respected scholar of Islam and a rabbi, he presents Judaism with a Muslim sensibility and frame of reference in mind, and his work thus establishes unprecedented intimacy between Jewish and Muslim consciousness and worldviews. Indeed, it represents the first work of its kind to offer a comprehensive introduction to Judaism with a special emphasis on issues of particular concern to Muslims. It explores with sensitivity and candor such difficult subjects as the "parting of the ways" between Abraham and his two sons Isaac and Ishmael, the role of the Jewish tribes of Medina in opposing the prophet Muhammad, the Zionist movement, and the emergence of the State of Israel.

Professor Durán's work, conceptualized in consultation with Professor Abdelwahab Hechiche, also breaks new ground in its ambitious introduction to Islam for Jews. A renowned Muslim scholar, he presents the majesty of the Muslim religion and Islamic history and culture. But he neither ignores nor rationalizes their more problematic aspects. His book offers a forthright and tough-minded treatment of Muslim fundamentalism and also offers a candid analysis of the situation of women in Muslim belief and practice, as well as an unsentimental assessment of the historical treatment of minorities within Islamic societies. Professor Durán's book is finally also a *cri de coeur* against intolerance, chauvinism, and religious triumphalism, as well as a passionate argument in favor of mutual respect and reconciliation between Muslims and Jews.

The American Jewish Committee's major project in Muslim-Jewish relations—the present volumes and those to follow, including a book on the two religions aimed at high school students as well as translations into Arabic of all the volumes—would never, could never have been undertaken except for the extraordinary vision and generosity of Harriet and Robert Heilbrunn. Their devotion to interreligious understanding, and particularly to the improvement of Muslim-Jewish relations, is being advanced through the pioneering work of the Harriet and Robert Heilbrunn Institute for International Interreligious Understanding of the American Jewish Committee, founded through their support. Their commitment has been the indispensable cornerstone of this agenda within the American Jewish Committee.

Several of my colleagues at the American Jewish Committee have participated in this ambitious undertaking. I would particularly like to acknowledge the efforts of Dr. Stephen Steinlight and Rabbi A. James Rudin, as well as Shula Bahat, Ralph Grunewald, Robert Rosenbaum, Linda Krieg, Mel Leifer, Yehudit Barsky, Larry Grossman, Aleida Rodriguez, and Brenda Rudzin. Moreover, Bernie Scharfstein of Ktav Publishing, as always, has been a wonderful partner.

The late and beloved Cardinal O'Connor of New York once said: "No organization I know in this city, in this country, in this world, has done more to improve Christian-Jewish relations than the American Jewish Committee."

Let us hope that, with the far reaching initiatives made possible by Harriet and Robert Heilbrunn, the same will one day be said by religious leaders of our desire to forge an era of enhanced understanding and strengthened ties between Muslims and Jews around the world.

David A. Harris
Executive Director
The American Jewish Committee
February 1, 2001

Preface by Martin E. Marty

For Muslims and Jews in the United States this is a time of reconnoitering, of anxious probing, cautious testing. One of intense mutual curiosity mingled with deep apprehension. For the huge Christian majority, the moment constitutes a unique vantage point from which to observe the incipient American encounter of two communities laden with the heavy weight of historical antagonism and the baggage of suspicion stemming from conflicts in faraway lands. For Americans outside the fascinating and traditionally fractious Abrahamic family of Jews, Christians, and Muslims whether they belong to other faiths or to none—it is a time to watch how Jews and Muslims begin to interrelate and speculate how their embryonic relationship will ultimately impact the greater national life.

In some respects these are gloomy times for Jewish-Muslim relations. The conflict in the Middle East between Arabs, chiefly Muslim, and Israelis, chiefly Jewish, has heightened precisely when, for the first time, these two sets of "Children of Abraham" live together in America in substantial numbers and have an opportunity to interrelate. The conflict casts a long shadow and inevitably clouds mutual perceptions, especially those of American Jews and Arab Americans. How far it conditions the outlook of the largest segment of American Muslims, those who emigrated from the subcontinent (India, Pakistan, and Bangladesh), is harder to gauge.

In other respects the times are, at least, relatively hopeful: some American Muslims and some American Jews have begun to build positive relationships. These twin books are one of the more formal and visible signs of the good intentions shown among a small but growing set of thinkers and leaders within both peoples, and the "ordinary folk," often neighbors, are also showing affirmative signs. They want to get along, keep foreign feuds and ancient rivalries outside the American equation, minimize conflict among each other in the United States, learn about each other, and make contributions together to a national life that had been so often identified simply with Christianity.

These books are not only signs of the intention to do so, but helpful and encouraging evidences that the learning can go on, indeed, that it is going on.

By and large, American religious leadership is not only adjusting intellectually to the new terrain, but it is also beginning to traverse it. The phrase "Judeo-Christian," which only recently became the semiofficial usage to characterize America's religious culture—and represented an advance over an older Christian triumphalism embodied in language that described America as a "Christian nation"—is, in turn, losing its capacity to encompass a far more diverse and complicated religious landscape.

In community after community formal dialogue goes on and "trialogue" becomes increasingly common. I was involved in a recent Muslim-Christian encounter in Houston, where the basketball star Hakim Olajuwon, a knowledgeable Muslim, hosted a presentation by a scholar of Islam and me. There was an overflow audience. The atmosphere was cordial. The questions were challenging. There was no superficial "feel good" interfaith blather about how "nice" everyone was. Instead, people spoke frankly, and thus there was a genuine chance that progress might result.

In interfaith meetings in Detroit and Milwaukee, I saw Christians and Jews now in open relation to Muslims. Many of the Christians and Jews were surprised to learn of the varieties of Islam and of the differences within the Muslim community. Too often Muslims are perceived as a monolithic bloc who agree not only on Qur'ân—which they do—but also on politics and economics—which they do not—or, as their enemies charge, as united in common support of terrorism.

As Khalid Durán's book convincingly demonstrates, it is Islamic nations and governments that are most threatened by radical Islamists. He also shows a very different and very accurate picture of an infinitely more expansive and inspiring Islam than one learns of in the popular media or in the folklore of the suspicious. As his book underscores, a great many non-Muslims in America and elsewhere confuse the political ideologies of the radical Islamic fundamentalists with the religion of Islam. His book permits us to encounter Islam the way most Muslims understand it—not as it is understood by the radical extremists whose perverted concept of Islam is widely reported in the media, causing widespread hostility toward and fear of Islam.

Jews in the United States, loyal to Israel though they may be, are also hardly monolithic in their attitudes. Nor do they line up automatically in defense of policies many Muslims regard as not only anti-Arab but also as anti-Islamic. On the contrary, American Jews have multiple agendas, including the need for the Jewish community to live in harmony with the Islamic children of Abraham as they have done in recent decades with their Christian counterparts. Indeed, Jewish organizations such as the American Jewish Committee, sponsor of these books, largely pioneered the field of human relations in the United States, working to foster democratic pluralism and mutual respect and understanding among religious, racial, and ethnic groups. It has also gone on record as strongly opposing discrimination against Arab Americans.

Both books of the *Children of Abraham* are serious, friendly, accurate, and helpful presentations of the history and practices of the two faiths. It is my earnest hope that they get used in schools, synagogues, mosques, and churches, as clear and fair-minded introductions to subjects too often still treated prejudicially. I end this Foreword with words of applause. These books will greatly benefit our nation, one in which Muslims and Jews share space and place, time and energies, policies and hope. They are a timely, thoughtful response to an urgent need.

Martin E. Marty
Fairfax M. Cone Distinguished Service Professor Emeritus
The University of Chicago

Author's Preface

Advanced technology has brought the nations of the world physically closer together than ever before. Dramatic advances and cost reductions in transportation and in global communication have made it possible for widely dispersed people to meet and talk in person or via satellite or e-mail and to interact in a host of ways never dreamed possible even a generation ago. Our growing physical closeness has not been matched by a commensurate closing of human distance in spiritual terms, however. Our technology has enabled us to buy more goods and to acquire unprecedented wealth; and it has also expedited the transfer of more diseases and pollutants across the mountains, deserts, and oceans that separate us. But it has not enabled us to live together more securely or with greater mutual trust and respect.

During the many centuries when different peoples lived separately and in relative isolation from one another, foreigners were naturally considered strange and threatening. They tended to enter one's territory only in order to take land or wealth, to plunder or conquer. It was customary to disparage other ethnic, racial, and religious groups in order to protect the familiar way of life of one's own group and stiffen resistance to the feared outsiders. Suspicion of the other naturally became a part of the human condition; even today most people are conditioned to suspect the outsider.

Today, however, the traditional relationship between insiders and outsiders is rapidly changing. As globalization advances and the proportion of new immigrants and transnational people soars in virtually every permeable society, human populations are mixing in ways never considered possible only a few decades ago. Hoary notions of nationhood are yielding to more complex social and political arrangements, and historic national patriotic allegiances are in many places giving way to more ambiguous, attenuated, and transient notions of belonging and group loyalty. "Homelands" are often populated with significant ethnic, racial, or religious minorities. As a result, many people are beginning to realize that the "other" is often the "self." Yet despite our forced proximity to many different peoples, we have few models for learning to live in a diverse world. Fast-paced and breathtaking global social change has far outpaced our capacity to respond to its implications in coherent and meaningful ways, and it has resulted in heightened anxiety about our own identities and greater fear of the other. The other is not safely removed at a distance; we feel the other impinging ever more palpably upon our most basic phenomenal realities—our economic, cultural, social and political lives.

Even our religious wisdom, so steeped in God's guidance of Scripture and tradition, has tended to view other religions with suspicion. This is partly the logic of monotheism. If God is One, good, merciful, and all-knowing, why would God give different and often-conflicting revelations to different peoples? The traditional answer to this question assumed that if more than one revelation were true, then God is either not

One, not good, not merciful, or not all-knowing. But the traditional answer is not necessarily logical, for as the Qur'an suggests, God in his great wisdom may have given the divine message to different peoples (Yunis 10:47; Al-Nahl 16:36), each in their own language and according to their own cultural norms to enable them to understand. The problem arises when different Scriptures, records of the divine will given in different cultural contexts, appear to be in conflict. The traditional response to this problem has been to accuse the Scriptures of the "other" of being inaccurate, no longer valid, or distorted. Such accusations encourage a similar response from the adherents of the other religion, thereby plunging the respective religions and their followers into conflict. Sometimes these conflicts have led to war.

Throughout history established religions have accused emerging religions of falsehood. Thus Judaism did not accept the Scripture of Christianity, and neither Christianity nor Judaism accepted the Scripture of Islam.[1] Conversely, while an emerging religion may acknowledge the Scripture of its predecessor, it also seeks to diminish its validity and authority, thereby protecting its own emerging revelation from the discrepancies between them. Thus Christianity considers God's laws promulgated in the Torah to be superseded by the coming of Christ, and Islam considers the revelations of the Torah and Gospel to have been corrupted and therefore made invalid as Scripture. These positions preserve the integrity of the insiders' religious systems, but in so doing, encourage a

---

[1] It should be added that Islam, too, does not accept the Scriptures of later emerging religions, such as the revelations of the Ahmadiyya and Baha'i movements.

great deal of interreligious conflict, some of which, both in the past and even now, has led to horrific bloodshed and suffering. With today's increasingly mixed world and the acquisition of weapons of mass destruction by more and more nations that are engaged in historic quarrels founded in large measure upon religious differences, this approach to other religions is no longer justifiable or even tenable. New thinking about the relationship between the three peoples of Scripture is necessary, and it can come about only when we know more about one another's religious teachings and traditions.

The purpose of this book is not to encourage conversion. No effort is made to convince the reader that Judaism has any more truth or value than Islam. Likewise, it is not its purpose to make excuses for aspects of Judaism that are problematic or difficult. On the other hand, the author does not wish to perpetuate false stereotypes or distortions of Judaism that might impede dialogue and better understanding.

Often, similarities or parallels between Judaism and Islam are pointed out for the interest of Muslim readers. The purpose in doing so is to help them to better understand Judaism by observing it through the lens of Islam. Noting similarities and parallels sometimes helps to highlight subtle differences as well. There is no attempt here to suggest that Judaism and Islam are the same or that they teach the same lessons. The fact is that Judaism and Islam are separate religious civilizations that have evolved in different places, among different peoples, in different periods of history, and in response to different sets of social and historical forces and conditions. By noting the similarities and parallels between the two religions, the Muslim reader will not only better understand Judaism, but may also appreciate why Jews value it.

Judaism has evolved over many centuries, and contemporary Jews acknowledge that the kinds of Judaism practiced today differ substantially from the Judaism practiced in the ancient era of the Bible. There are also a variety of expressions of Judaism today. As in all periods of Jewish history, there are different schools of interpretation of the Bible, different schools of law, and different attitudes toward practice and theology. The Muslim reader will immediately note that this aspect finds its parallel in Islam. The Judaism described in this book is what might be called "mainstream" Judaism— not the radical practice of the ultra-Orthodox or the equally radical practice of the ultra-Reform, although in many cases neither would disagree with the perspective articulated here. I try to take a middle road in my description of Judaism with which most practicing Jews would agree.

The reader will note that references to God, Muhammad, and the prophets use typical English conventions. While I respect all the prophets of Judaism, Christianity, and Islam, I use the typical Jewish mode of reference. I therefore refrain from the usual pious Islamic custom of writing "May God's prayer and peace be upon him" after every mention of the Prophet Muhammad or "Peace be upon him" in reference to other prophets. This is simply a matter of English prose style and does not imply disrespect.

Let me conclude the preface with this observation: Improving Muslim-Jewish relations by building greater mutual understanding and respect is the paramount purpose

of this book. This goal is particularly urgent at a time when
the enmity and violence associated with the Israeli-
Palestinian conflict, so bloody and dispiriting at present,
threatens to further alienate Jews and Muslims across the
world. At the heart of the conflict, and impeding the peace
process, is the difficult and tremendously sensitive issue of
sovereignty over the holy places of Judaism and Islam, especially in Jerusalem. Thus the religious dimension of the struggle cannot be ignored; indeed, it must be seen as core, and its
impact on Jewish-Muslim relations as a whole cannot be overstated. This book, and its companion volume on Islam, represent an effort to help build understanding between the two
faiths through truth-telling about our histories and religious
systems and motivations, an especially critical task in the
bleak present circumstances. But this is a moment to seize,
and that is why I was pleased to take up the offer of Rabbi A.
James Rudin and Dr. Stephen Steinlight of the American
Jewish Committee to contribute to this series on Jewish-
Muslim relations. The AJC has played a leading role in chart-
ing the relatively new terrain of modern Jewish-Muslim relations. Those of us who are dedicated to bettering Muslim-
Jewish understanding must not cease in our labors now.

R. F.

Part I
A Survey of Jewish History

Jewish history emerges out of the mists of the ancient Middle East, a region that produced some of the earliest literatures of humankind. Much of this ancient literature is mythic, and the early material of the Bible finds literary and linguistic parallels with some of the mythic Middle Eastern literature of the most ancient period. Historians do not rely on any Scripture as a source of history without corroboration from other sources, such as ancient artifacts, royal chronicles or archives of neighboring kingdoms, or archaeological studies. Accordingly, there is no definitive corroboration for much of the history found in the early books of the Bible, so although it may in fact be historically accurate, historians do not accept its representation as *necessarily* factual. Rather, they tend to see the early history of Judaism and the Jewish people as emerging out of an ancient world where history and myth merge.[1] The merging of history with myth is sometimes

---

[1] When I use the word *myth* here, I am not referring to its common meaning as "untruth," but to its primary meaning as given in *Webster's Unabridged Third New International Dictionary*: "a story that is usually of unknown origin and at least partially traditional, that ostensibly relates historical events usually of such character as to serve to explain some practice, belief, institution, or natural phenomenon" (2:1497).

called "sacred history," and it is clear that the *academic* history of Judaism emerges out of the *sacred* history of Judaism.

For our purposes, the distinction between sacred and academic history is not of great importance. Whether or not Abraham or Moses or King David actually did or said all of the things portrayed in the Bible is less important than noting *how* these figures are portrayed in Jewish tradition and examining the *content* of their words and actions. If, for example, the Jewish portrayal of a character found also in the Qur'an differs from the portrayal in Islamic tradition, we are not concerned with making a judgment as to which is "correct" and which "false," nor can we "prove" whichever judgment we make. Jewish believers will believe their own Scripture over others, and Muslim believers will do the same. On the other hand, the similarities and differences between the biblical and qur'anic portrayals will help us to understand the similarities and differences between the two religions, and it is this knowledge that will help to bring us understanding, wisdom, and brotherhood.

NAMES FOR THE JEWISH PEOPLE

The Jewish people have referred to themselves by a variety of names, and this multiplicity sometimes causes confusion: Hebrews, Israelites, Children of Israel, Judeans, and Jews. To a certain extent, these names correspond to periods in Jewish history. The Qur'an itself distinguishes between *Banu Isra'il* and *Yahud* (or *alladhi hadu*), the former referring to the Israelites of the Bible and the latter to Jews (or "those who have become Jews") who were contemporary with Muhammad.

The term *Hebrew* refers to the ancient patriarchs Abraham, Isaac, and Jacob, and the matriarchs Sarah, Rebecca, Rachel, and Leah and their children. Jacob, the last of the great patriarchs, is depicted in Genesis 32:25–33 as engaging in a mysterious struggle with an angel who blesses him with the following: "Your name shall no longer be Jacob, but Israel, for you have striven with beings divine and human, and have prevailed." The name "Israel" (Hebrew: *Yisra'el*) can mean "one who struggles with the divine." Jacob's twelve children represent the twelve tribes of Israel, and the members of the tribes are referred to in the Bible as the Children of Israel (Hebrew: *benei yisra'el*) or, simply, Israel.

Many centuries later after the death of King Solomon, Israel was divided into two kingdoms. The northern and larger comprised ten of the tribes and took on the name Israel. The southern kingdom was dominated by the large tribe of Judah (Hebrew: *Yehudah*), and took on its name. In 721 B.C.E.,[2] the Assyrian Empire destroyed the northern kingdom of Israel and its people, leaving only the southern tribe of Judah with its inhabitants, the Judahites or Judeans (Hebrew: *yehudim*). From that time onward, the people have been referred to as Judeans, which through linguistic variation became "Jews" in English. However, despite the loss of most

---

[2] The abbreviation B.C.E., meaning "before the common era," is a universal, as opposed to Christian, way of citing dates on the Western calendar. Thus, B.C.E. rather than B.C. ("before Christ"), and C.E ("common era") rather than A.D. (*anno Domini*, "the year of our Lord").

of the tribes, Jewish tradition tends to this day to refer to the Jewish people as Israel.

In Jewish tradition, therefore, the term *Israel* does not refer to a land or a modern nation-state but to a people. The official name of the modern Jewish state is the State of Israel (Hebrew: *medinat yisra'el*), meaning "the State of the People of Israel," though it is usually shortened for convenience to Israel. The lands of the Bible, many of which are not included within the borders of the modern State of Israel, are called, according to Jewish tradition, the Land of Israel (Hebrew: *eretz yisra'el*). In this book we will use *Jews*, *Jewish people*, or *Israel* to refer to the Jews of any period, while *Israelites* and *Children of Israel* refer only to the period of the Bible.

1

Origins

CREATION

The Bible begins with God's creation of the universe and all the worlds within it. The biblical story of creation is the story of God's unity as creator of all matter, all energy, and all life. There is no creative power aside from God; God has no associates. Just as God's unity is determined in the Bible through the ultimate mercy of creating the universe and all that is therein, so too are the universe and all of its creatures a unity as the product of God's creative power.

The unity of the universe is realized through the laws of physics and nature, whose origin is the divine will. All non-sentient created things—whether animal, mineral, or vegetable, and whether gas or liquid or solid—exist within the divine unity because they function according to these natural laws. The only exception to this unified system is humanity, a race of sentient beings that has always demonstrated a limited ability to bend the laws of nature.

According to the biblical perspective, the unique nature of humankind may be seen as both a blessing and a curse. From the outset, the Bible portrays humankind as unable to live up to its potential without divine assistance. The story of Adam and Eve in the Garden of Eden first establishes this principle (Genesis 3), and the tale of human sin and error continues through the next three biblical narratives: the stories of Cain and Abel (Genesis 4), Noah (Genesis 6–9), and the Tower of Babel (Genesis 11). Although each of these stories centers on specific characters, they offer a generic portrayal of the state of uncontrolled human nature. The creative power within humanity and our independent nature may lead to our downfall, our continual inability to live up to the divine expectation. Having established this as a truth, the Bible then demonstrates how the Jews in particular and humanity generally can live up to their potential. This can be achieved only by means of divine intervention. From Genesis 12 and onward, and throughout the remainder of the Bible, God provides instruction and guidance through the Jewish people to humanity. This takes place first through personal intervention with the family of Abraham, and then by giving the Torah (literally, "instruction"), the rules of behavior by which human beings are expected to live.

ABRAHAM: HIJRA AND COVENANT

God calls to Abraham to leave his native land and promises him great blessing (Genesis 12:1):

> The Lord said to Abram, "Go forth from your native land and from your father's house to the land that I will show you. I will make of you a great nation, and I will bless you; I will make your name great, and you shall be

a blessing. I will bless those who bless you and curse him that curses you; and all the families of the earth shall bless themselves by you."

This call marks the beginning of monotheism and the beginning of the history of the Jewish people, who derive from the seed of Abraham. Abraham's journey in response to God's call is not referred to as a *hijra* as it is in Islam, but Judaism sees it quite similarly as a watershed that marks his transition to the new spiritual state of being in personal relationship with God. Why God calls Abraham is never explained in the Bible, although later Jewish literature from the fourth or fifth century C.E. provides answers in narrative form that closely parallel what is said in the Qur'an:

Rabbi Hiyya, grandson of Rabbi Ada of Yaffo said: Terah was an idol-maker. He once went out and had Abraham sell them for him. When a man came to buy one Abraham said to him: "How old are you?" He answered: "I am fifty" [or sixty]. Abraham exclaimed: "Woe to a man who is sixty years old and who wants to worship something that is only a day old!" So the man was ashamed and departed. Then a woman came with a plate of flour and asked of Abraham: "Take this and offer it to them." So he got up and took a stick and broke all of the idols, after which he put the stick into the hand of the biggest idol. When his father returned he cried out: "Who did this to them?!" He answered: "I will not conceal it from you. A woman came with a plateful of

fine flour and said to me: 'Take this and offer it to them.'
I offered it to them, and they all argued over who would
eat first. Then the biggest one got up, took a stick in his
hand, and destroyed them." His father said: "Why are
you mocking me! Do they have any knowledge?"
Abraham answered: "Your ears should hear what your
mouth is saying."[1]

Abraham is portrayed as having already known of the unity
of God prior to his being called by God, thereby providing an
answer to the question. God calls Abraham because, as the
only and quintessential monotheist, he has used reason to
demonstrate God's unity.

This may be the source of Abraham's being chosen by God,
but Abraham must prove that he remains worthy by showing
his obedience to the divine will, and this he does. As in
Qur'an 2:124 ("And remember, when his Lord tested
Abraham with commands [*bikalimat*], and he fulfilled them"),
God notes after Abraham dies that "Abraham obeyed Me and
kept My charge, My commandments, My laws, and My
teachings" (Genesis 26:5). In Islamic terminology, Abraham is
a proto-Muslim because he submitted himself (*aslama*) entirely to the divine will.[2] In Jewish terminology Abraham feared
God and obeyed the divine commands.

Of deep importance to Judaism, God establishes an eternal
covenant with Abraham (Genesis 17):

---

[1] Genesis Rabbah 38:13. See Qur'an 19:41–50, 21:51–67, 26:69–86, 29:16–18.
[2] See Qur'an 2:128, 3:67. See also 16:120: "Abraham was a nation obedient to God, a
monotheist. He was not an idolater."

When Abraham was ninety-nine years old, the Lord appeared to Abraham and said to him: "I am God Almighty. You will be blameless if you walk in My ways. I will establish My covenant between Me and you, and I will make you exceedingly numerous. . . . You shall be the father of a multitude of nations. . . . I will maintain My covenant between Me and you and your offspring to come as an everlasting covenant. . . . I assign the land you sojourn in to you and your offspring to come, all the Land of Canaan, as an everlasting holding, for I am [also] their God."

This covenant is essentially a contract. God promises many good things to Abraham and his descendants, and Abraham and his descendants are obligated to obey God's commands ("walk in My ways").

God further said to Abraham: "As for you, you and your offspring to come throughout the ages shall keep My covenant . . . every male among you shall be circumcised. You shall circumcise the flesh of your foreskin, and that shall be the sign of the covenant between Me and you. And throughout the generations, every male among you shall be circumcised at the age of eight days."

Like the Qur'an, the Bible sometimes seems to repeat itself when it articulates ideas or commands with slightly different nuances or wording. The terms of the Abrahamic covenant include numberless offspring for Abraham and the promise of a homeland in the Land of Canaan, later to be called the Land of Israel.[3] Abraham and his family, in turn, are obligated to be obedient to God's will. No specific laws are given here aside from the commandment of circumcision as the sign of the covenant, because God is in an ongoing relationship with Abraham and his family and can personally inform them of what is required of them. Later, however, God prepares Israel for a time when God will no longer be as easily accessible. This preparation occurs at Mount Sinai, where God reveals the Torah, meaning "teaching." From Sinai onward, the covenant is governed by obedience to a formal code of law.

ISAAC AND ISHMAEL

Meanwhile, Abraham's wife, Sarah, despite the divine promise of innumerable offspring, remains childless. She therefore presents her maidservant, Hagar, to Abraham as a second wife. Ishmael is born of this union and is circumcised in response to the covenantal command. God blesses Ishmael but promises Abraham and Sarah that their future son, Isaac, will be the only child of Abraham who remains in covenantal relationship with God (Genesis 17:20): "As for Ishmael, I have heeded you and I hereby bless him. I will make him fertile and exceedingly numerous. He shall be the father of twelve tribal princes, and I will make of him a great nation. But My

---

[3] 1 Samuel 13:19, Ezekiel 40:2, etc.

covenant I will maintain with Isaac, whom Sarah shall bear to you at this time next year."

Why Ishmael is excluded from the covenant is never explained in the Bible. Scholars tend to believe that the purpose of this story, as of many of the other tales in Genesis, is to explain the close ethnic and linguistic relationships between the Israelites and the peoples among whom they lived. Ishmael serves in the Bible as the patriarch of the Arab peoples. Some of his sons listed in Genesis 25, such as Hadad in 25:15, have Arabic names. Others have names that sound like the names of known places in Arab lands, such as Duma (Dumat al-Jandal in the desert of Syria) or Tema' (Tayma' in Arabia). Ishmael's son Kedar has the same name as an Arab tribe that lives in the Wadi al-Sirhan in present-day Jordan.[4] According to this view, the kinship relation between Ishmael and Isaac would explain the similarities that Israelites noticed in the ancient Arab peoples with whom they had social and economic contacts. Similarly, Genesis describes the relationship between the Israelites and their Edomite neighbors as having originated through Isaac's two sons: Jacob, who represents Israel, and his twin brother Esau, who represents the tribes of Edom.[5]

In Genesis 21, Hagar and Ishmael are sent away from the Abraham tribe, and little more is heard about Ishmael and his descendants in the Bible. According to Jewish tradition,

---

[4] Fred Winnett, "The Arabian Genealogies in the Book of Genesis," in *Translating and Understanding the Old Testament: Essays in Honor of Herbert Gordon May*, ed. H. T. Frank and W. L. Reed (Nashville: Abingdon Press, 1970).

[5] See Genesis 25, 27. So too, the Moabites and Ammonites derive from Lot, Abraham's nephew (Genesis 19:29–38).

Abraham maintains contact with his son Ishmael, but Judaism knows nothing about Abraham and Ishmael building or purifying the Ka`ba and Abraham establishing Ishmael and his offspring there.[6]

THE BINDING OF ISAAC

The climax of Abraham's life was his response to God's command in Genesis 22 to sacrifice Isaac in the land of Moriah. Unlike the Qur'an, the biblical rendering of this story specifically identifies the intended sacrifice as Isaac, and Jewish tradition refers to the episode as the *Akedah* or the *Akedat Yitzhak*, the "binding" or the "binding of Isaac."[7] Having passed the supreme test of obedience and faith in God, Abraham receives the divine promise and blessing once again and for the last time. His descendants will be as numerous as the stars in the heavens and the sands on the seashore, they will seize the gates of their enemies, and all the nations of the earth will bless themselves through his offspring.

Abraham serves as a paradigm in Jewish tradition for certain valued human traits. He is patient in suffering, a lover of peace (Genesis 13:8–9), hospitable to strangers (18:1 ff.), concerned about the welfare of others (18:23–33), committed to transmitting the ideals of justice and righteousness to his offspring (18:19), and always obedient to God and His commands.

---

[6] Qur'an 2:125–128, 3:95–97, 14:37.

[7] See Qur'an 37:99–113, which names neither son. The identity of the intended sacrifice (*al-dhabih*) is identified by later commentators and traditionists.

JACOB AND THE DESCENT TO EGYPT

Isaac's son Jacob, also known as Israel in the Bible,[8] is the father of twelve sons who represent the tribes of Israel. The story of Jacob's son Joseph and his betrayal by his brothers, his being sold into slavery in Egypt, and his rise from the depths to the very pinnacle of power and wealth is told both in the Qur'an (surat Yusuf) and Genesis (chaps. 37, 39–50). In Judaism as in Islam, the Joseph story is greatly beloved, and many commentaries and books have been written in response to it. More important, however, for our purposes here, is the meaning of the redemption of the Children of Israel (*benei yisra'el*) from Egyptian bondage.

THE EXODUS

Abraham is referred to in the Bible as a Hebrew (Genesis 14:13), as are his descendants until the Exodus from Egypt. From the Exodus until the division of the unified nation into two kingdoms after the death of Solomon, the people are called Israel or the Children of Israel. The change of terminology corresponds with a change in the nature of the people. The descendants of the Abraham tribe merge with other unfortunate Egyptians when they all escape from Pharaoh (Exodus 12:38) and form a unified community based on the experience of suffering.

---

[8] See Genesis 32:29, 35:10, 37:13, etc.

Israel's redemption from Egyptian bondage is considered one of God's great acts of mercy, for God heard the cry of the oppressed when they called out in anguish about their lot (Exodus 3:9–10).[9] The story of the redemption is recalled every year during the festival of Pesach (Passover), which commemorates this great act of divine mercy. The Exodus from Egypt symbolizes the potential for complete human redemption, for it serves to prove that just as God redeemed Israel and others suffering from Egyptian bondage, so too will God bring final redemption to the entire world in the End of Days.

THE COVENANT AT SINAI

The Exodus marks the beginning of the formation of the nation of Israel, but it is completed only when God gives the Torah at Mount Sinai. The Sinai experience, as it is often called, marks one of the great watersheds of Jewish history, for it is at Sinai where all the Jewish people, whether living or not yet born according to the tradition, witnessed the giving of the commandments, or Torah. All were there amid the thunder and lightning, and every single individual agreed to obey God's commandments by calling out together, "We shall obey" (Exodus 19:8, 24:3, Deuteronomy 5:24, 29:9–14). The Torah itself is the sign of the expanded covenant at Sinai, for the Torah is referred to as the "Book of the Covenant" (Exodus 24:7). In the covenant established by God with

---

[9] For qur'anic renderings of this, see 7:103–138, 10:76–91, 20:9–79, 26:10–66, 28:3–40.

Abraham, circumcision and its observance served as the living sign of God's relationship with Abraham's offspring. In the covenant's reaffirmation at Sinai, the entire Torah and obedience to it became the living sign of God's relationship with the refugees from Egypt who became the nation of Israel.

The nation of Israel was formed when the people accepted God's Torah as the central institution of life. All of the people accepted the responsibility of trying to live by it, and in doing so they unified themselves as a people and a nation under God and God's commandments. The Sinai experience marks the formation of `am yisra'el*, the "people of Israel," also referred to as the *ummah*. This word conveys the same meaning as the Arabic term *umma*, for the Jews regard themselves as a religious nation governed by the commandments of the Torah, which affect every aspect of human behavior from the ritual to the ethical, social, family, and civil.

At Sinai, for the first time in human history, a portion of humanity was afforded the real possibility of living up to the expectations of the divine will because it had a record of the divine will in the form of covenantal law. It would not be easy to do, of course, and the Torah itself often refers to the difficulty the Israelites had in fulfilling the divine demands. From the perspective of Judaism, however, although backsliding was deplorable, it never invalidated the covenant. That is, the covenant between God and the Jews was eternal and never to be revoked. Those who would not or could not live up to the terms of the covenant would be punished, but the covenant would never be dissolved (Deuteronomy 4:31).

Jewish thinkers have struggled with the question as to why the Bible singles out Israel as the only recipient of the Torah. Is this exclusivist and exclusionary? Does it mean that Jews are inherently better than any other nation or people? Are the Jews a superior people for having been given the Torah? The Bible gives no definitive answer. On the one hand, it states, "You are a people holy to God. God chose you among all other peoples on earth to be His treasured people" (Deuteronomy 14:2). On the other, it says in Amos, "To Me, O Israelites, you are just like the Ethiopians. True, I brought Israel up from the land of Egypt, but also the Philistines from Caphtor and the Arameans from Kir" (9:7).

Like the Bible itself, the rabbis of the Talmud were uncomfortable with an exclusivist image of Jews and Judaism.[10] The Talmud sometimes directly interprets biblical verses, and in the talmudic tractate Avodah Zarah 2b, it asks:

> Is it not written [in the Torah], "The Lord came from Sinai and rose from Seir unto them, He shined forth from Mount Paran" (Deuteronomy 33:2)? And it is also written: "God comes from Teman" (Habakkuk 3:3). What did God seek in Seir, and what did He seek in Mount Paran? Rabbi Yohanan says: "This teaches that the Holy One, blessed be He, offered the Torah to every nation and every tongue, but none accepted it, until He came to Israel, who accepted it."

---

[10] The Talmud, which dates from about the fifth or sixth century c.e., will be discussed in greater detail below.

Elsewhere in the Talmud (Shabbat 88a) we find an interesting parallel with Qur'an 2:63, 93, and 4:154:

"Moses led the people out of the camp toward God, and they took their places at the bottom of the mountain" (Exodus 19:17). Hama b. Hasa said: "This teaches that the Holy One turned the mountain over above them like an [overturned] cask and said to them: 'If you accept the Torah, good. But if not, this shall be your grave.'"

Both of these interpretations recognize and underscore that Israel is not inherently better than any other nation or people. The only thing that distinguished Israel was its willingness to accept God's commandments and attempt to live by them. In ancient days, no other people forswore idolatry and lived according to God's law. Israel always remained a small nation surrounded by idolatrous peoples, so it is not surprising to observe the Israelites living apart from the peoples among whom they dwelt. This behavior was designed to preserve their monotheism, but it was interpreted in the Greco-Roman world as elitist. Rather than elitism, Israel's desire to separate itself from other peoples was a survival trait intended to avoid backsliding into the rampant idolatry practiced by the Greeks and Romans and other ancient civilizations.

THE TORAH AS RULES FOR HUMAN BEHAVIOR

The Hebrew word *torah* literally means "teaching," and the teachings of the Torah encompass almost every possible human behavior. In the modern world we divide the Torah into ritual law, civil law, criminal law, and moral and ethical requirements. These range from detailed instructions about such diverse subjects as how to offer animal sacrifice, when to eat certain ritual foods, acceptable marriage partners, fair mercantile practice, rules for fair and proper judgment, rules for admitting evidence in a trial, treatment of non-Israelites, care for the poor and indigent and orphans and widows, when and how to observe religious holidays, which foods may be eaten and which are forbidden, how to treat certain diseases, how property may be inherited, and so forth. The instruction is given in different sections of the first five books of the Bible, collectively termed the Pentateuch in English, but in Jewish usage referred to as the Torah (and sometimes as the *Ḥumash,* or "Five"). Instruction is given in the form of positive commandments (what one is required to do) and as negative commandments (what one is forbidden to do). These five books are Genesis, Exodus, Leviticus, Numbers, and Deuteronomy; they are the only books of the Bible that Jewish tradition claims were revealed by God at Mount Sinai. The other nineteen books of the Hebrew Bible are also sacred, but they do not reach the same level of sanctity as the first five.

2

Consolidation and Dispersion

ENTERING THE LAND

After receiving the Torah, the Israelites are depicted as remaining in the desert for forty years before entering the Land. This chapter in the history of the Jewish people is worthy of some discussion because it raises an important issue about the meaning of history and Scripture in Judaism. The Bible often depicts the Israelites as unable to live up to the divine commandments. In the desert they worship the Golden Calf (Exodus 32),[1] fail to trust in God enough to enter the Promised Land after hearing the report of the twelve scouts (Numbers 12–13), and repeatedly complain about their lot.[2] The Israelites are fully human; they are morally weak and tend to succumb to temptation; they often fail to do the proper thing. Here, biblical history functions both as a national epic and as a moral tale. Even with the divine law, Israel cannot always live up to the divine requirements. Human failure is a part of life, but in every case of failure there is also the light of hope, because God forgives, and because right-

---

[1] See Qur'an 2:51–54, 92–93, 4:153, 7:152.
[2] Exodus 5:21, 14:11–12, 15:24, 16:28, 17:2–7; Numbers 11:4–6, 14:1–4, 20:2–5, 21:4–5, etc.

eous individuals demonstrate heroic leadership and moral behavior. Therefore, Israel survives and eventually enters the Promised Land, even as a flawed people.

According to the Bible, it is not only the common folk who err, but prophets and kings. Even Moses fails God when, in anger and frustration at the complaints of the people, he strikes a rock in order to bring forth water in the desert rather than speak to it as commanded by God (Numbers 20:7–13). Nevertheless, despite their complaints and failings, a new generation of Israelites emerges from the desert, united by the revelation of Torah and a sense of common destiny, ready to enter the land promised to Abraham and his descendants as the Land of Israel.

The entry into the Land after forty years in the desert is often referred to as a conquest because the biblical Book of Joshua depicts Israel as taking the Land by military force. Hardened by living forty years in the desert, a generation of toughened warriors overruns the local inhabitants through God's will. Modern archaeological excavations in the area do not confirm this depiction, however, because there are no traces of the universal destruction or burn layers found in other places where a major conquest is known to have occurred. Historians suggest that the Israelites may have entered the Land in a large migration that eventually dominated the local religions and cultures of the area, sparking occasional battles where they were resisted, but mostly succeeding through strength of numbers and a successful religious civilization.

FROM JUDGES TO KINGS

The subsequent period is one in which the twelve tribes of Israel controlled their own individual territorial holdings under tribal chieftains usually called judges. In this period, as depicted in the biblical Book of Judges, the twelve tribes lived separately and sometimes squabbled or even fought one other. The lack of unity became such a problem that the people called upon the head priest to give them a king. This was considered impious at the time, since no single human had been allowed to amass great power in Israel. Until that time, God was the only king and ruler of the Israelites. God relented to the wishes of the people, however (1 Samuel 8), after warning that human kings would abuse power and exploit their subjects, which indeed occurred. Saul was anointed king, but failed miserably as a ruler, was defeated militarily, and died in battle. He was succeeded by the great King David, a mighty hero but nevertheless a flawed personality according to the Bible. David unified the tribes into a single kingdom and created a great Israelite empire that stretched from the borders of Egypt into Mesopotamia. His military prowess was matched by his sublime composition of psalms and devotion to God, but, the mortal that he was, he succumbed to his carnal desires and abused the power of kingship for his own personal gain, for which he was severely punished (2 Samuel 11–12).

David's son Solomon continued to rule a united Israel. He built the great Temple in Jerusalem, outwitted the Queen of Sheba, and in other ways ruled wisely and successfully.

Despite his great wisdom, however, Solomon revealed his
human frailty by backsliding from absolute monotheism
when he allowed his foreign-born wives to worship according to their native idolatrous ways. Solomon even built
shrines for their gods, and some claim that he worshiped
them himself, for which he and his descendants were also
severely punished (1 Kings 11:1–13).

Throughout the Bible, the great heroes of Israel are always
depicted as mortals plagued with the problems and human
failings of real people. Jews are proud of their ancestors and
the great achievements they realized, but Judaism does not
idolize its ancestors or its past. Lessons and caution must be
garnered even from the heroes of Israel, for no mortal is without failure or sin.

Among David's accomplishments was the establishment
of Jerusalem as the capital of the kingdom around 1000 B.C.E..
Prior to David's capture of the city from the Jebusites, it was
one of the few parts of the Land that was not under the control of one or another of the twelve tribes. Jerusalem was
known as a holy place even before Abraham, for it had a
sacred spring and a temple to a deity known as *El Elyon*, the
"Most High God" (Genesis 14:17–20). It was a perfect capital
for David's unified kingdom because it was situated outside
the tribal areas and therefore politically neutral, was central-
ly located, was already known as a holy city, and was emi-
nently defensible. David built a royal palace there, but
because of his warrior status God forbade him to be the one
to build the Temple (1 Chronicles 22:7–9). This privilege was
given to his son Solomon, who built the great Temple in

Jerusalem (1 Kings 6–7). The period of the united monarchy marked the beginning of a golden age, for art, literature, and commerce all flourished. Solomon built strong and beautiful cities and fortifications in many parts of the land, and Israel was proud and unified under a strong central government and religious system.

THE DIVIDED KINGDOM

As in most modern countries, where there is always some tension and competition between the central government and regional interests, the united monarchy faced tension between the royal government and the needs and interests of the tribes. David and Solomon were able to hold the divisive forces at bay, but Solomon's son Rehoboam failed to keep the kingdom unified (1 Kings 12). The ten northern tribes rebelled and formed their own independent kingdom with its capital in Samaria. This marks the period of the divided kingdom, during which, for some two hundred years, the people of Israel were divided between Israel, the northern kingdom, and Judah, the southern kingdom.

Larger and more powerful, the northern kingdom was ruled by nineteen kings representing a number of family dynasties. Strong externally, the northern kingdom was internally weak, with much infighting, and given to immorality. Growing class distinctions bred injustice and corruption, and many abandoned their religious obligations by worshiping in local shrines. This was the era when the great prophets of Israel arose to demand true worship and social justice, but despite the righteousness of many individuals, the nation as a whole is depicted in the biblical books of 1 and 2 Kings as persisting in its wayward behavior. The northern kingdom was finally destroyed in 721 B.C.E. by the Assyrian army.

The southern kingdom of Judah was ruled by the dynasty of King David. Although it, too, knew rebellion and dissension, in comparison with the north it enjoyed greater internal peace. Judah remained small but more cohesive. Nevertheless, despite its greater unity around the institutions of the Davidic dynasty and the Jerusalem Temple, it also suffered from social and religious corruption. Judah, therefore, had its own prophets who denounced evil behavior and warned of God's coming judgment.

This is an appropriate opportunity to comment on the Bible's view of history and the role of Israel in it. According to the Bible, God is actively involved in human affairs and represents the force that determines all historical events. The economic, social, and political forces now seen as influencing history are modern constructs unknown to the Bible. Therefore, the biblical writers—and here it is possible to speak of biblical writers, such as the chroniclers of the books of Kings and Chronicles or the writers of the many prophetic books—interpreted all events in terms of God's reaction to Israel's behavior. Every disaster, whether epidemic, drought, invasion, or bureaucratic ineptitude, is interpreted as God's direct punishment for evil behavior, while great successes, such as military victories or brilliant governmental policies, are understood as divine rewards.

Historians read biblical history with different analytic tools than religious believers. From the standpoint of academic history, whether Jewish or Muslim or Christian, the decline of the united monarchy of Israel occurred as a result of economic, cultural, and political developments in the monarchy and throughout the Middle East. The Davidic Empire arose when the two great Middle Eastern world powers, Egypt and Mesopotamia, were weak. It declined as these great powers recovered and again dominated the region. There were certainly periods of greater and lesser corruption, social inequity, and religious backsliding within the polities of Israel and Judah, but the prophets and chroniclers viewed all of world history as resulting from the behavior of Israel. Thus they prophesied that the kingdoms would be destroyed if the people did not behave in exemplary fashion, obey the divine law fully, and faithfully observe the rituals and rites of monotheistic Judaism. Israel's decline was associated with evil behavior, and improvements in the lot of Israel with righteous behavior. When the Assyrians destroyed the northern kingdom in 721 B.C.E., its destruction was viewed as divine punishment. Judah, the southern kingdom, survived due to its loyalty to God's law and will.

Judah, however, eventually fell in 586 B.C.E. The dominant power in the Middle East at this time was Babylonia, and the prophets of Judah saw Babylonia as an instrument of God. The prophets were pious reformers who attempted to keep Israel on the right path. Although they condemned many aspects of Israelite behavior, they also proclaimed a message of hope that survived the destruction of Jerusalem and the Temple: The kingdom might be destroyed, but a core of the covenanted people would survive and would be brought back to Jerusalem and the land by God (e.g., Isaiah 37:30–32, Jeremiah 31:7–9, Micah 2:12–14). The prophets' reliance on and trust in the eternal covenant gave them the confidence to rally the survivors to continue to live according to the Torah, even in exile outside of the Land of Israel.

EXILE AND RETURN

When the northern kingdom was destroyed, the victors dispersed the tribes throughout the Assyrian Empire in such a way that they were unable to retain their religious and cultural identity. The result was the assimilation and annihilation of the northern kingdom of Israel. Its people are remembered as the "Ten Lost Tribes" that are no more, for they did not survive the Assyrian conquest. The two tribes of Judah and Benjamin, which survived in the southern kingdom for another 150 years, were collectively called Judeans because the large tribe of Judah was by far the dominant one. The prophets of Judah, from which we get the word *Jew*, worked hard during this time to instill the religion, values, and ethics of Judaism deep into the hearts of the people. When Babylon eventually conquered Judah in 586 B.C.E, destroying the Temple and carrying off a great many of its inhabitants, the Jews were able to retain their religious and cultural identity even as a tiny minority in a foreign land. Psalm 137 records the feelings of the Jewish exiles in Babylonia:

By the rivers of Babylon,
there we sat, sat and wept, as we thought of Zion.[3]
There on the poplar trees we hung up our lyres,
for our captors asked us there for songs,
our tormentors for amusement, [saying,]
"Sing us one of the songs of Zion."
How can we sing a song of the Lord on alien soil?
If I forget you, O Jerusalem,
let my right hand wither;
let my tongue stick to my palate
if I cease to think of you,
if I do not keep Jerusalem in memory
even at my happiest hour.

The forced captivity in Babylon lasted about fifty years. In 539, King Cyrus of Persia defeated the Babylonians and allowed those who wished to return to the Land of Israel to do so (Ezra 1–2). Tens of thousands returned the following year, but many others chose to remain in Mesopotamia. The returnees, together with the Judeans who had remained in the Land, rebuilt the Temple in Jerusalem. The rebuilding was completed in 515 B.C.E. However, all was not well, for the country remained poor; Jerusalem was unfortified and vulnerable, and the people were disorganized. Without a strong religious and governmental organization there was growing intermarriage with neighboring unbelievers, and religious commitment weakened.

---

[3] Zion is another name for Jerusalem (1 Kings 8:1, Isaiah 1:27, etc.).

Ezra and the Restoration

Ezra, a Judean born in exile, learned of the difficult conditions in Jerusalem. He petitioned the Persian king (probably Artaxerxes I) to allow him to return with a group of exiles, and his request was granted. The Persians were very tolerant and had no objection to strengthening the province of Judah, so Ezra was allowed and even enabled by the Persian crown to establish a system to teach and enforce both Jewish law and the laws of the Persian king. Most scholars fix the date of Ezra's arrival in Jerusalem at 457 B.C.E. Ezra reorganized the community, publicly read aloud the entire Torah, and required the Judeans to again bind themselves to observe the commandments of Jewish ritual and tradition (Nehemiah 9–10).

At about the same time, a Jewish official at the royal court named Nehemiah asked Artaxerxes for permission to join in the rebuilding of Jerusalem and was appointed governor of Judea, the name by which Judah was now known. While Ezra restored the religious and social system of Judaism, Nehemiah restored the economic and political infrastructure. Together, they were able to strengthen the Jewish community of Jerusalem and Judea and ensure a strong and successful Jewish revival.

The period of Exile and Restoration had a major impact on the development of the Jewish religion. First, it changed Judaism from a local ethnic religion to a universal religion. Prior to the Exile, all human religions were localized. It was assumed that if one moved to another land, one would have to worship a new set of gods. The concept of a universal God only came into being when the exiled Judeans insisted on continuing to worship their Israelite God even in the foreign land of Babylonia. The "God of Israel" proved to be just as real in Babylon as in Jerusalem, thereby demonstrating the unity and universality of the One God. Second, the Exile proved to the Judeans that they could worship God even without the formal sacrifices in the Temple that had been destroyed. Prior to the Babylonian Exile, divine worship in all religions was conducted through sacrifices in temples or holy places. The first possibility of formal worship other than animal sacrifice seems to have been born of necessity in Babylon, far from the Jerusalem Temple. Since Jews were forbidden to make sacrifices to God outside of the Jerusalem Temple, they had to devise other means of divine worship. Thus a new form of worship that took the form of communal prayer and later became standardized in the synagogue, church, and mosque was established by the Judean exiles in Babylon. Their experience demonstrated that prayer and supplication were efficacious anywhere, that God would respond to worship even outside the framework of animal sacrifice and sacred places.

The experience of religious exile widened the Judeans' religious horizons in multiple ways that would eventually exert a profound influence on all the monotheistic traditions. Not only did it prove the universality of God and the ability of human beings to worship anywhere and without sacrifices, but it also universalized the sense of responsibility for monotheism. Before the destruction of the First Temple, the

Israelites tried to remain faithful to their religious teachings in the face of near-universal idolatry, but they did not consider it their responsibility to influence others to become monotheists. By the time the Jews returned from the Babylonian Exile, they regarded idolatry as bad for all people everywhere.

THE SECOND TEMPLE PERIOD AND HELLENISM

The nearly four hundred years between Solomon's construction of the Temple and its destruction by the Babylonians is referred to as the First Temple period. The nearly six hundred years from its rebuilding in 515 B.C.E. to its second destruction by the Romans in 70 C.E. is called the Second Temple period. Very little is known about the time between Ezra and Nehemiah's restoration and the coming of Alexander the Great to the Middle East in the 330s B.C.E. Alexander's conquest, however, was a watershed in Middle Eastern history because it marked the large-scale introduction of Greek ideas into the region. *Hellenism* is the term used to describe the impact of Greek (Hellenic) ideas on the indigenous Middle Eastern cultures, all of which were forever altered by these events.

Hellenism, first of all, brought together the many varied cultures and religions of the region. There was a great exchange of goods and of ideas, and for the first time many people considered themselves citizens of the world. One of the greatest questions for the Jews was how much Hellenistic influence was permissible in Judaism without jeopardizing

Jewish identity and Jewish faithfulness to God's will. To what extent did Greek ideas and customs clash with God's requirements to remain true to the Torah? Various answers were proposed and a variety of Jewish expressions developed. The range of the Jewish responses to Hellenism stretched the fabric of Jewish society to the breaking point in the second century B.C.E. During a period of forced Hellenism perpetrated by Jewish radicals and their Greek supporters under a despotic Greek ruler named Antiochus IV, Judea suffered from a civil war that very nearly destroyed the Jewish people. The conservative faction known as the Maccabees won by throwing out the radical Hellenists in about 168 B.C.E. and carving out an independent Jewish state that preserved the old ways. This victory for tradition is marked by the holiday of Hanukkah, which commemorates the rededication of the Jerusalem Temple, which had been defiled by the Greeks and their radically Hellenistic Jewish allies.

For the next century Judea was governed by the Hasmonean dynasty of Jewish kings, but as time passed the Hasmoneans became more and more culturally Greek. Jerusalem eventually became a Greek city, or *polis*, filled with places of Greek learning, art, language, culture, and religion. Jews and Judaism would never again be isolated from the intellectual and political trends of the rest of the world. This amalgamation was threatening for Judaism, but at the same time it was a source of stimulation and development. Judaism was much influenced by foreign ideas, but in turn it influenced the many foreign peoples with whom it came into contact. As a result, the Jewish religion was freed from its boundaries in Judea. Some Greeks and Romans formally converted to Judaism, and many others adopted certain elements of Jewish practice or belief, a process known as judaizing. Through the many Greek, Roman, and local Middle Eastern converts, as well the many judaizers who learned about Judaism but did not actually convert, Judaism spread throughout the Hellenistic world and became a major world religion—the first universally recognized expression of monotheism. This was a period during which groups representing different expressions of Judaism began to emerge. Some of them, such as the Sadducees and the Pharisees, are mentioned in the New Testament. Jewish, Greek, and Roman writings from the period mention other groups, such as the Essenes and the Zealots.

JUDAISM AND CHRISTIANITY

The century leading up to the destruction of the Second Temple in 70 C.E. was one of the most turbulent for the Jews of Greco-Roman Palestine. The Roman Empire had taken control of Judea. There were Jewish communities throughout the Middle East and North Africa, including Egypt, and in Greece and Italy, France, Spain, Germany, and even England. The old community in Babylon had grown as well, and Jewish settlers had penetrated Arabia as far as Yemen.

The Bible promised the Jews that if they obeyed God's Torah they would be rewarded in this world with peace, prosperity, good health, and a good life (Deuteronomy 7:9–15, 11:13–27). But most Jews did not feel that their lot in this world reflected their piety and faithfulness to God and the covenant. Jews observed their own righteous brethren suffering from poverty, disease, and violence at the hands of Roman soldiers and officials; they saw, too, that the powerful infidels seemed to be enjoying the best that life could offer. The idolatrous Romans oppressed the Jews in their own land but enjoyed all possible earthly pleasures.

Biblical passages, especially from the books of the prophets, alluded to or even promised a time when God would right all the inequities of this world. God would bring back the Israelites from throughout the dispersion to Jerusalem and the Land of Israel, where they would be governed with justice and peace and blessed by God's love (Isaiah 11:11–12, Amos 9:14–15). Other passages indicated that the human figure who governed the righteous and redeemed Israel in the End of Days would derive from the family of David, the ancient unifier of Israel (Isaiah 9:1–6; Ezekiel 37:21–28). God alone, however, would accomplish the miracle of redemption; the Hebrew Bible teaches nothing about a heroic messianic figure who will miraculously redeem Israel. Nevertheless, during the terribly difficult period under Roman rule, and after it had become clear that prophecy had ceased, many Jews in the Roman Empire began to believe that a divinely guided messianic figure would bring God's redemption. As the messianic idea developed in this period, its various expressions were enshrined in the Talmud and Midrash, the collection of Jewish tradition comprising the "Oral Torah."[4]

---

[4] The Talmud and the Midrash will be discussed below in chapter 7.

Messianic expectation was high during the Roman period, and at various times, and in different circles, several individuals were thought to be the awaited messiah. The most famous of these was Jesus, son of Joseph of Nazareth. While some Jews believed in his status as the redemptive messiah, most did not. Those Jews who did believe in his messianic status became the founders of Christianity, which eventually accepted and required belief in Jesus' messiahship as theological truth. Soon thereafter, Christianity began to require the belief that Jesus was not only the awaited messiah, but the very Son of God. Most Jews refused to accept the messiahship of Jesus because, according to Judaism, the true messiah will bring immediate redemption and not require a "Second Coming." When the followers of Jesus began to require the belief that Jesus was also God's son, Christianity moved beyond the pale of acceptable Jewish belief. Judaism considers the Christian concept of the Trinity to be a violation of God's unity.

Given the absolute unacceptability to Judaism of the Christian belief that Jesus is the Son of God, Surat al-Tawba presents an interesting problem. In 9:30, the Qur'an says: "The Jews say: Ezra is the son of God, and the Christians say: The messiah is the son of God. This is what they say from their mouths, resembling the speech of unbelievers of old. God fight them, for they lie." The problem presented by this verse was clear to Muslim scholars from the earliest times, because they lived among Jews and therefore observed that Jews did not believe that Ezra was the Son of God. Virtually all of the classical Muslim Qur'an commentators write that this verse does not refer to all Jews, but rather to certain individuals or groups living in Arabia. Surat al-Tawba is a Medinan verse, and the commentators provide traditions that shed light on it in the context of the prophet Muhammad's life in Medina. Muhammad b. Jarir al-Tabari, for example, offers the following traditions in his commentary:[5]

> Al-Qasim related to us [in a chain of tradition going back to] the authority of Abdallah b. Ubayd b. Umayr: One man said this [that Ezra is the Son of God], and they say that his name was Finhas.[6] Abu Kurayb related to us [in a chain of tradition going back to] the authority of Ibn Abbas: Four men came to the Apostle of God and said, "How can we follow you when you have abandoned our direction of prayer [*qibla*] and you do not claim that Uzayr is the son of God?" Because of what they said, this verse was revealed.

While it is clear that Judaism as a religious civilization does not accept the view that God has partners or children, it is probable that some fringe groups pushed the limits of acceptable belief with the important figure of Ezra. Two ancient and originally Jewish books, for example, associate a near-divine or angelic status to the biblical personages of Ezra and Enoch. These are 4 Ezra, also known as 2 Esdras 14:9, 50[7] and 2 Enoch

---

[5] Jami` al-Bayan `an ta'wil ay al-Qur'an (1405; Beirut, 1984), on 9:30 (pt. 10, pp. 110–111).

[6] This same Finhas is known in the Sira of Ibn Ishaq to have said other blasphemous things, such as that God is poor and we are rich, which precipitated the revelation of 3:181: "God has heard the words of those who said: 'God is poor and we are rich.' ..."

[7] This verse is found only in the Syriac, Ethiopic, Armenian, and Arabic recensions of the book, but not in the Latin.

22:11. Although composed by Jews, both of these books were rejected by Judaism and did not become part of its canonical literature. However, because of their parallels with Christian beliefs, some Christian groups adopted and preserved them. It appears as if some members of a Jewish sect espousing these beliefs were living in Medina at the time of the Prophet and expressed such views, which were immediately rejected and countered through the revelation of the qur'anic verse.

Both Christianity and Judaism claimed the Jewish Scriptures as their own. In addition to accepting the Hebrew Bible (which it calls the "Old Testament"), Christianity believed that Jesus himself, as God's son, epitomized God's will. Since Christians believe that God sent His own son to earth for a divine purpose, every moment of the life of Jesus on earth must have reflected the will of God. Jesus, as it were, is consequently the living revelation of God. The written stories of Jesus' life, therefore, are considered to be divine Scripture. They are the Gospel, meaning "Good Story," the core of the Christian Bible, or "New Testament." Generally speaking, Christianity believes that the great prophecies of the Hebrew Bible are actualized in the life of Jesus as messiah and divinity in human form. Judaism, however, believes that the great prophecies have not yet been actualized. Jews and Judaism do not accept the New Testament as divine Scripture, while Christians and Christianity do not accept the commandments of the Old Testament as binding, because they consider them to have been superseded by the coming of Jesus. There are many differences between Judaism and

Christianity, of course, but the core distinction lies in the disagreement over the messiahship and divinity of Jesus and the role of the divine commandments in life.

DESTRUCTION AND DISPERSION

By the first century C.E., Rome had firmly established its rule over Judea. The Roman governors and procurators became increasingly harsh and unjust until, in the year 66, the Jews revolted, led by zealots who believed that God would assist them in their war against the Roman infidels and bring about the expected End of Days. The Jews, however, were not all of one opinion regarding the revolt. Many believed either that it was not the appointed time or that war was not the proper means of realizing the Redemption. The Jewish revolt against Rome caused major disruptions in the Roman Empire, and legions were brought from many parts of Europe and the Middle East to quell it. Rome finally succeeded in regaining control of Jerusalem in 70 C.E., and destroyed the Temple in the process. The last Jewish fortress to fall to the Romans was Masada near the Dead Sea, which fell in 73 C.E.

When the Temple was destroyed, sacrifices ceased, the functional priesthood ended, and Jerusalem no longer served to unify the scattered Jewish nation. With the end of the priestly leadership, learned sages, or rabbis, began to fill the void. The Sanhedrin, or scholarly assembly, served as a central judiciary and legislature, and its head (the patriarch, or *nasi*) became the central Jewish authority in relations with Rome. The destruction of the Temple marks the end of

Biblical Judaism and the beginning of the ascendance of Rabbinic Judaism.

There was one final and terribly destructive Jewish rebellion against Rome. It was again precipitated by oppressive Roman rule and was led by a messianic military figure named Shimon Bar Kokhba and his religious supporter, Rabbi Akiba. They seized Jerusalem from the Romans in 132 C.E. and attempted to restore the Temple. The Bar Kokhba revolt, however, failed. The Roman emperor, Hadrian, razed the entire city of Jerusalem in 135 and built a heathen city named Capitolina in its place. From this Latin name comes one of the Arabic names for the city, *Ilya*. Jews were forbidden to be within eyeshot of Jerusalem upon pain of death, and the entire area around the city lay in ruins. The Romans practiced a form of "ethnic cleansing" in order to keep Jews away from Jerusalem, and were so determined to prevent further rebellions that they ceased calling the region Judea in order to dissociate it entirely from the Jews. They changed the name of Judea to *Palestina*, taken from the vanished ancient people known as the Philistines. Judea lay in ruins. The survivors fled northward to Galilee or out of the area entirely. Until the coming of Islam in the seventh century, Jews were prohibited from entering Jerusalem except on one occasion each year, the ninth day of the month of Av, which was a universal Jewish day of mourning.

3

Rabbinic Judaism, the Talmud, and the Medieval World

FROM BIBLICAL JUDAISM TO RABBINIC JUDAISM

The Romans destroyed the Jerusalem Temple, but they destroyed neither Judaism nor the Jews. In fact, although the loss of the Second Temple caused great trauma, as did the loss of the First Temple, the net result of both tragedies was to strengthen the people and their religion as they entered into an exile that would last thousands of years. By the second destruction, no longer would the religion be centered on a sacrificial system run by a hereditary priesthood, nor would it be bound to a single holy city and holy land. Henceforth, the unity of God and the moral-ethical system that belief in it demanded would be carried within a religious system where study and communal and personal prayer replaced sacrifice, and where good deeds sustained a community that had formerly been sustained by a political system. Learned rabbis replaced hereditary priests as leaders of the community, and the home and synagogue replaced the Holy Temple as the center of Jewish ritual and spiritual life. These major structural changes followed the historical transition from Biblical

Judaism to Rabbinic Judaism. Despite these changes, however, the heart of Judaism remained always the same. The absolute unity of God framed Jewish theological beliefs, and Jewish life continued to be governed by Torah—God's teachings and divine commandments. Judaism, however, would henceforth always be a more easily portable religious system than during the biblical period. In exile and dispersion, its only truly sacred objects would be the scrolls and books of the Torah.

The Mishnah and Talmud

Rabbinic Judaism had been developing quietly in the Land of Israel for centuries while the Temple was still standing, but its early development ran in parallel with the ancient service in the Temple. In addition to the written texts of Scripture—the Torah, the books of the prophets, and the various other books, such as Psalms, Proverbs, and Chronicles—there developed a vast repertoire of oral wisdom that was handed down from sage to disciple for many generations. This large pool of wisdom remained in oral form for hundreds of years, but much of it was collected and written down during the tragic aftermath of the abortive Bar Kokhba rebellion. This body of tradition, consisting largely of the sayings and actions of great Jewish sages over several centuries, was called the Mishnah, the Hebrew term for "collection of learning." The Mishnah was collected and committed to writing around the year 200 C.E. It was compiled into six books, or orders, that contained the sages' wisdom regarding how the

Torah should be applied to the human activities of daily life. Written in Hebrew, each order of the Mishnah covers a different aspect of life. *Zera'im* ("seeds") treats agricultural issues and daily prayer, *Mo`ed* ("set feasts") treats the ritual requirements of the Sabbath, festivals, and fasts. *Nashim* ("women") treats matrimonial law, women's rights and responsibilities, laws of divorce, and vows. *Nezikin* ("damages") treats many types of civil and criminal law along with a popular ethical guide. *Kodashim* ("sacred things") records much of the formal ritual of the Jerusalem Temple, and *Tohorot* ("ritual cleanness" [Arabic *taharah*]) treats various aspects of human, ritual, and food purity. The Mishnah was collected in Palestine, reproduced, and then sent throughout the Jewish world. It became the most common vehicle for applying the divine law of the Torah to the daily lives of Jews wherever they lived.

The Mishnah became a core text that was studied faithfully by Jews along with the Bible. It was considered the highest honor to become the student of a sage, and the curriculum of instruction centered on knowing the Torah and discussing the Mishnah. Many generations of Mishnah discussions, especially in Palestine and in the Jewish communities of Babylon, extended the topics of discussion greatly. In fact, after the destruction of Judea by the Romans, the center of the Jewish world began to shift back again toward Babylon (today's Iraq) as it had after the destruction of the First Temple centuries earlier. Members of the ancient Jewish community of Iraq continue to refer to themselves as Babylonians to this day, even though the Babylonians of the Bible were defeated and driven from power more than twenty-five hundred years ago.

By the time of the collection of the Mishnah in 200 C.E., the language of the Jews had changed from Hebrew to its sister language Aramaic, the lingua franca of much of the Middle East at this time. Most Jews in the region still knew Hebrew and prayed in the holy tongue, but Aramaic became their daily language. As a result, Aramaic also became the language of Jewish learning. Sages and their disciples continued for another two or three centuries to discuss and apply the rules of the Mishnah and the laws of the Torah, and these discussions grew into a large volume of oral tradition that was painstakingly recorded in human memory. As this library of oral literature became too vast even for the most gifted people to retain in their memories, two versions were eventually written down. One was collected in Palestine around the beginning of the fifth century, and the other was collected in Babylon about a hundred years later. They are both organized around the Mishnah and contain much overlapping material, but the Babylonian collection is far more complete and comprehensive. These collections, written in Aramaic, are called *Gemara,* or "completion," because they form the supplementary commentary on the Mishnah. Together, the Mishnah and Gemara form the Talmud, the "book of learning" par excellence of Rabbinic Judaism. The Talmud is a vast sea of Jewish tradition that applies the laws of Torah in intricate detail to the daily ritual and spiritual, civic, social, personal, and moral life of the Jew.

Some scholars have compared the Talmud to the Islamic

Hadith. There are indeed a number of similarities, although there are also significant differences. Both remained oral for generations before they were committed to writing. Both preserve a great deal of information about how to live according to God's design that is not directly discernible from the text of Scripture, whether Hebrew Bible or Qur'an. Both are authoritative even though they are not the same as the written text of Scripture. Both provide the names of the human recorders or witnesses of the tradition. One of the major differences between the two pertains to the source of the tradition. In the Hadith, the source of all authoritative tradition is the Prophet. In the Talmud, the great sages of Judaism are the sources of the tradition, which, ultimately, is said to go back to Mount Sinai. While Judaism and Islam, respectively, consider the words and actions of the sages and Muhammad to be divinely inspired and therefore authoritative, neither religious system accepts the authority of the other's tradition. This should not be surprising, given that each system grew up independently of the other.

Despite the differences, however, the many similarities between Talmud and Hadith naturally resulted in religious systems that possess many structural and phenomenological parallels. Both Judaism and Islam, for example, are governed largely by a system designed to regulate human behavior. In Judaism this system is called *halakhah*, and in Islam it is called *shari`a*. Although the two words are linguistically unrelated, semantically they give the same meaning: *shari`a* means "the way to the waterhole" or "the way to the source," while *halakhah* means "the way to go" or "something to go by." Both are systems of governance of human behavior derived from God through Scripture and tradition. They do not teach precisely the same conduct, but they both require that we take care to live our lives according to the divine will. This extends from the foods we put into our mouths to the words we allow to come out of our mouths, how we treat our families and friends and strangers, how we conduct our businesses, how we pray, and so forth. The range of similarities and differences should not surprise us. Both Jews and Muslims have dedicated themselves for many centuries, and have devoted enormous, painstaking effort, to seeking out the divine will in the simple daily lives of human beings. The particulars of each system must vary, but the desire and intent are the same.

JUDAISM IN ARABIA AND THE EMERGENCE OF ISLAM

According to Islamic sources, Jews penetrated Arabia and settled there as early as the time of Moses. The great *Kitab al-Aghani* of Abul-Faraj al-Isfahani records a number of legends that postulate the historical origins of Arabia's Jews. One of these legends touches on the origins of the two great Jewish tribes that Muhammad knew in Medina:

> The Banu Qurayza and the Banu al-Nadir were called *al-Kahinan* [the two priestly tribes] because they were descended from al-Kahin, the son of Aaron, the son of `Amran, the brother of Moses b. `Amran, may the prayers of God be upon Muhammad, his family, and the two of them. They settled in the vicinity of Yathrib

[the pre-Islamic name for Medina] after the death of Moses, upon him be peace.[1]

Another tradition suggests that a second wave of Jews migrated to Arabia after the Roman conquest of Judea:

> Then Rome rose up over all the Children of Israel in Syria, trampled them underfoot, killed them, and married their women. So when Rome conquered them in Syria, the Banu al-Nadir, the Banu Qurayza and the Banu Bahdal fled to the Children of Israel [already residing] in the Hijaz. When they departed from their houses, the king of Rome sent after them to bring them back, but it was impossible for him because of the desert between Syria and the Hijaz. When the pursuing Romans reached al-Tamr, they died of thirst, so that place was named Tamr al-Rum, which is its name to this day.

The Jews of Yemen in southern Arabia had still other traditions. One traced the origins of Yemenite Jewry to the union of King Solomon and the Queen of Sheba, known as Bilqis in Islamic sources. According to the legend, Solomon and Bilqis had a son together whom Solomon wished to be raised in proper Jewish fashion, and therefore he sent Jews from Jerusalem to Bilqis's land, where they settled and established a fortress near San`a.[2]

---

[1] This and the following legends may be found in Gordon Newby, *A History of the Jews of Arabia* (Chapel Hill: University of South Carolina Press, 1988), pp. 14–23.

[2] Ibid., p. 33. See also Reuben Aharoni, *Yemenite Jewry: Origins, Culture and Literature* (Bloomington: Indiana University Press, 1986).

Whatever its origins, there was a well-established Jewish community living in Arabia by the time of Muhammad's birth, just as there were also Christians in the peninsula. Exactly what kind of Jews lived in Arabia is not clear, however. The evidence suggests that they practiced a form of Judaism that did not always reflect the standards and norms of Rabbinic Judaism as we know it. The qur'anic verse cited above in chapter 2, witnessing that at least some of the Jews of Medina considered Ezra to be the son of God, is an example of the unorthodox ideas that had crept into Arabian Jewish beliefs. Other qur'anic references to strange beliefs lend additional evidence of their untraditional practices and beliefs. Surat al-Ma'ida (5:64), for example, has "The Jews say: 'The hand of God is fettered.' [But] their hands are fettered! And they are cursed for what they say!" The Qur'an here is probably responding to Lamentations 2:3, a biblical passage mourning the destruction of the First Temple: "[God] has withdrawn his right hand in the presence of the foe." This verse is a poetic statement claiming that it was God's will to destroy Jerusalem at the hand of the Babylonians by refusing to defend the city against them. God punished Israel by withdrawing His right hand[3] from defending Jerusalem. This verse does not suggest that God is in any way limited or weak, but rather that God *chose* to withdraw the divine protection.

---

[3] The term *God's right hand* (Hebrew: *yemino*) is a metaphor for God's power and might in many passages of the Hebrew Bible and does not imply that Jews consider God a corporeal being.

An interpretation of this verse in the midrashic book called Lamentations Rabbah (end of 2:6) says:

> "The right hand [of God] is fettered."[4] I have determined an end [for the fettering] of My right hand. When I have redeemed My children [the Children of Israel] I will redeem My right hand, as David said [in Psalm 60:7]: "So that those whom You love might be rescued, release Your right hand and answer me."

This interpretation suggests metaphorically (not literally) that God purposefully fettered His right hand in order to cause the destruction of Jerusalem as punishment for the sins of Israel. There is nothing in this interpretation that would be unacceptable to either Judaism or Islam.

Another interpretation, however, in an old collection of writings that was rejected by Judaism, has the following statement: "Rabbi Ishmael said to me: Come and I will show you the right hand of the Omnipresent One [i.e., God], which has been banished behind him because of the destruction of the Temple."[5] The first interpretation understands the fettering of God's hand as a metaphor for God's refusal to protect Jerusalem on account of its sins. The second interpretation ignores the metaphor and claims outright that God's hand is weakened or useless because of the destruction of the

---

[4] The biblical text reads *otah ha-yamin shehi meshu`abedet*, and the term *meshu`abedet*, which means "subjugated" or "enslaved" in Hebrew, has the meaning of "being bound or responsible" in Aramaic, the language of the Midrash.

[5] 3 Enoch 48a as cited by Newby, *History of the Jews of Arabia*, p. 59.

Jerusalem Temple. The first is acceptable to Judaism, whereas the second is not, and in fact the second interpretation is found in a book that was rejected from Jewish tradition. The Qur'an appears to be condemning the latter interpretation, which must have enjoyed a certain following among the Jews of Medina in the lifetime of the Prophet.

Why would Jews stretching and straying beyond the limits of acceptable Jewish belief have been living in Medina? The answer is that the isolation of Arabia served regularly as a refuge for people seeking freedom from oppression. We know, for example, that early Christian communities found asylum from Roman persecution in various Arabian desert regions, and later groups escaped the theological compulsion of the Orthodox Byzantine Empire in the safety of the Arabian Peninsula. These were nonorthodox Christians who sought sanctuary in Arabia in order to live out their beliefs without interference. Although we have less documentation for Jews of this period than for Christians, it is quite likely that marginal Jewish groups did the same in order to escape the pressures of the Jewish establishment, and that one or more settled in Medina.

In addition to the Qur'an, the biography of the Prophet known as the Sira sheds some interesting light on the Jews of Medina and the Judaism they practiced. Some readers may be surprised to learn that the Jews of Medina actually motivated some and perhaps many idolatrous Arabs to follow Muhammad and become Muslims. The great biographer of the Prophet, Muhammad Ibn Ishaq, gives this tradition in the Sira:

`Asim b. `Umar b. Qatada said on the authority of some elders of his tribe, who said: When the Messenger of God met them he said: "Who are you?" They answered: "From the Khazraj [tribe of Medina]." "Are you allies of the Jews?" "Yes," they answered. So he said: "Will you not sit with me so I can talk with you?" "Of course," they replied. So they sat with him, and he called them to God, expounded to them Islam, and recited for them the Qur'an. Now God had prepared them for Islam in that the Jews, who were people of the Book and knowledge while they themselves were polytheists and idolaters, lived with them in their towns. They used to raid [the Jews] in their settlements, and when [bad feelings] arose between them the Jews would say: "A prophet is being sent soon. His time has come. We will follow him and kill you with his help [just as] `Ad and Iram were destroyed."[6] So when the Messenger of God spoke with this group and called them to God, some of them said to the others: "By God, this is the very prophet about which the Jews had threatened us. Do not let them get to him before us!" So they responded to his call, believed him, and accepted his teaching of Islam.[7]

---

[6] Ad and Iram are names of ancient Arabian tribal groups that had long since disappeared by the emergence of Islam but still lived in the memories and oral traditions of the Arabs.

[7] Al-Sira al-Nabawiyya (Beirut, n.d.) 1:428–429, in Alfred Guillaume, *The Life of Muhammad: A Translation of Ishaq's Sirat Rasul Allah* (New York: Oxford University Press, 1967), pp. 197–198.

This interesting tradition notes the Jewish expectation of a messianic savior whom they referred to as a prophet. Although the Jews did not purposefully encourage their pagan Arab neighbors to become Muslims, their religious influence in Medina created an environment in which pre-Islamic Arabs had become open to the idea of an Arab prophet. That Muhammad successfully fit the role is clear from the overwhelming success he attained in Medina. Ibn Ishaq preserves another tradition that sheds more light on the Jewish view of Muhammad, given on the authority of Salama Ibn Salama Ibn Waqsh:

> We had a Jewish neighbor among the [clan of the] Banu `Abd al-Ashhal who came out to us one day from his home. . . . He spoke of the resurrection, the [divine] reckoning, the [heavenly] scales, the Garden and the Fire. . . . [They asked] "What would be a sign of this?" He said, pointing with his hand to Mecca and the Yemen [i.e., southward]: "A prophet will be sent from the direction of this land." They asked: "When will he appear?" He looked at me, the youngest person, and said: "This boy, if he lives his natural term, will see him." And by God, a night and a day did not pass before God sent Muhammad, His messenger, and he was living among us. We believed in him, but [the Jewish neighbor] denied him. . . . When we asked him, "Aren't you the man who said these things?" he said, "Certainly, but this is not the man."[8]

---

[8] Ibid. 1:212, in Guillaume, *Life of Muhammad*, pp. 93–94.

Medina's Jews taught many religious tenets shared by Judaism and Islam. These include a Day of Judgment and a heaven and hell in the world-to-come, and at least some of them anticipated the coming of a prophetic figure who would be a harbinger of the Day of Judgment. And yet, when Muhammad came to Medina, most Jews refused to accept his prophethood. There were some very notable exceptions, such as the famous Abdullah Ibn Salam, but as a community, the Jews of Medina overwhelmingly refrained from giving up their ancient tradition and becoming Muslims. Given Muhammad's great success and the awesome authority vested in him by nothing less than the revelation of the Qur'an, how could this have happened?

It is probably impossible to recover the precise reasons for the Jews' refusal as a community to follow Muhammad; specific reasons are hard to extract from the sources available to us. The Qur'an and the Sira note how the Jews stubbornly refused to believe that he was a prophet, but specific reasons beyond obstinacy are not given. Thus we can only conjecture here. Perhaps, as the tradition cited above suggests, Muhammad did not fit their specific expectations about the awaited one. It is also clear from the Qur'an that although the revelations recited by Muhammad to the community in Medina were similar to the revelation of the Torah, they were different enough in detail that the Jews suspected their authenticity. The Qur'an was revealed in Arabic and in an Arabian cultural context, while the Torah was revealed in Hebrew and in an Israelite cultural context; this difference in the style of discourse may explain much of the disagreement.

But the discrepancy was apparently enough for the Jews, who
were already wary of what they considered to be distortions
of the meaning of the Hebrew Bible found in the New
Testament and Christian interpretations.

Whether or not the Jews' insistence on remaining true to
their ancient tradition should be commended or condemned
must remain a matter of opinion. Suffice it to say here that
Muhammad and the Jews of Medina did not, in the end, find
a common ground. Certain verses of the Qur'an condemning
the Jews of Medina were revealed in response to the real historical discord, arguments, and hostility that ensued between
them. Some early Muslim commentators and scholars composed a collection of books called *Occasions of Revelation* (*asbab
al-nuzul*) that tied qur'anic revelations with historical
episodes in the life of the Prophet. These scholars note that
many of the verses negatively portraying Jews were revealed
specifically in response to Muhammad's conflict with them.
These verses respond to specific incidents and either condemn the behavior of certain Jews of Medina or assuage the
hurt and anger that Muhammad felt in response. So, for
example, Surat al-Ma'ida (5:85): "You will definitely find that
the strongest in enmity against the believers are the Jews and
the idolaters, and you will find those closest in love to the
believers being those who call themselves Christians
(*nasara*)." This verse points to the fact that Muhammad never
lived among Christians and therefore never suffered rejection
by them as he did by the idolaters of Mecca and the Jews of
Medina. It was only after Muhammad's death that the
Muslims entered into open conflict and war with the

Christians in Arabia and with the Byzantine Empire. Similarly, for example, Surat al-Ma'ida (5:49) condemns the Jews for attempting to entice Muhammad away from God's revelations of the Qur'an. Some of these verses were mistakenly applied to the Jews as a whole in later generations, thereby perpetuating a certain amount of anti-Jewish stereotyping among Muslims.

Not only in the Qur'an, but also in the Hadith and the Sira did the brief conflict between Muhammad and the Jews of Medina become immortalized and generalized, and it formed the earliest basis for determining the treatment of Jews in Islam. Toward the end of his life the Prophet received the revelation of al-Bara'a (9:29): "Fight those who do not believe in God or the Last Day, and who do not forbid what has been forbidden by God and His Messenger, nor acknowledge the religion of truth from among the People of the Book, until they pay the poll tax [*al-jizya*] out of hand [`*an yadin*], having been brought low [*wahum saghirun*]."

On the one hand, the great similarities between Jewish and Islamic scriptural texts and religious practices ensured that Jews (like Christians, for similar reasons) were considered a religious minority whose religious and economic rights were absolutely protected by the Muslim state. On the other, the differences and the ultimate refusal of the Jews (and again, of the Christians also) to accept Islam as their own religion caused their social position in Islamic society to remain always at a disadvantage. Their protection (*dhimma*) was predicated on their paying the special *jizya* tax and accepting a secondary status in Islamic society. Still, the situation of

protected religious minorities (*dhimmi* peoples) in Islam was
certainly as good as or better than that of religious minorities
under any other contemporary religious or political system,
and as we shall soon learn, Jewish life flourished in many
parts of the Islamic world.

THE ISLAMIC CONQUESTS AND THE JEWS

Unlike Christians and Zoroastrians, Jews were nowhere in
control of an army or a state at the time of the Islamic conquests. Wherever they lived, Jews were religious minorities
with certain social, religious, and economic disabilities
imposed upon them by the state and the official state religion.
When the Muslim armies advanced against the Byzantine
Romans and the Persians, therefore, they were not attacking
the Jews directly, although some Jews chose to join their hosts
in fighting against the invaders. In most cases, however, the
Jews either did not resist the Muslims or else actively collaborated with them. In Hims (Emesa), Jews helped prevent the
Byzantine army from entering to defend the city. In Hebron
and Caesarea, Jews helped the Muslims penetrate the cities'
defenses. And in Spain, the Jews rose up in armed revolt
against their Christian overlords and were appointed by the
Muslims to garrison certain Spanish cities and keep them
under Muslim control.[9]

The Jews were better off under the Muslims than under the
Byzantine Christians, and it is likely that they also fared bet-

---

[9] Norman Stillman, *The Jews of Arab Lands* (Philadelphia: Jewish Publication Society,
1978), pp. 22–28.

ter than under the Zoroastrian Persians. However, the
medieval world did not share the modern Western values of
pluralism and religious equality. Jews were free to practice
their religion without interference, but a number of restrictive
conditions applied that were codified in the Pact of `Umar
(*ahd `Umar*).[10] Jews were not allowed to hold any public reli-
gious ceremonies, could not build new synagogues or repair
existing ones without special dispensation from the governor,
and were prohibited from raising their voices so loud during
prayer as to attract the attention of passersby. In addition,
Jews (and Christians) were forbidden to carry weapons, ride
horses, or use saddles, and were not allowed to build homes
larger than Muslim ones. They were also required always to
show deference to Muslims, such as by rising from their seats
when Muslims wished to sit down or by dismounting from
their mules or donkeys when passing a Muslim pedestrian.
Jews could not be appointed to government offices and other
key public posts, and were not allowed to strike Muslims.

Many of these rules were observed in the breach, especially in times of social, economic, and political stability.
However, if Jews were deemed to have violated their responsibility to accept a secondary status in Islamic society (by, say,
building a new synagogue, taking a position in a public
office, or not showing enough deference to Muslims), their
protection (*dhimma*) could be withdrawn, and then they
would be left defenseless against the mob. An example of
how the system worked may be observed in the case of the
famous Jew named Shmuel ben Yosef ha-Levi, also known in

---

[10] Ibid., pp. 157–158.

Jewish history as Shmuel ha-Nagid ("the prince") and in Arabic as Isma`il Ibn Naghrela. He was a rabbi who was both vizier and army commander for Habbus and his son Badis, the Muslim kings of Granada. As Badis grew older, he gave Shmuel more and more authority, and Shmuel carefully wielded his power and influence in the kingdom with great wisdom and circumspection. When Shmuel died in 1055, his son Yosef was appointed to replace him. Although exceptionally talented, like his father, Yosef was arrogant and disliked. His lack of *dhimmi* comportment contributed to his downfall, and he was eventually murdered in 1066 and the Jewish community of Granada slaughtered. Technically, both Yosef and his father had broken the pact by accepting high public office and authority over Muslims. This fact was ignored when Shmuel comported himself with exceptional humility and when the kingdom as a whole was happy. However, when stress arose and Yosef refused to be self-effacing, his *dhimma* was breached. He was killed and his community devastated.

Life for Jews under Islam was probably better than under any other political or religious system in the premodern period. It was, nevertheless, precarious and sometimes dangerous, and Jews as well as other religious minorities always knew their place. Second-class citizenship of this kind would be legally unacceptable in today's true democracies, as would the periodic riots against and massacres of Jews or Christians in the medieval Islamic world.

The second-class status of minorities in the Islamic world clearly had an influence on conversion, for during the first few centuries following the Conquest, most of the Christian,

Zoroastrian, and Jewish subjects of the Islamic empires became Muslim. Given the freedom, the social, economic, and political opportunity, and the respect afforded Jews in modern-day democracies, it may be easy to overlook the relatively good position Jews and other religious minorities enjoyed under Islam.

THE TRIUMPH OF RABBINISM UNDER THE ABBASID CALIPHATE

The Jewish communities of Arabia were a very small minority of the Jewish world, and, as mentioned above, their practice of Judaism seems to have been different from the mainstream's. By the time of the Prophet's death in 632, the major center of Judaism had shifted from Palestine to Babylonia, largely because the Persian Empire was far more welcoming to Jews than the Christian Byzantine Empire. The Jewish communities of the Persian Empire were represented at the royal court by a Jew with the official title of *resh galuta,* or exilarch, meaning the "head of the exile." The Babylonian Jews had great academies of learning, primarily in the cities of Sura and Pumbeditha, not far from the future site of Baghdad. Each academy was headed by its most learned scholar, who carried the title of gaon. By virtue of their knowledge and wisdom, it was the geonim (plural of gaon) who eventually assumed the leadership of the Jewish world.

The structure and organization of the Jewish community in Babylon did not change significantly with the Islamic conquest, but its relative strength rose at a meteoric rate once the Abbasid empire established its capital in Baghdad in 762.

Baghdad, the capital of an Islamic empire stretching from the Indus River to the Atlantic Ocean, was located at the very center of the world's largest Jewish community. The roles of the exilarch and geonim, therefore, took on universal status throughout the Jewish world. The exilarch was in attendance at the court of the caliph, and the geonim sent official interpretations of Jewish law, known as *teshuvot,* to Jewish communities throughout the empire. The *teshuvot* were "responsa" (Arabic: *fatawa*) dealing with questions posed to the great sages by learned rabbis elsewhere who were, in effect, appealing to the "supreme court" of Jewish law in Babylon/Iraq. The geonim became the highest authority on Jewish law, which, like Islamic law, encompassed all aspects of life, and geonic religious authority was supreme because it was based on the knowledge and interpretation of divine law. The legal decisions of the geonim were based on the Talmud and talmudic interpretation of the Bible, and it was during this period of great Abbasid power, coinciding with the great centralization of Jewish authority in the geonim, that the Talmud and its interpretation of the Torah became the central authority for Jewish life.

The Talmud might not have attained this centrality if the status of the geonim had not been enhanced by their association with the world power and prestige of Abbasid Iraq. The capital of the empire became so important for the Jews that the great academies of Sura and Pumbeditha, though still referred to by their places of origin, eventually moved to Baghdad. The unity of the Abbasid empire allowed for the easy transportation of people, goods, capital, and ideas from the Jewish center in Baghdad to most of the Jewish world, and in fact, some 90 percent of world Jewry lived in the Islamic world at this time. They were free to govern their internal affairs with little interference from the Muslim authorities as long as they paid their taxes and acknowledged the dominion of Islam through certain behaviors, some more or less humiliating. Their Muslim masters did not much care what the Jews did as long as they kept the peace, paid their taxes, and remained in their place.

FROM GOLDEN AGE TO DECLINE

Medieval Islamic civilization developed into its most productive period between the years 900 and 1200, and Jewish civilization in the Islamic world followed suit. During this period, some of the greatest works of Jewish philosophy, grammar, law, philology, and lexicography were written, in parallel with great advances in these fields in the Islamic world. Jewish poetry in Hebrew found a renaissance during this period as well, and its meters, styles, and contents parallel those of its Muslim Arabic counterpart.

During this period Iraq began to lose political control of the empire; and perhaps not surprisingly, the Jewish leadership in Baghdad similarly lost its hegemony over most of world Jewry. The rise of Umayyad Spain and Fatimid Ifriqiya and Egypt was accompanied by the rise of the Jewish communities in these areas, and the economic and political success in these new and growing centers attracted scholars and intellectuals.

Nowhere was this more pronounced than in Spain, where Jewish civilization flourished along with the flowering of the Islamic and secular sciences. Hasdai Ibn Shaprut (d. 975), a Jew, was physician and personal adviser to the Umayyad caliphs `Abd al-Rahman III and al-Hakam II. Not only did he serve his Muslim masters excellently, he also patronized the arts and sciences among the Jews. Just as Muslim caliphs, governors, and people of high standing had their own courts in which the Islamic and secular sciences were supported and encouraged, so too did high-standing Jews and Christians support their own artists and intellectuals. This created a great flowering of culture throughout Islamic Spain, known in Arabic as al-Andalus. The relatively open society of al-Andalus was reversed and then ended by the coming of North African armies to help defend against the Spanish Christians, who were pushing the Muslims southward from their strongholds in the north. Jews were highly restricted under the Islamist Berber regimes and eventually began moving northward to newly conquered Christian areas where, for the time being, they were treated better.

The reversal of Jewish good fortune in Spain was mirrored in other parts of the Islamic world, where by the thirteenth century the open and humanistic qualities of Islamic society began to give way to a more feudalistic mentality of rigidity and control. This was a period when Islam was on the defensive. The Crusaders had invaded the Levant in 1098 and remained for two centuries. Moorish Spain was losing badly to the armies of the Reconquista, and the Normans had captured Islamic Sicily and southern Italy. European Christians were sailing across the Mediterranean to raid and plunder the North African coast. And the Mongol horde wrought destruction on the Muslim East, eventually putting an end to the Abbasid caliphate in 1258.

During this time of political and economic decline, Islam began to turn inward and, among other things, restricted the freedoms and fortunes of the minority religions living in its midst. The actual situation varied considerably from place to place, but the general trend was to enforce the restrictions of the Pact of `Umar and even, in some cases, to add to them. Jews (and Christians) were squeezed out of civil service and increasingly isolated. Some communities were forced into ghettos. In some cases, Jewish and Christian communities were massacred. As the Islamic world declined, so too did the Jewish communities within it, and Jewish intellectual, cultural, and religious creativity tended to shift toward the Jewish communities of Europe. The Islamic world was far from unified by this time, so that treatment of Jews varied. There were temporary reversals in some places. One notable instance was the Ottoman Empire in the fifteenth and sixteenth centuries, but as a whole the position of Jews continued to decline into the modern period.

THE JEWS OF CHRISTIAN EUROPE

In the early Middle Ages, no more than 10 percent of the world Jewish population lived in Europe. Because it was largely undeveloped at the time, Jews preferred .to live in more highly civilized areas. By the high Middle Ages

(1000–1300), however, the European situation had improved considerably, and the Jewish population grew accordingly. As the Islamic world declined, the Christian European world improved. The situation for the Jews in Christian Europe, however, was always precarious. Christianity claimed to be the natural successor to Judaism, and Christians thought of themselves as the "true Israel" (thus suggesting that the Jews were not). Because Christianity saw itself as superseding Judaism, the Christian self-concept required public demonstrations that Jews and Judaism were degraded and inferior. It was of great importance that Jews living among Christians occupy an obviously degraded and inferior position. The Islamic view of *dhimmi*s offers clear parallels to this, but the Christian system, on the whole, was harsher and more consistent in imposing secondary status on the Jews.

The Jewish population of Europe increased as it declined in the Islamic world, and Jews enjoyed the economic and political improvements of Europe in the high and late Middle Ages. Unlike the Islamic world, however, as Christian Europe developed economically, intellectually, and scientifically, its treatment of Jews did not improve. And unlike the Islamic world, where there was always a place for Jews in the larger society, many of the states of Christian Europe sought to rid themselves of Jews altogether. The most famous case is that of Christian Spain, whose Jews were all forcibly expelled or converted in 1492 (and its Muslims only a few short years later). But the Jews were expelled from England, France, and many of the German states as well. Luckily, when they were expelled from one location, they were able to find refuge somewhere else in Europe, but the net result was often impoverishment and tragedy.

There was considerably less unity in the Christian world than in the Islamic world, and the Jews had excellent skills that made them attractive to certain Christian rulers and kings, even as the same skills made them threatening to others. In certain exceptionally bad situations, all the Jews in some regions were massacred, as during the First Crusade in 1096 or the German Armleder massacres in 1336–39. Thus the Jews survived in Europe, but their lot was not generally good until the coming of the modern period.

4

Judaism and Modernity: Western Europe

RELIGIOUS RESPONSES TO THE ENLIGHTENMENT
AND JEWISH EMANCIPATION

By the late 1700s, the majority of the world's Jewish population lived in Christian Europe. There is no single date, however, that marks the beginning of the modern era in Europe, for modern ideas evolved over time and became influential in various parts of the continent at different periods. The great watersheds that served as precursors to modernity were the Renaissance and the Christian Reformation. Both contributed greatly to the modern concept of Enlightenment and the resulting emancipation of the Jews and other European minorities. Two Enlightenment ideas had very important consequences for the Jews of Europe. The first insisted that every man should be judged according to his own merits and not, as was previously the case, according to his family, class, or religious status. This allowed the possibility for Jews to be accepted and integrated into European society for the first time without prejudice and discrimination. The second insisted that every individual is capable of applying reason and personal judgment to decision-making and need not rely blindly on tradition. This allowed the possibility for Jews to be welcomed into European civilization without the prejudice of traditional Jew-hatred. It also encouraged Jews, like their Christian neighbors, to reevaluate the meaning of their religious tradition for the modern age.

THE EMANCIPATION OF THE JEWS

European social philosophers took the new idea of universal laws in the physical sciences and began to apply it to the human condition. Since all members of any species of animals have the same environmental requirements to thrive, some asked, why should one class of humans have privileges that are denied to others? Until the modern period, family heritage, social class, and religious beliefs largely determined the physical happiness of Europeans. What moral argument could support the privileges of the nobility, for example, while peasants were deprived of many of the necessities for a proper civilized life? Every European state had its established church, and the adherents of other faiths, including Christian minority faiths, were denied equal status. The path to modernity meant limiting the privileges of the nobility, improving the condition of the peasants, breaking down regional separatism, and reducing the power of the established churches and their clergy. When equal rights and responsibilities were eventually extended to people of various class and religious backgrounds, Europe's Jews were among those emancipated, and they were allowed to take their place alongside Christians.

The process of emancipation was highly uneven, however. In many places Jews were not granted equal status until the twentieth century. In some, they were never accepted as equals; and in others, their emancipation was entirely reversed and worse, when millions were murdered during the Holocaust. Despite this unevenness, however, the emancipation forever altered the status of Jews in the West because it proved that, according to pure reason, there was no acceptable justification for denying them the rights and responsibilities of citizenship in the nations within which they lived.

Jews proved the correctness of this truth, for wherever they were allowed to participate in the same way as other citizens, they contributed far more to the benefit and welfare of their host countries than would be expected from their small numbers. In science, commerce, education, the arts, and even in politics, Jews demonstrated both an ability and a great yearning to advance personally and contribute to the welfare of the state as a whole. This sometimes unleashed a backlash among those who were less successful or who felt threatened by the quick and noticeable advance of the Jews, especially when one keeps in mind the many centuries during which anti-Jewish prejudice had become deeply ingrained in European culture and society.

JEWISH IDENTITY AND THE MODERN NATION-STATE

Without the creation of the modern nation-state, the Jews of Europe would perhaps never have been emancipated. Modern national identity successfully bridged the religious differences that had nearly crippled Europe for centuries with bloody wars and debilitating political and economic battles. The modern, secular nation-state that emerged toward the end of the eighteenth century was not concerned with the religious beliefs or practices of its citizens. Rather, it concerned itself with their willingness to contribute to the national cause through military and civic service, paying taxes, and generally working for the good of the nation.

Emancipation and integration into the new national identities of European society had a major effect on the development of Judaism, for Jews inevitably applied the ideas of modern Europe to their religious law, ritual, philosophy, ethics, and daily practice. The result was both a reduction in the degree of religious influence on their behavior and an increase in factionalism and divisions as they responded to the challenges of modernity.

JEWISH RESPONSES TO MODERNITY IN THE WEST

Jewish emancipation began in Western Europe. For the first time in thousands of years, Jews found themselves free of restrictive laws. They could live outside a ghetto, send their children to public schools, learn any craft or trade, employ Christians, and dress the same as other Europeans; they were not restricted to their homes on Sunday mornings and Christian holidays, and were allowed to go to public parks and places of amusement. For many, this was an invitation to abandon their Jewish identity and assimilate into the secular nation-state or even to convert to Christianity. The traditional Judaism that had been the basis of their culture for centuries had evolved in a different time and place, and it seemed quite at odds with the aesthetics, sensibilities, and ethics of modern Europe. One response to what appeared suddenly as a major incongruity between the old religious culture and the attraction of modern European culture was to modernize or reform Judaism to make it more compatible with the modern age. This was undertaken by a wide and varied group of rabbis and laity who are sometimes referred to as the early "reformers."

Reform Judaism

Some of the reformers were instrumental in developing what is today called Reform or Progressive Judaism. The earliest impulse to reform Jewish practice was in the area of prayer. Traditional Jewish prayer services had become longer and more complicated over the centuries, and the style, language, and musicality of the service had become exceptionally unappealing to the modern European aesthetic that was so attractive to Westernizing Jews. The earliest reformers began by reforming the prayer service to bring it into line with Western sensibilities. They also began to subject the study of Judaism to the same rigorous methods employed by other sciences. Other Jews reexamined the philosophical underpinnings of Judaism, and developed modern approaches and understandings of God, Torah, the role of the people of Israel in the world, and reward and punishment at the End of Time.

The new students of Judaism and the ideological reformers agreed that Judaism had never been static but was an evolving tradition. Judaism and Jewish practice had evolved over the millennia from the giving of the Torah on Mount Sinai through the destruction of the Temples and the exile, the medieval era, and up to the modern period. From Temple sacrifice to synagogue prayer, and from priestly to rabbinic leadership and practice, Judaism was always adapting in order to meet the religious, intellectual, and cultural needs of the Jewish people. The reformers considered it natural, therefore, that Judaism should continue to evolve, for innovation had always been very much a part of it.

As one of their major innovations, the reformers reexamined the place and meaning of the divine commandments. The Reform movement made a distinction between ritual commandments and moral-ethical commandments. Its exponents argued that the ritual commandments, such as the laws governing which foods are permissible, the use of Hebrew prayer, and other forms of ritual practice, were given to create a cohesive people and to separate it from a world populated entirely by idolaters. However, since the Western world was now essentially monotheistic, what with Christianity and Islam having joined Judaism as universal religions, there was far less of a need to keep the particularistic rituals that set Jews apart from other civilized peoples. The more important commandments, then, were those that required moral-ethical behaviors. By eliminating the kosher food laws, Sabbath restrictions, and other ritualistic commandments, while retaining the major theological distinctions, Reform Judaism lessened the cultural distance between Jews and other Europeans, enabling them to integrate completely into the greater Western world while remaining Jewish.

As part of this process, the reformers abandoned the idea that the Jews constituted a separate nation and instead began to conceive of Judaism as a religious denomination on the Christian model. Thus the Jews of France, for example, could now consider themselves entirely French from the national perspective, while practicing their own distinct religion, just as French Catholics and Protestants practiced different religions but were, in all other respects, national brethren.

Reform Judaism was a force of some importance in Europe but was never adopted by most of the continent's Jews. In the United States, however, it grew rapidly and became a powerful religious movement. One of its American hallmarks was the emphasis that every individual Jew, rather than merely obeying the dictates of his rabbi, had the right and the obligation to learn Bible and tradition and then make his own decisions about Jewish practice and observance based on his own knowledge. The result of this "democratization" of Judaism was to encourage a great variety of religious practices. Many Reform Jews chose to pray in English rather than in Hebrew and to observe only a very few commandments.

Orthodox Judaism

The reformers of the early nineteenth century were a small minority of Europe's Jews. Many others abandoned their heritage entirely, seeking to assimilate into the modern European nation-state and assume a national identity to replace their Jewish identity. Both the reformers and the assimilationists or secularists were viewed with great alarm by those who believed that the modernists failed God by refusing to punctiliously observe the Torah's commandments. They sought, in the first instance, to challenge what they perceived as the watering down of the commandments by emphasizing the importance of strict adherence to Jewish law and ritual. As a reaction to the modernizing trends, groups of Jews began to close themselves off from the danger modernity posed to group coherence and continuity by forming tightly knit communities that rejected its temptations. Some argued that the privileges offered by emancipation should be rejected. Others insisted on the complete social and cultural segregation of Jews from modern society. All together, these groups formed what is today called Orthodox Judaism. The Orthodox imposed restrictions on social and cultural interaction with non-Jews that were far more stringent than anything known to the Judaism of the ancient and medieval worlds. The slightest tampering with tradition was condemned, and new restrictions were enacted in order to protect Jews from the temptations of modernity, thereby moving Orthodox Judaism in the opposite direction of secularization or Reform Judaism.

But Orthodoxy should not be caricatured or oversimplified as representing a rejection of acculturation in toto: while resisting change in religious thought and practice, the Orthodox in Germany, for example (self-described as "Neo-

Orthodox"), embraced Westernization in dress, language, and culture. And over time, in Western Europe and particularly in the United States, significant elements within the Orthodox movement sought to balance their allegiance to Jewish traditionalism and separatism with greater participation in the national life and the broad culture of modernity. This branch of Orthodoxy, currently experiencing strong growth in the American Jewish community, is called "Modern Orthodoxy," and its acculturated adherents believe in combining commitment to the tenets of Orthodox Judaism and learnedness in Scripture with worldly knowledge and participation in the national cultural, social, and political life. This branch of Orthodoxy is perhaps best represented by Yeshiva University, founded in 1928 to train a new type of Orthodox rabbi, one capable of integrating the worlds of Orthodoxy and contemporary American thought and life.

Conservative Judaism

Conservative Judaism has taken a middle path between Reform and Orthodox Judaism. The founders of Conservative Judaism agreed with the reformers that the entire history of Judaism was one of change and development; Jews and Judaism had always responded creatively to the challenges of history. However, they disagreed with the more radical reformers about how far it was possible to go in allowing the modernization of Judaism. Three areas stand out as sacred in the Conservative position on Jewish observance: devotion to the Hebrew language in prayer services and other ritual activities, observance of the dietary laws (*kashrut*), and traditional Sabbath observance. Conservative Judaism, like Orthodox Judaism and contrary to Reform, insists on strict observance of the ritual commandments of Judaism, but it is more lenient in its interpretation of how to do so. Thus, Conservative Jews are permitted to eat some foods that are forbidden to Orthodox Jews, while their Sabbath observance is far more observant than that of Reform.

The overwhelming majority of practicing Jews in the United States is almost equally divided between adherents of Reform and Conservative practice. Orthodox Judaism represents a strong and influential but small minority. In the State of Israel, however, the overwhelming majority of practicing Jews are Orthodox, with Conservative and Reform Jews a very small but growing minority. About half the Jewish population of the United States is unaffiliated with any religious movement. They are often called "secular" Jews, meaning that they retain a feeling of Jewish identity but engage in little or no religious practice, such as prayer or holiday observance. In Israel, much more than half the Jewish population is secular. Although the majority of religiously practicing Jews in Israel is Orthodox, they make up only about 20 percent of the total Jewish population.

5

Judaism and Modernity: Eastern Europe

JEWISH NATIONALISM

Until the modern period, Jewish identity was based on religious nationhood. This sense of nationhood was not that of modern nationalism as defined by the modern nation-state, but rather a feeling of identity and camaraderie with all Jews anywhere in the world. Whether in Baghdad, Jerusalem, or Paris, Jews considered themselves to be different from their non-Jewish neighbors, and were so considered by the non-Jews among whom they lived. What bound Jews together, whether they lived in China, Yemen, Morocco, or Poland, was a common religious belief and practice, and a common way of conducting their daily lives, whatever language they spoke and whatever regional variations were reflected in their local cultures.

This sense of religious nationhood is closer to the Islamic *umma* than the Christian fellowship, because the religious precepts of Judaism go far beyond matters of acceptable belief. The position of Jews as second-class citizens wherever they lived helped to form a powerful universal identity over the centuries and millennia, so that the sense of Jewish nationhood may surpass even that of Islam, although such an observation would be impossible to prove. Suffice it to say here that Jewish identity remains a powerful force, even among Jews who define themselves as agnostic or atheist. Even atheism does not invalidate a person's Jewish identity according to Jewish law.

EMERGING EASTERN EUROPEAN NATIONALISMS AND JEWISH EXCLUSION

Prior to the modern period, a person's identity was based primarily on class, religion, gender, and region. With the development of the modern nation-state, religion became, theoretically, only a private matter. The modern nation-state became the primary locus of identity. Although the Jews of Western Europe were largely included in the transition from premodern to modern determinations of identity, in Eastern Europe, where the overwhelming majority of Jews lived in the nineteenth century, Jews were not emancipated. Particularly in the Russian Empire, the Jews suffered even more than other national and ethnic peoples under the yoke of the czar. Toward the end of the nineteenth century many of the ethnic peoples living in the Russian Empire attempted to free themselves from czarist rule and form modern nation-states. In contrast with the situation in Western Europe, however, the Jews of Eastern Europe were not accepted as participating members of the newly evolving nations. Whether in Poland, Ukraine, Romania, or Russia, and even where they spoke and dressed like the local people, they were excluded from the national liberation movements. Not only did they suffer from pogroms or massacres under the czar, but they were afforded the same treatment by the activists in the national liberation movements.

Eastern European Jews responded to their miserable life in the nineteenth and early twentieth centuries in a number of ways. Many tried to escape by emigrating to Western Europe and the Americas, and well over a million came to the United States between 1880 and 1920. Others hoped to find solace and even redemption by delving ever more deeply into Judaism. An important portion of Eastern European Jews became active in universalistic political movements that hoped to end prejudice and inequality by creating a world of economic and social equality through socialism or communism. Another substantial segment of Eastern European Jewry responded to their misery, including their rejection by the national liberation movements, by agreeing that the peculiar nature of Jewish nationhood prevented their integration into the modern European nation-state.

Wherever they were, these Jewish nationalists concluded, they were rejected as Jews. Even secular Jews who had completely abandoned religion were excluded from the nationalist liberation movements because of their Jewish identity. What exactly was it about their identity that made them unfit for the nationalist movements? Certainly not religion, for many of the anti-Jewish nationalist leaders were also secularists. Some of Eastern Europe's Jews began to feel, quite logically, that their rejection was based, not on their *religious* identity, but on their *national* identity. Their own personal experience showed them that even overcoming religious prejudice did not enable Jews to be accepted fully as people. Moses Hess, one of the earliest Jewish nationalists, concluded:

"We shall always remain strangers among the nations. . . . Religious fanaticism may cease to cause hatred of the Jews in the more culturally advanced countries; but despite enlightenment and emancipation, the Jew in exile who denies his nationality will never earn the respect of the nations among whom he dwells."[1]

JEWISH NATIONALISM AND ZIONISM

There was no hope for the Jews to join the nationalist movements of Eastern Europe, and they were suffering heavily from the violence of robbery, rape, and even massacres at the hands of their peasant neighbors and even the regional and national governments that should have protected them. Jewish nationalists therefore called for the creation of a Jewish nation where, under their own government and police force, they would no longer be victimized by the hatred and prejudice of other religions and nationalities. Long before the Holocaust, Jewish nationalists came to the logical conclusion, given their own historical experience, that living at the mercy of peoples who hated them was no longer tenable. In the modern period, many national peoples were ridding themselves of the yoke of foreign control by forming their own

---

[1] Quoted in Arthur Hertzberg, *The Zionist Idea* (New York: Atheneum, 1959), p. 121.

nation-states where they could decide their own destiny. This would also be possible for the Jews, they declared, because Jews, too, made up a national people.

The European theorists of nationalism at the time defined so-called national peoples as groups sharing a common history, language, land, and vision. Jewish nationalists claimed that the Jews had all these criteria of nationhood. Their common history was well known and obvious, and their common language was the ancient tongue of Hebrew, learned by Jews throughout the world. But not all Jews had the same vision. Many were piously awaiting the coming of the Messiah; others sought to modernize Judaism, while still others wished to secularize and assimilate. The nationalists aspired to a Jewish state. An additional problem was the one of a common land, for Jews had been living all over the world for many centuries and had not controlled their own political destiny for nearly two millennia. Some Jewish nationalists were content to build a Jewish nation-state anywhere, so long as the land involved became an exclusively Jewish possession. Most of the nationalists, however, insisted that there was only one land that truly qualified as a Jewish national territory, and this was the land that had been settled, farmed, governed, and defended by Jews for over a thousand years: the Land of Israel. The Jewish nationalist movement became the Zionist movement, so named because of its insistence that only Zion, one of the biblical names for the ancient Jewish capital of Jerusalem and therefore symbolic of the whole Land of Israel, must be the location for the rebirth of the Jewish people in a modern nation-state.

Zionists remained a minority movement among the Jewish people until the Holocaust, when those who hated the Jews perpetrated a nearly successful genocide, and most of Europe simply stood by without interfering. The fact of world complicity through indifference, if not direct involvement, in the destruction of European Jewry convinced the Jewish people, with only a very few exceptions, to support the establishment of a modern Jewish state in the Land of Israel. There Jews would finally be able to govern and defend themselves, no longer at the mercy of peoples that did not care for their welfare, or that sought to oppress or destroy them.

ZIONIST VIEWS OF ARABS

Any discussion of Zionism would be incomplete if it did not treat the problem of the indigenous Arab population already living in what Jews call the Land of Israel, also known as Palestine. Mostly, the Zionists were so desperate to find a solution for the misery of Jewish life in nineteenth- and early twentieth-century Eastern Europe that they tried to ignore the very serious problem of non-Jews living in the land where they wished to create a Jewish state. The Arabs, of course, resented the large immigration of Jews and their quick domination of the local economy of Palestine, and many reacted actively and violently in attempting to prevent further immigration. This was countered by Jewish force, which further heightened the tension. The history of the conflict is much too complicated to examine in detail here, and Jews and Arabs have very different positions on this issue. Suffice it so say

here that the Zionists did not agree among themselves about
how to live side by side with Arabs within or without the
Jewish state, and their views ranged widely. Some called for
the expulsion of all Arabs from what they wanted to be an
exclusively Jewish state. Others insisted on a binational state.
Still others felt that a Jewish state could offer absolute and
complete equality to all its citizens, regardless of their religious, ethnic, or cultural heritage. The outbreak of violence
and, eventually, war complicated the situation between Jews
and Arabs in Palestine and radicalized the positions of both
sides, leading to subsequent wars and political attempts to
resolve the conflict. Most Jews today believe that history has
proven that only a modern nation-state governed and
defended by Jews can guarantee the security of the Jewish
people.

JEWISH VIEWS OF ARABS AND MUSLIMS

What does Judaism teach about Arabs and Muslims and
about living together in the modern Middle East? It must be
noted, first of all, that the Bible and Talmud, the most sacred
books of Judaism, were collected and canonized before the
birth of Muhammad, so there is no reference in them to
Muslims. As noted in chapters 1 and 3, the Hebrew Bible
records the close kinship relationship between Israelites and
ethnic Arabs through their common father, Abraham, but
there seems to have been relatively little direct and ongoing
contact between the two groups in the biblical period. One
major exception is the story of Moses, who married the

daughter of a wise Midianite Arab pagan priest called Yitro (Jethro) in Hebrew, but whose Arabic name was probably Watru. Jethro assisted Moses and helped him establish a proper system of government for the Israelites during their period of wandering in the desert (Exodus 18). In the biblical Book of Nehemiah (2:19, 6:1–6), an Arab named Geshem (Arabic: Gashmu) tries to prevent the Judeans from returning and rebuilding Jerusalem, despite their having received the permission of the Persian king. The Jewish Hasmonean kings had good relations for a time with the Arab civilization of the Nabateans, whose capital was Petra in today's kingdom of Jordan. The Talmud refers occasionally to Arabs along with other ethnic peoples, but does not have much to say about them, either negatively or positively.

The view of Islam held by Jews living under Muslim domination tended to reflect the treatment they received at the hands of their Muslim masters. Mostly, they wrote about other things. Interestingly, the early Zionists were very favorably inclined toward Arab culture and the generally neutral treatment Jews had received under Islamic rule. Partly in response to the terrible violence the Jews of Eastern Europe were suffering at the hands of their Christian neighbors, the Zionists looked toward Arab and Islamic culture and religion as an ideal civilization that could tolerate the existence of a Jewish homeland or state within it. The conflict and eventual violence between Jews and Arabs in British Mandate Palestine ended this outlook, however, and the intractable conflict that has plagued Jews and Arabs in the Middle East ever since has contributed to prejudicial attitudes on both sides. It should be noted, however, that Jewish religious texts from the Bible onward have nothing particularly negative to say about Arabic culture or Islamic religion. They remain quite neutral. Judaism, therefore, has no particular teaching regarding either Arabs or Muslims that might differentiate them from any other human population. As should be expected, Judaism does not regard Christianity and Islam as its religious equals, but neither does Judaism suggest that good and moral Christians and Muslims would be excluded from entering heaven in the world-to-come. Current negative attitudes toward Arabs and Islam in modern Israel are a direct result of the many wars and terrible violence that Israeli Jews have endured for the past century. This is not to suggest, of course, that Palestinian Arabs have not also suffered terribly from these wars and other acts of violence. Israeli prejudice against Arabs and Islam is likely to change within a generation or two if and when a real and just peace effectively ends the overwhelming fear and anger that most Israelis have, whether considered justifiable or not, toward their Arab Muslim neighbors.

THE HOLOCAUST

The Holocaust left an indelible mark on the soul of the Jewish people. Although there were attempted genocides of other peoples before World War II, and further attempts since, never in the history of humankind were such careful planning, huge expenditure of resources, and monumental human effort devoted to the destruction of a single group of humans. Jews then and now have responded to the Holocaust in a variety of ways. Some have abandoned any religious commitment, maintaining that the destruction of European Jewry proves that God abandoned the Jewish people. Conversely, others have become more pious and committed as a result of the horrors of the Holocaust. In secular terms, the memory of the enormity serves to strengthen a sense of peoplehood among Jews and underscores their near universal support for a secure State of Israel.

Jews have also responded differently to the Holocaust in terms of their relations with the non-Jewish world. Some are determined to work diligently to prevent genocidal hatred and violence from ever again being directed at any group of human beings. They argue that because Jews were victims of the most horrendous and unprecedented crime in history, they have the awesome responsibility to help ensure that no such act ever again occurs.

Another response to the Holocaust has been to turn away from the world and concentrate only on Jewish survival. The exponents of this view argue that as innocent victims of the most horrendous crime in human history, and as sufferers of indescribable horrors inflicted upon them by some of the world's nations while the others stood by without interfering, the Jews owe the world nothing. Many Jews regard the leaders of the Arabs of Palestine in the 1930s and 1940s as guilty of complicity in the Holocaust. The mufti Hajj Amin al-Husseini, for example, long-time leader of Arab nationalism in Palestine, collaborated with Nazi Germany as one of its chief propagandists to the Arabs. He recruited and organized

Muslim volunteers for the Nazi cause, supporting and aiding the Nazi program for the extermination of the Jewish people. Therefore, according to this position, Palestinians and Muslims cannot claim that they had nothing to do with the Holocaust.

The Holocaust has cast a certain shadow over the relations between Jews and Arabs because Jews tend to see Arabs as yet another group that stood by and allowed the destruction of European Jewry. Conversely, Arabs tend to consider themselves innocent of the Holocaust, which they claim was purely a European phenomenon. Given the position of the Muslim mufti, al-Husseini, along with other Muslim religious leaders who acquiesced or even sometime collaborated with Nazi Germany and its designs in the Middle East, the position of Islam is sometimes questioned by Jews. Muslims, on the other hand, tend to consider the Holocaust a purely European and Christian phenomenon with which they had absolutely nothing to do. In their view, the Palestinians living in Israel and Palestine, and more so those who were exiled from the region, have been made to bear the punishment for crimes against the Jews perpetrated by Europeans and Christians. The pain of victimization, accusation, and blame is deep and not easily forgotten. It may be transcended in part through honest dialogue and discussion, but people can and must learn to live together even when there cannot be a full understanding between them.

THE STATE OF ISRAEL

The State of Israel was established in 1948, only three short years after the end of the Holocaust, and it was established through war and blood. As mentioned previously, few Jews today do not completely support the right of Jews to have a Jewish state. The religious teachings of the Bible and the Talmud, however, have been interpreted both in favor of and against the establishment of a modern Jewish state. The argumentation of both positions is complex and sometimes obscure, but from a religious perspective the issues revolve around the idea of the messiah.

After the destruction of the Second Temple and the dispersion of Jews by the Romans in its aftermath, the rabbis came to the conclusion that the Jewish people were destined by God to remain in exile until the coming of the Messiah. They taught that it was no longer possible or even desirable for Jews to control their political destiny, and this would continue to be so until the Messiah came and redeemed not only the Jews but the entire world. The Zionist movement, on the other hand, was begun and organized almost entirely by people who did not adhere to the theological and religious principles of traditional Judaism. They neither agreed with the rabbis nor sought their guidance. On the contrary, they called for the establishment of a modern, secular state in which Jews would be safe from persecution and oppression and the constant fear of violence. As a result, Jewish religious leaders opposed the Zionists from the outset. The religious opposition to Zionism was partially a response to previous Jewish attempts to gain political independence in ancient times and in the medieval ages. These attempts had all ended in failure and the subsequent destruction of large Jewish populations. The lesson Jewish religious leaders took from these disasters was that humans must wait until God decided that the time for redemption had come. According to their understanding, only God can decide when it is time for redemption. The attempt to "force the hand of God" by working through political channels to create a Jewish state would only bring the divine wrath and another horrible destruction. The Zionists therefore remained almost exclusively secularists.

By the 1930s, however, a new religious interpretation of Zionism began to evolve with the thinking of Rabbi Abraham Isaac Kook, an influential leader of the Jewish community in Palestine.[2] He suggested that the secular Zionists were not forcing the hand of God, but were actually, if inadvertently, carrying out God's divine plan by creating a Jewish state, thereby beginning the process of redemption. According to Kook, God's will was and is inscrutable, but the signs suggested that the final redemption was near at hand. Thus religious Jews were obligated to assist the Zionists, or at least not to condemn them for their work in building up the Land of Israel.

The horror of the Holocaust was interpreted by some anti-Zionist Orthodox Jews as a terrible punishment for attempting to force the hand of God. For most others, however, whether Orthodox, Conservative, Reform, or secular, the

---

[2] Ibid., pp. 416–431.

Holocaust confirmed the belief that only a Jewish state could protect the world's Jews from some future disaster.

Israel's victories in the War of Independence in 1948 and, even more so, in the 1967 war were interpreted by many Orthodox Jews as divine signs that the redemption was finally at hand. As a result, Orthodox Judaism became more and more Zionist during the second half of the twentieth century, for it tended to place Israel fully within the process of reaching a final redemption that was near at hand. Zionism itself, however, has undergone many changes and developments. While some Zionists continue to call for Jewish political control over all of the biblical Land of Israel, the overwhelming majority are moving increasingly toward accepting a much smaller state that is in close and cooperative relationship with its Arab and Muslim neighbors.

Postmodern Judaisms

The current age is increasingly referred to as "postmodern." The connotations of the term are numerous, but for Judaism and Jewish practice and ideas, it means that Jewish living and thought have begun to transcend the boundaries of modern thinking. There are "postdenominational" forms of Judaism that incorporate aspects of Jewish life deriving from sources as varied as strict Orthodoxy and liberal Reform, and even movements that combine elements of Judaism with Buddhist or native American religious traditions. There are also Jewish "post-Zionists" who support the State of Israel but call for far more arabized or even partially islamized forms of national culture. What is most important to remember is that although most Jews feel very closely connected to other members of their religious-national civilization and culture, there are a wide variety of expressions of Judaism and Jewish culture. Some are religious, and some secular, but all relate to the peoplehood or nation of Jews as a unity.

Part II
God, Torah, and Israel

Judaism and the Jewish people, including Jews who do not define themselves as believers or practice the religious traditions, may be fully understood only in relation to God and Torah and the history of the relationship between them. It is therefore common when examining Judaism to organize thinking about it in terms of God, Torah, and Israel.

6

God

In every religious civilization, the details of the human understanding of God vary in different eras and schools of thought. However, despite this necessary variety, every religion nevertheless retains a distinctive central view of God around which its institutions and ideas revolve. In Judaism, it is God's unity and singularity, God's role as creator and therefore "owner" or controller of the universe, and God's role as the divine lawgiver.

The Bible and later Jewish literature are absolute in their insistence that God is One and there is no other (e.g., Deuteronomy 6:4, Isaiah 45:21, 46:9). Acceptance of a multitude of gods (polytheism) or worship of images (idolatry) is absolutely forbidden throughout the Bible, the Talmud, and all subsequent Jewish writings. Such biblical passages as the rhetorical question in Exodus 15:11, "Who is like You, O Lord, among the gods?" do not imply that the Israelites assumed that other gods existed. On the contrary, the question underscores the absurdity of worshiping pagan images.

GOD AS DEPICTED IN THE BIBLE

God is often described in human terms, with "hands" or "eyes," and can "hear" the cries of those who call out to Him, in contradistinction to idols, all of which are devoid of life. But these attributes are understood metaphorically. The Bible contains many anthropomorphisms, or descriptions of God in terms that are humanlike. These were intended to express abstract ideas in concrete rather than obscure philosophical ways. They do not mean that God *has* hands, eyes, or ears. As the Talmud points out, the "Torah speaks in human language" so that we humans can begin to understand, in our own imperfect way, what is truly beyond human comprehension.[1] Maimonides, the great Jewish thinker and philosopher who lived in Islamic Spain and Egypt, pointed out that God is beyond depiction and therefore has no descriptive attributes, because every attempt to do so by humans only applies limitations to God. The attributes applied to God in the Bible, therefore, actually represent our own human emotions evoked by our experience of God's existence. They cannot characterize God's actual attributes; these are truly beyond our ability to describe.[2]

GOD AS CREATOR

Because God created the world, established its natural laws, and gave it its order (Jeremiah 33:25), God transcends the world of nature. God is eternal. All else must perish, but God preceded the universe and will outlive it (Isaiah 40:6–8, 44:6; Psalm 90:2). Since the entire cosmos is the work of God, the

---

[1] Anthropomorphic expressions in the Qur'an were also a major problem until al-Ash`ari (d. 935) developed a formula known as *bila kayf* ("without modality") to alleviate it.

[2] *Guide for the Perplexed* 2:54.

beauty and awesome majesty of nature are a declaration of God's glory, and thus nature itself is depicted as praising God (Psalm 19:2, 13 ff.). All things belong to God, and God is the Lord of all (1 Chronicles 29:11–12). The very last act of divine creation was the conscious cessation of creation on the seventh day (Genesis 2:1–3). This was the origin of the centrality of the Sabbath, which, as creative pause, brings rest and refreshment to the world.

Biblical expressions of God always represent the historical reality of the ancient world, in which the people of Israel alone recognized God's oneness and unity. With the possible brief exception of the Egyptian pharaoh Akhenaton, for the entire biblical period stretching more than a thousand years, only Israel recognized true monotheism. No other people on earth realized the truth of God's unity and remained loyal to that truth. The Bible therefore directs its message almost exclusively to Israel, for there was no other people that could effectively understand and respond to it. This is sometimes seen as exclusivist, since God is portrayed in the Bible as designating Israel to be God's "treasured people" (`am segullah). This approach should not be surprising, given the historical reality of the period. Because of the historical context, idolatry is not necessarily regarded as a sin for non-Israelite peoples (Deuteronomy 4:19) since it was the reality of human existence apart from Israel. The people of Israel, however, are warned never to succumb to its temptation.

Therefore, just as the Bible depicts Israel having been "chosen" by God to be given the Torah, so too must Israel forever be a "choosing people" that remains loyal to the divine commandments despite the many temptations represented by the surrounding human civilizations. Jews, like all humans, however, are weak and succumb to temptation. The Bible depicts Israel as having failed to live up to the demands of the Torah, for which it was always punished. Other peoples were not punished for the same infractions, but because Israel had the Torah it was obligated to live it fully. But like all other mortals, Jews are human and prone to error. The Bible therefore depicts a long cyclical history of Jewish failure to live up to the divine command. Failure brings divine punishment, followed by Israel's repentance, to which God responds with love and mercy. But being human, Israel eventually errs again. This is a major theme in the historical theology of the Jewish people. Yet the fulfillment of the divine purpose is never in doubt. The people of Israel will not perish (Jeremiah 31:26–27). It will, according to Jewish theology, be restored to complete faithfulness, and in its final redemption at the End of Days it will bring salvation to the whole earth by leading everyone to God (Jeremiah 3:17–18). Until that time, however, Israel will remain God's witness (Isaiah 44:8) and will continue to suffer whenever it errs.

GOD AS LAWGIVER

God is the divine lawgiver. The covenant at Sinai binds all Jews to observe the law God gave. The rabbis of the Talmud counted 613 divine commandments stated explicitly in the Torah, meaning the first five books of the Bible: 248 positive commandments (obligations to do certain things) and 365 negative commandments (obligations *not* to do certain things). These commandments are better understood as rules of behavior than as "laws" in the Western legal sense of the term, because they include rules about human moral and ethical behavior and religious ritual as well as what we today would call civil and criminal law. They might best be thought of as rules by which a civilized people should live, and there is no separation into the Western categories of religious, social, and criminal behavior. So, for example, in the brief list of behavioral rules found in the thirty-seven verses of Leviticus chapter 19, all of the following may be found: honor your mother and father (v. 3), observe the Sabbath (v. 3), do not make idols (v. 4), offer sacrifices to God properly (vv. 5–8), allow the poor and the non-Israelite stranger to gather the dropped produce in your fields after your first harvest and leave the corners of your fields unharvested for them (vv. 9–10), do not steal or lie to one another (v. 11), do not swear falsely by God's name (v. 12), do not defraud your neighbor (v. 13), do not hold back from paying your workers their wages daily (v. 13), do not insult the deaf or place a stumbling block before the blind (v. 14), do not favor either the rich or the poor when rendering judgments in court (v. 15), do not take vengeance against your neighbor (v. 18), love your neighbor as yourself (v. 18).

God commands all these things to the Jewish people. Even when not living in their own country and without a police force and judiciary to enforce the law, the Jewish people has felt itself obligated to live out the divine commandments at all times and in all places. God is the divine lawgiver. Because of our human weakness, God would be justified in exacting terrible punishment against us for our many sins. But God is also merciful and forgiving for our all-too-human shortcomings. Thus, God is depicted in the Bible as being strict in judgment but also greatly merciful and loving. The Hebrew words for God's biblical attributes of justice and mercy are *din* and *rahamim*, which correspond to the similar terms in Arabic: *din* as in *yawm al-din*, or Day of Judgment, and *Rahman* ("Mercy"), one of the ninety-nine names of God found in the Qur'an. The complex combination of divine justice and mercy is expressed in God's words to Moses: "The Lord passed before him and proclaimed, 'The Lord, the Lord, God merciful and gracious, slow to anger, and abounding in steadfast love and faithfulness, keeping steadfast love for thousands, forgiving iniquity and transgression and sin, but who will by no means clear the guilty'" (Exodus 34:6–7).

While the Bible requires the Jews to obey a great number of commandments, non-Jews are required to observe only seven basic laws. These are derived from the story of Noah and the Flood, and are called the Noahide Commandments.[3] They include prohibitions of robbery, murder, adultery, and cruelty (expressed as not eating the flesh of a living animal), and a requirement to establish courts of justice.

God the lawgiver articulates the divine requirement to live according to moral-ethical rules. However, while God repeatedly warns that obedience to the divine commandments is absolutely necessary, blind obedience without attention to the spiritual and moral-ethical underpinnings of the com-

---

[3] They are listed in the Talmud, Sanhedrin 56a.

mandments is also unacceptable. The hypocrisy of obeying the letter of the law while transgressing its purpose is not sufficient in Judaism. Thus the biblical prophets said in the name of God: "I cannot endure iniquity along with solemn assembly" (Isaiah 1:13); "God has told you, O human, what is good and what the Lord requires of you: to do justice, to love loving-kindness, and to walk humbly with your God" (Micah 6:8); "Learn to do good; seek justice, correct oppression; defend the fatherless, plead for the widow" (Isaiah 1:17). The underlying motive of the commandments is to purify and elevate humankind (Psalm 119:29, 40, 68).

THE PROBLEMS OF EVIL AND FREE WILL

The problem of evil is raised in the Bible, and no simple answer is given. It should be noted, first of all, that Judaism not only allows but also encourages difficult questions and even challenges to God. Abraham challenged the divine justice with his words, "Shall not the Judge of all the earth do right?" (Genesis 18:25). The later prophets ask, "Why does the way of the wicked prosper? Why do the treacherous thrive?" (Jeremiah 12:1), and the Book of Job concentrates entirely on the problem of evil. The biblical answer is not simple. It points out the limitations of human understanding of the workings of the world. While human life is short, history is extremely long, so the human ability to understand the deep meaning and function of God's universe is fragmentary at best. "Just as the heavens are higher than the earth, so are My ways higher than your ways, and My thoughts than your thoughts" (Isaiah 55:9). On the other hand, the Psalms teach, "Though the wicked sprout like grass and all evildoers flourish, they are doomed to destruction forever" (Psalm 92:8–10). Exactly how this destruction works itself out remains a mystery according to Judaism, but humans are not forbidden to attempt to understand it.

If God is the creator of the universe and all that fills it, then is not God's power limited by the fact that humans are free to resist the divine will? God commands obedience (Deuteronomy 30:16), but true obedience is impossible without free will. Therefore, God may be said to have voluntarily established a kind of divine self-restriction to allow humans the freedom to choose between good and evil. In the Talmud the rabbis attempt to explain the divine self-limitation: "Everything is in the power of heaven except for the reverence of heaven" (Berakhot 33b).

Jewish religious literature is familiar with the story of God's punishment of an angel who refused to respect the authority of God's creation in the first Adam (see in the Qur'an, Al-A`raf 7:11–18, Al-Hijr 15:26–43, Al-Isra' 17:61–63). According to Jewish versions found in the Midrash and even earlier in 2 Enoch 29:4 and 5, the fall of Satan was caused by his jealousy of Adam and, according to some versions, even of God. As a result Satan was flung down from heaven, after which he became the source of humankind's tendency toward sin.

In later Jewish thinking, God's omnipresence in the universe is depicted as God *being* the universe. But God's *being* the universe did not allow room for the world to exist as a system and for humankind to function in complete freedom. God therefore contracted, thereby allowing the universe to function, and in doing so allowed also for imperfection and evil to develop. This imperfection and potential for evil are the necessary results of exercising human freedom. There is no single answer in Judaism to the problem of evil, and the variety of responses has resulted in a continuing discussion to this day. Whatever one's personal response to the problem, the Jew is never absolved from the responsibility not only to strive for the good, but also to hinder evil (Leviticus 19:17).

GOD AND HUMANITY

The relationship between God and humanity is exemplified by the covenant between God and Israel. Even though Israel cannot always live up to the letter of the divine commandments and is punished accordingly, the covenant or relationship never ends. God's loving-kindness or grace governs the divine side of the relationship, while human love and devotion to God govern the human side. Twice every day, the Jew recites the witnessing affirmation: "Hear, O Israel, the Lord God is One!" This affirmation continues with the following command: "And you shall love the Lord your God with all your heart, and with all your soul, and with all your might" (Deuteronomy 6:4–5). This daily statement is one of complete surrender to the divine will, corresponding to the Islamic understanding of *Islam.* Jewish love of God does not mean that Jews are forbidden to question God's acts and the ways of the universe. In Judaism, questioning God is neither forbidden nor rebuked. In the biblical Book of Job, Job's friends, who blindly take sides with God, are condemned, while Job is ultimately rewarded despite his critical indictment of God's actions.

The relationship between God and human is never static but always evolving, developing. It is both as formal and fearful as the relationship between an emperor and his slave, and as intimate as that between familiar lovers. The two biblical words that most clearly demonstrate the complexity of the relationship are *ahavah*, "love," and *yir'ah*, "fear, awe." *Ahavah* expresses the intimacy, whereas *yir'ah* expresses the terror of a mortal standing before the greatest power in the cosmos. These two words correspond to the two words cited earlier in relation to God's attributes of mercy (*rahamim*) and justice (*din*).

GOD AS DEPICTED IN RABBINIC LITERATURE

The essential nature of God as a unity and the relationship between God and the universe and between God and Israel do not change in the Talmud. The Talmud and its related literature developed mostly after the destruction of the Temple by the Romans in 70 C.E. This marked the beginning of the loss of Jewish national existence and the long period of exile from the Land of Israel. The Talmud emphasizes that, despite the destruction of the Temple and the hardships of exile, God has not abandoned the Jews. On the contrary, God joins the people in mourning the loss of the Temple, grieves with them over the punishment He pronounced upon them, and even goes into exile with His children. If there is any change in the depiction of God, it is that God appears in the Talmud as nearer to the masses, the brokenhearted, and the ordinary person in need of help.

God's attribute of justice required the destruction and exile, but God's attribute of mercy mourned these along with His people, just as parents mourn the necessity for stern consequences meted out to their children. God is now even closer than before, for God has observed the human need for divine accessibility after the Temple's destruction. When the priests could no longer offer sacrifices on behalf of the community after the destruction of the Temple, every individual became obliged to engage in personal prayer. Now each and every person may commune personally with God, and indeed is required to do so.

In dispersion and in exile even in their own land under Roman control, the Jews were confronted with the new and emerging religions of the Roman and Persian empires. Some Jews were attracted to the dualism of gnosticism, which believed in a god of light and goodness on the one hand, and a god of darkness and evil on the other. Other attractions included new forms of messianism and secret religious rituals practiced by Roman soldiers in caves and by others in various mysterious settings. The rabbis were vigilant in not allowing such popular heresies to penetrate Judaism and steer Jews away from the absolute ethical monotheism of the tradition. Perhaps partially in response to the destruction and exile, and partially to the threat of dispersion into the new and popular heretical religious systems that were growing up around them, the Jews of this period experienced God in a closer and more personal way than was known from the Bible. In the literature of the rabbinic period, God loves and remains intimate with Israel even in exile. God will answer His people whenever they seek Him.

GOD IN MEDIEVAL JEWISH PHILOSOPHY

Medieval Jewish philosophy was strongly influenced by Greek ideas and systems as studied and analyzed in the medieval Islamic world. When Greek philosophy first came to the attention of Jews in Greco-Roman times, it was rejected entirely as being too closely associated with paganism. Centuries later, however, Jews living in the Islamic world realized that philosophy could be an acceptable endeavor when they observed Muslims adopting Greek modes of thinking yet remaining thoroughly monotheistic. Jewish systematic theology was strongly influenced by the Kalam school of thought that developed in the Islamic world and by Arabic versions of Neoplatonism and Aristotelianism. The most basic goal of medieval Jewish philosophy was to demonstrate that biblical theology is rational and that human reason, within certain limits, can demonstrate the reality of God and the truth of Jewish religious tradition. These goals were virtually identical with those of their Muslim philosophical colleagues, who were simultaneously working through the problems of human reason, divine revelation of the Qur'an, and God's reality in an Islamic context. Many Christian thinkers living under Islam were engaging in the same basic quest.

Early Jewish philosophers like Sa`adia (Sa`d Ibn Yusuf al-Fayumi, d. 942) and Bahya Ibn Pakuda (late 11th cent.), following the work of the Muslim Mutakallimun (adherents of the Kalam school of philosophy), sought to demonstrate the existence of God through proofs of the creation of the world. Based on the common observation that simple artifacts require an artisan to make them, the extremely complex and delicately balanced order of the universe must have required a Creator to fashion it. Abraham Ibn Daud and Moses Ibn Maimun (Maimonides) followed an Aristotelian system of demonstrating the existence of God. One of their proofs argues from motion. Since things in the world are in motion and no finite thing can move itself, every motion must be caused by another. However, if every motion depends on a prior cause that in turn depends on a cause prior to it, there must be one ultimate cause that puts the entire system into motion. This is the "unmoved mover," who is God.

For Judaism, any proof of God's existence is incomplete if it does not also establish God's unity, and the medieval Jewish philosophers agreed that the absolute unity of God requires that God be incorporeal, meaning without body or material existence. The Bible, however, as noted above, often describes God in quite physical terms with human or bodily characteristics, so medieval Jewish philosophers demonstrated how these descriptions did not imply the corporeality of God. They eventually determined that the biblical descriptions of God were actually descriptions of negative attributes. That is, God is so great that the reality of God is beyond human ability to comprehend, let alone describe. Therefore,

every seemingly *positive* description of God is really only
describing, in a somewhat roundabout way, what God is *not*.
For example, the statement "God is wise" can only mean that
God is not ignorant, because any human attempt to understand the nature of God's wisdom is impossible. Similarly,
statements that God is just or merciful do not *describe* God,
who is beyond description. Rather, they describe the *effects* or
results of God's reality that are experienced by us, and do not
account for a property or aspect of God, which, by definition,
is impossible for us to experience or describe using human
language.

The medieval Jewish philosophers engaged in and solved
many of the intellectual challenges that they faced in the
world of science and interreligious conversation. In doing so,
however, many Jews felt that these highly intellectual explanations deprived them of an intimate and personal relationship with a loving and compassionate as well as stern and
commanding God. One response to the systems of the
philosophers was a series of mystical formulations of God
that allowed, within a unity, a God who is at once unknowable and intimate.

GOD IN THE KABBALAH

The mystics of the Kabbalah observed through their own
experience that God is unknowable and yet reachable. That is,
God is hidden to us in the depths of God's very being, yet
God is revealed to us through acts of creation and the ongoing preservation of that creation. These two essential aspects

of God are not contradictory to kabbalists, but actually complement each other.

The essential God is beyond description or even a name. In fact, the Hebrew name most often used in Judaism in reference to God is *Adonai*, which simply means "our Lord." This is the name recited instead of the actual name of God written in the Bible, which is made up of four consonantal letters with entirely different sounds from *Adonai*. It is forbidden to pronounce these four letters aloud, and in any case, since the ancient alphabetical system of Hebrew did not include vowels, the actual pronunciation of the divine name has been lost.[4] The reason that Judaism has forbidden any attempt to actually pronounce God's name derives from a combination of respect and awe in relation to God. A name is a label. One who knows another's name knows something about that person and is therefore in a position of relative power over that person. This aspect of relationship becomes apparent if one thinks of a situation where two people meet and one knows the other's name but not vice versa. The person not knowing the other's name usually feels awkward until the other person's name is known, thereby making the relationship equal. Our relationship with God is unequal, and not knowing God's name is one of the many reminders of that reality.

To the kabbalistic mystics, the only thing that can be said of God is that God *is*. This absolute divinity is usually called

---

[4] This is not considered a problem in Judaism. The divine name was pronounced aloud only by the high priest of the Jerusalem Temple and only on the most sacred day of the year, Yom Kippur. Some Christians pronounce it Jehovah, Yehovah, or Yahweh, but Jews continue to avoid uttering the name in respect for the overwhelming majesty that is God.

the *Ein Sof*, meaning "without end" or "the infinity." The life of the *Ein Sof* is concealed within itself and is not revealed, but religious people seek the revelation of this concealed life. This revelation is available through the emanation of the *sefirot*, or divine spheres. The *sefirot* are the domain of the life of the revealed God. They are heavenly configurations which, although described almost as distinct regions, are completely within the divine unity. Sometimes the *sefirot* are depicted as divine attributes, but they are actually the various states in which God has constantly revealed Himself from the time of creation to this day. Each individual *sefirah* points to a special aspect of the revealed God that can be known by the trained mystic. Traces of the *sefirot* may be found in everything created and are discernible in everything by the mystic who knows how to interpret the symbolic language of outer reality. God as *Ein Sof* is outside of creation and the soul of souls that exists at the center of all, while the *sefirot* are the "souls" and inwardness of everything in creation. While no created object, animate or inanimate, is divine, an aspect of the divine exists in every creation.

The world of the *sefirot* is therefore the region of divine revelation to which the mystic may plug in, for the flow of divine life rises and descends in the stages or emanations of the *sefirot*. The unity of God in the *sefirot* is dynamic, not static. There is a unity in the stream of life flowing eternally from the *Ein Sof*, the hidden essential everything out of which all creation extends through the stages of emanation.

The Kabbalah, like all other areas of Jewish thought, encompasses a variety of schools. Similar to mysticism in

Islam, a variety of approaches and techniques were developed to find personal unity or attachment with God. Thus a range of thinking and practice is subsumed under the category of Jewish mysticism.

THE MODERN PERIOD

In the modern period, new ways of comprehending God evolved under the influence of modern science, mathematics, and philosophy. Thinkers articulated these new ideas using a variety of conceptual tools and language. God was imagined by some as the "world-soul," for example, the ultimate ground of the unity of all reality. God as world-soul does not equal the world, but is prior to and independent of it, is absolutely spirit and otherwise beyond human knowledge.

Many modern thinkers imagined God as absolutely associated with morality and ethics. The term "ethical monotheism" developed as a means of understanding the concept of God's unity as essentially ethical. Some modern thinkers envisioned God as so far beyond all positive descriptions that one could only consider God as an "idea." The existence of God, according to this view, cannot necessarily be proven through arguments based on absolute logic, but God's existence must be assumed nevertheless as the absolute ground of morality. The reality of God is affirmed because the alternative of denying morality cannot be accepted.

Partly in reaction to such highly abstract notions of God articulated in the modern period, there developed a school of thinking known as existentialism. According to the existentialists, God is not known through philosophic inquiry or rational demonstrations, but through personal encounter, which is a kind of revelation. Such an encounter is deeply personal. God may be encountered as an all-powerful and loving father, or as simultaneously the "wholly Other" and the "wholly Same," the "wholly Present." This conception of God is very close and available, as close to the individual as one's own breath, available always when the individual is open to the relationship.

Most Jews today live their lives largely outside the framework of traditional Jewish concepts of God. On a daily basis, very many Jews function essentially as agnostics who refrain from observing most of the cultural-ritual commandments of Judaism. They tend to choose which commandments to observe based on personal and highly individual criteria. Many attend synagogue and fast on Yom Kippur, the holiest day of the Jewish calendar, and observe the commemoration of the Exodus from Egypt on Pesach (Passover) but choose not to observe most other ritual commandments. Such behavior suggests not only ambivalence toward the commandments but uncertainty about God's role and demands. According to recent surveys, most Jews consider themselves believers, but their belief in God does not necessarily fit the traditional concepts offered by Jewish tradition. As will be noted below, absolute belief in God is not a requirement for good standing in the Jewish community. Judaism has concluded that one's personal belief cannot be legislated. One can be encouraged but not forced to believe, since belief is so personal and idiosyncratic an experience. Proper behavior, on the other hand, can be expected and critiqued. The divisions between the various streams and interpretations of Judaism stand mostly on how they understand the Jew's responsibility to act in response to God's commands.

7

Torah

The word *torah* literally means "instruction" or "teaching." The term is sometimes used generically in the Bible as "instruction,"[1] but *the* Torah refers to the revelation given to Israel through Moses at Mount Sinai (Deuteronomy 4:44): "This is the Torah that Moses set before the Israelites: these are the exhortations, laws, and rules that Moses addressed to the people of Israel after they left Egypt." In this sense, the Torah, sometimes also called the Torah of Moses (*Torat Moshe*), consists only of the Pentateuch (Hebrew, *Ḥumash*), the first five books of the Bible: Genesis, Exodus, Leviticus, Numbers, and Deuteronomy. It is about the same length as the New Testament and the Qur'an. The entire Hebrew Bible is called the *Tanakh*; this term is an acronym made up of the initial letters of the names of the three sections that comprise it: *Torah* (the first five books), *Nevi'im* (the Prophets), and *Ketuvim* ("Writings," the last section of the Bible). Today, the word *torah* or *sefer torah* ("Torah scroll") also refers to the handwritten parchment scroll containing the five books of the Pentateuch that is housed in a special receptacle in every synagogue. This scroll is read aloud at every Sabbath morning

---

[1] See Leviticus 6:7, 7:1, Numbers 6:21, etc.

service during the year as part of the synagogue prayer ritual. Each week a different portion is read, beginning with the first verse of Genesis and ending with the last verse of Deuteronomy, so that the entire Torah (i.e., the Pentateuch) is read completely through every year. The Hebrew Bible is considered sacred Scripture in its entirety, but the first five books are the most holy because they represent the direct revelation given by God to the Israelites at Mount Sinai.

TORAH AS SCRIPTURE

Despite the fact that the Torah scroll only includes the Pentateuch, the Hebrew Bible, in toto, is considered sacred writ. The most ancient and most sacred part of the *Tanakh* is the Torah (Pentateuch), which in addition to the 613 traditional divine rules of behavior, also tells the history of the world, of humankind, and of the origins of Israel. The Torah begins with the creation and ends with the Israelites poised to reenter the Land of Israel after having received the Torah at Mount Sinai and having wandered in the desert for forty years.

THE PROPHETS

The books included in the *Nevi'im* ("Prophets"), the second division of the *Tanakh*, are historical in nature and describe the unfolding of Israel's history from the conquest of the Land of Israel under Joshua to the destruction of the First Temple. The Book of Joshua describes the Israelites entering

the Land of Israel. The Book of Judges (Hebrew: *Shoftim*) contains material about the twelve tribes of Israel during the
period when they lived in separate tribal areas. The two
books known as 1 and 2 Samuel contain the history of the rise
and consolidation of the Israelite monarchy, first under Saul
and then under David. 1 and 2 Kings continue the history of
the Israelite kingdom from the end of David's reign. They
include the narrative of Solomon's succession, the disruption
of the kingdom at his death, the division into the kingdoms of
Judah and Israel, and their histories through the destruction
of Israel by Assyria in 722 and the destruction of Judah by
Babylon in 586. In addition to these works, the *Nevi'im*
includes the books of Isaiah, Jeremiah, Ezekiel, and twelve
other prophets.

THE WRITINGS

The third division of the *Tanakh*, known as *Ketuvi*m
("Writings), is a varied collection. The Psalms and Book of
Lamentations are personal and liturgical poetry. The Song of
Songs (sometimes called the Song of Solomon in English) is a
collection of love poetry. A series of books sometimes collectively referred to as "wisdom literature" address ancient
ideas about morality and social ethics, the place of
humankind on earth, and similar subjects. These include
Proverbs, Job, and Ecclesiastes. The Writings also contain historical works, such as Ruth, Ezra, Nehemiah, and Esther, and
official chronicles of the kingdom of Israel in 1 and 2
Chronicles. The Book of Daniel is a blend of history and

prophecy and is probably the last book to have been included in the Hebrew Bible.

THE NATURE OF JEWISH SCRIPTURE

In English, the *Tanakh* is called the Bible; Jews refer to it as the Hebrew Bible. Christians, however, generally refer to it as the "Old Testament." The latter term reflects a fundamental element of Christian theology, because it labels the *Tanakh* as representative of an *old* covenant that, since the coming of Jesus, only has meaning in relation to the *new* covenant or New Testament. According to this theology, the "old" covenant with the Jews is no longer functional, while the "new" covenant applies only to the Christians—those who believe in the saving power of Christ. Christianity maintains that since the coming of Christ, there can be no other truly divine relationship with God except through Christ. The old covenant was realized through the observance of commandments, but the old commandments have been canceled since the coming of Christ. Since the Old Testament does not explicitly refer to Christ, but rather to a covenant based on divine commandments, it is no longer valid in and of itself. The Old Testament, according to Christianity, has meaning only insofar as it is related to the birth, mission, and passion of Jesus.

Jews, on the other hand, do not believe in the virgin birth of Jesus, or that Jesus was the Son of God, or that Jesus was the Messiah. According to the Jewish view, the coming of the Messiah will bring redemption to the entire world. Because

Jesus did not bring the world to redemption, he cannot, according to Judaism, have been the Messiah. While some Jews are more observant than others of the commandments found in the Torah, no Jews believe that the saving power of Christ can bring personal salvation. Since the entire New Testament is devoted to the story and meaning of Jesus as savior, Jews do not accept the New Testament as part of their Scripture.

TANAKH AS NATIONAL LITERATURE AS WELL AS REVELATION

The *Tanakh* is a very large collection of books that span about a thousand years. All of it is considered sacred, but only the Torah, according to tradition, was the direct revelation of God at Mount Sinai. The remaining sections of the Bible were revealed to the biblical prophets or were divinely inspired in other ways, but except for the Torah, most of the Bible is not considered the *direct* words of God. The books included in the Prophets and Writings form part of the extensive ancient national literature of the Jewish people, much of which was written by humans acting in response to what they understood as God's demands and will.

The stories, history, poetry, and songs found in the Bible express the human frailties, yearnings, failures, and victories of flesh-and-blood people, and they express them in very human terms. Even the greatest heroes of the Bible are depicted with the drives and frailties that are so much a part of human life. The great King David, who unified Israel to defeat the Philistines, who established Jerusalem as the capital and sang the most beautiful songs to God, is nevertheless forbidden to build God's Sacred House because of his warrior status and the blood on his hands (1 Chronicles 22:8, 28:3). And he is soundly condemned and punished for causing the death of a man because of his infatuation with the man's wife. The wise King Solomon is criticized in the Bible for his laxness in allowing idolatry to creep into the royal compound in Jerusalem (1 Kings 11). And even Moses, the great lawgiver and the only biblical prophet to witness God face to face, is condemned never to enter the Land of Israel for his weakness when carrying out God's commands (Numbers 20). The lessons that Judaism derives from these failures is not that God cannot protect His prophets from error, but rather that even the greatest humans remain human and therefore prone to weakness. No human can be a god. We are flesh and blood, and we are destined to struggle with the difficulties of real life. We are always free to err and perhaps to overcome our errors. The struggles of the ancient heroes and prophets provide inspiration and hope for today. They had to struggle. Therefore, so can we. The imperfections of the figures in the Bible teach, further, that even the great power of kingship, royalty, or prophethood does not relieve a person of the responsibility of trying at all times to live up to the divine will.

Canonization and Other Scriptures

Canonization is the act of officially determining what is authentic to a body of Scripture and what is not. Every col-

lection of Scripture represents a canon. That which is officially determined to be Scripture is *canonical*. Books, verses, or
even words that are not considered Scripture are *outside* of the
canon. Every scriptural religion, relatively early in its history,
is confronted with the task of fixing its official scriptural
canon. Once revelation to the community has ended, the leaders collect everything that purports to be a record of the
divine voice, whether written down fully, in note form, or
preserved in the memories of witnesses. They analyze and sift
this material, in the process determining what is authentic
and authoritative revelation, and what is not. Once canonization has taken place there can be no more authentic revelation.[2] Thus every scriptural religion rejects subsequent claims
of divine revelation, whether they arise from within its tradition or from other religions. Judaism officially denies the status of authoritative revelation to the New Testament and the
Qur'an, Christianity denies it to the Qur'an, and Islam denies
the status of revelation to all post-qur'anic claims made by
such groups as the Baha'i or the Ahmadiyya.

The foregoing process does not work in reverse. While earlier religions officially reject all subsequent revelations, later
religions tend to assign a certain value to prior revelations,
although they never accept them as completely authoritative
or accurate. Thus, Christianity accepts the Hebrew Bible (i.e.,
the Old Testament) as accurate revelation but no longer
authoritative except inasmuch as it serves as a prophecy of the
coming of Jesus. Similarly, Islam accepts the New Testament

---

[2] The one possible exception to this rule is the Church of Latter-day Saints (the
Mormons), who have a doctrine of limited continuing prophecy.

and the Hebrew Bible as authoritative in that they both derive from God, but regards neither of them as accurate. Only those parts of the New Testament and the *Tanakh* that fully correspond to the meaning and message of the Qur'an can be treated as truly accurate and authoritative revelation.

These observations about how religions relate to one another's Scriptures are not usually acknowledged in debates between adherents of different faiths. The usual polemical position maintains that there are profound differences in content, meaning, and interpretation among the three great monotheistic Scriptures, and since all claim to be accurate records of God's will, only one of them can really be true. This position has generally been taken by all three monotheistic religions. Despite the existence of this *institutional* trend, however, *individual* Jews, Christians, and Muslims have sometimes accepted the basic worth and truth of the other Scriptures, and have sometimes attracted followings for this view. As the Qur'an itself teaches, a revelation or prophet was sent to every human civilization, each message given in the specific cultural and linguistic setting that would be best attended to by that civilization.[3] Thus it is not surprising that different religious civilizations have *different* records of their revelations, but the differences are not necessarily contradictory. Every individual is different, and we are all motivated by different things and in different ways. Why shouldn't God have understood this truth about human nature and therefore laid out different paths to the same goal of obedience to the

---

[3] See Qur'an 37:71 ff., 57:25 ff., etc.

divine will? This possibility seems to be the thrust of surat al-Ma'ida 5:48.[4]

According to Judaism, Jews are not the only people entitled to enter the world-to-come (paradise or heaven). Provided they are not pagans, righteous persons of all religions have the same opportunity, whether or not they obey all the commandments as enumerated in the Torah. In a discussion recorded in the Talmud, the great sages Rabbi Eliezer and Rabbi Joshua disagree over the meaning of Psalm 9:18, "Let the wicked return to She'ol,[5] all the nations who forget God!" Rabbi Eliezer understood the verse to mean that the wicked among Israel are in the same category as non-Jews ("the nations") whose future in the afterlife is the underworld. This interpretation is rebutted by Rabbi Joshua, who argues that the most significant phrase in the psalm is "who forget God." Only those who forget God are destined to the underworld. Therefore, all non-Jews who are mindful of God merit the world-to-come, just like righteous Jews.[6]

TORAH AND TRADITION

After the giving of the Torah at Mount Sinai, there evolved a parallel tradition of Jewish wisdom that is often referred to as the Oral Law or Oral Torah. This is the sea of knowledge that

---

[4] See also al-Hujurat 49:13. Even surat al-Kafirun is read by some Muslim scholars as an early divine statement to the effect that idolatry, although wrong, is a matter of personal belief that cannot be legislated.

[5] She'ol is a biblical term denoting a shadowy underworld to which the dead are sent.

[6] Tosefta, Sanhedrin 13:2; Babylonian Talmud, Sanhedrin 105a.

was passed down orally from generation to generation over many centuries. This oral tradition was not written down for many hundreds of years, but was passed on by word of mouth from sage to disciple and from parent to child. It is a large compendium of wisdom that includes stories and legends, discussions of the sages about morals and ethics, conversations between rabbis about legal issues, proverbs and moral lessons and tales, and legal arguments that analyze fine points of the divine law. The oral tradition was eventually collected, written down, and codified over the centuries from about 200 to 600 C.E. in the Land of Israel and also in Babylon (modern Iraq), where there was a very large Jewish community.

THE TALMUD AS ORAL TORAH

The most authoritative oral tradition was gathered into two collections, the Mishnah and the Gemara, that together comprise the Talmud. We noted above in chapter 3 how these works evolved historically. The Talmud is called the Oral Torah both because its contents are ancient, reaching back into the earliest periods of Jewish memory, and because it carries an authority second only to that of the Torah (Pentateuch). According to Jewish tradition, Moses learned a great deal of wisdom directly from God when he spent forty days and nights on Mount Sinai (Exodus 24:18), but this wisdom was not set down in the Written Torah that was revealed directly to all of Israel at the mountain. Moses passed this wisdom down orally to his successor, Joshua, who then passed it to the tribal elders, who in turn passed it on to the prophets. The prophets gave it to the great sages, who eventually recorded it in the Talmud (Mishnah, Avot 1:1). There is some discrepancy, however, as to whether all or part of the Talmud derives from God at Mount Sinai. According to some, the entire content of the Talmud was given to Moses orally at Mount Sinai. According to others, only certain rules of scriptural and legal interpretation were passed down and learned by the ancient sages, allowing them to develop their own opinions and ideas within a divinely established framework. Still other Jews do not consider any parts of the Talmud to have originated directly from God, but see it as reflecting the attempts of humble but wise humans to comprehend and live out their own understanding of the divine will.

The Talmud is an extraordinarily dense and difficult work, written in the two different languages of Hebrew and Aramaic (often mixing them in the same line), and containing many layers of argumentation and levels of meaning. One of the very interesting aspects of the Talmud is that it records the discussions and opinions of the sages without usually coming to a final and definite conclusion about which is the "correct" answer to the question at hand. Neither are the principles or theoretical underpinnings of the various arguments usually articulated. Therefore, one who studies Talmud must attempt to work through the complex arguments in order to understand the issues and their implications; the process is extremely complicated and difficult. It is considered an honor to engage in the difficult endeavor of studying Talmud, for not only is such study respected as an effort to come to a better understanding of the divine will, it is also a means of sharpening one's wits and developing one's intellect.

THE MIDRASH

Although the Talmud does not stray from the general parameters established by the Written Torah, it is organized independently and thus is not a direct commentary on the Bible. Judaism, however, is so very closely connected to the Written Torah that from ancient times there evolved direct commentaries on important parts of the *Tanakh*, and many of these were also passed on orally from generation to generation. The most ancient commentaries were compiled into works that are collectively called Midrash, a term from the same root as the Arabic *darasa*, meaning "to learn." The Midrash is a series of collections of ancient commentaries on all parts of the Bible. Each part of a book of Midrash may be quite short, some as short as a few words or a sentence. Often a number of small parts are joined together to form larger paragraphs, and these paragraphs are then organized into chapters and entire books. Many of the smallest parts of the Midrash are recorded on the authority of a rabbi or sage, but some are anonymous. They comment on the Bible from a wide variety of perspectives and treat everything from ancient legends to laws, poems, and moral lessons. Although the Midrash originated in the same era as the Talmud, the midrashic process has never completely ceased; additional midrashim were compiled and written in the medieval period, and modern collections of Midrash continue to be written. Although it is of great interest and has deep moral and theological value, the Midrash does not have the same high status as the Talmud in Jewish eyes. This is the case even though part of the Talmud is in the form of Midrash and some midrashic elements can be found in the Talmud.

HALAKHAH AND AGGADAH

The Bible, Talmud, and Midrash contain a wide variety of material that can be roughly divided into halakhah and aggadah. *Halakhah* refers to the legal material in all of these works, and is similar in content and meaning to the Islamic *shari`a*. As noted above in chapter 3, the two words convey the same basic meaning: *shari`a* means "the way to the waterhole" or "the way to the source," while *halakhah* means "the way to go" or "something to go by."

Aggadah is a term used to designate nonlegal materials. These include legends, moral aphorisms and tales, theological discussions and debates, poetry, folklore, and even medical advice and other information.

JEWISH VIEWS OF TORAH

In the Jewish view, it is impossible for human beings to live properly without divine guidance, and this is provided by the Torah, meaning the broadest range of Jewish learning. In fact, the creation of humanity is understood by Jewish tradition to have occurred for the explicit purpose of living out God's

Torah. According to this assumption, the Torah apparently existed even before humanity or the rest the world was created, because the Torah serves as a kind of blueprint for the life of this world. Jews differed over whether or not the Torah existed before creation, but the issue did not become as great a controversy as the ninth-century Islamic *mihnah* about the createdness or uncreatedness of the Qur'an begun by the Mu`tazilites. Rabbis are quoted in the Talmud as teaching that the Torah, written in black fire upon white fire, preceded the world by two thousand years.[7] The medieval philosophers tended to disagree with the idea of an uncreated Torah, but the controversy continued for centuries. This issue, like most other theological controversies in Judaism, always remained "academic," however, with no consequences meted out against anyone holding either position.

Since the beginning of the modern period, the nature of the Torah has continued to be the subject of discussion and controversy. The traditional view holds that God gave the Torah to the Jewish people at Mount Sinai, that the remainder of the Bible was divinely communicated or inspired, and that the Oral Torah, in its roots if not its entirety, also derives from the original revelation at Mount Sinai. Many other views have developed in the modern world. Some Jews consider only the Pentateuch divine and the other parts of the *Tanakh* as works by humans inspired by love for God and an interest in carrying out the divine will. Others maintain that none of the Torah is a direct and unadulterated revelation of God, and

---

[7] Jerusalem Talmud, Shekalim 6:1; Leviticus Rabbah 19:1.

that it is a record of human attempts to understand and act out God's will in history. Jews have often argued these positions, sometimes with great vigor and emotion. Whatever one's personal opinion about the nature and divinity of Torah, however, and even when insults and anger have overruled reasonable discussion, Jews have rarely come to blows about such issues or attempted to expel anyone from the community because of their views. The general cultural value of Judaism is to argue one's opinions forcibly but not to attempt to impose belief. Ultimately, God determines our fate in this world and the next, judging us according to our behavior, not our opinions.

8

Israel

Israel remained a very small community in the biblical period and was always surrounded by other peoples, all of whom were idol worshipers. The Bible therefore designates Israel as `am segulah ("a treasured people"), the only people that stands in partnership with God through a covenant. This special relationship is sometimes referred to as Israel's "election," and it implies much greater responsibility than is expected of other nations, with corresponding penalties as well as rewards: "You only have I singled out of all the families of the earth; therefore I will visit upon you all your iniquities" (Amos 3:2). Israel's special position did not result from its having special power or even inherent merit; it was rather an act of divine love and the fulfillment of a promise given to Abraham and the patriarchal ancestors. The Book of Deuteronomy (7:6–8) makes this point quite clearly:

> You are a people consecrated to the Lord your God: of all the peoples on earth the Lord your God chose you to be His treasured people. It is not because you are the most numerous of peoples that the Lord set His heart on you and chose you—indeed, you are the smallest of

peoples; but it was because the Lord loved you and kept
the oath He made to your fathers.

Despite Israel's special position in relation to God, many of
its neighbors had more advanced material civilizations and
Israel was attracted to them. The Bible occasionally depicts
Israel as being tempted by the neighboring peoples and their
gods, because in ancient times adopting a foreign culture
required worshiping its gods.

Most ancient idolatrous cultures, from Mesopotamia to
Greece, Egypt, or England, believed in gods of the same
generic categories: a god for the weather, for the sea, for fer-
tility, for war, and so on. Each culture, however, had its own
names for its various deities, and the images of deities of the
same general type, as well as specific aspects of their myths
and rituals, also differed from culture to culture. Daily life in
all these civilizations included formal acknowledgments
through worship of the beneficence and power of the gods.
Since the various pagan gods were more or less associated
with specific regions and cultures, and usually did not differ
fundamentally from gods of the same category in other
regions and cultures, idol worshipers assimilating into a new
culture did not find it very difficult to assimilate its gods.
Monotheists, in contrast, found it impossible to give respect
to another nation's gods and yet remain loyal to the One God
of the universe. Israel, therefore, was under great pressure for
many centuries to remain distinct from all other peoples and
civilizations in order to remain loyal to God. The Bible contains many episodes depicting groups of Israelites succumb-

ing to the temptation of foreign cultures and their gods, and being punished accordingly: It promises, though, that despite the punishments, the people of Israel will never perish (Jeremiah 31:26–27). Israel will do penance and be redeemed, and its ultimate redemption will bring salvation to the whole earth (Jeremiah 2:17–18).

The great effort needed to remain faithful to an unseen God without resorting to the use of images encouraged Israel to avoid involvements with foreign peoples and keep to itself. Remaining separate from other peoples became very much a part of Jewish culture over the many centuries when the Jews were the world's only monotheists. This trait relaxed somewhat with the development of the monotheistic systems of Christianity and Islam. During the Middle Ages, whenever Jews were welcomed into Christian or Islamic society, they freely intermingled socially and economically with their monotheistic neighbors. However, the original internal inclination to keep separate, reinforced externally by the ghettoizing and discriminatory legislation of the great Christian and Muslim empires, inculcated a tendency to remain apart from others. While the liberalizing forces of modernity have worked to weaken this tendency, the unforgotten horrors of the Holocaust have strengthened the psychological barrier, as has the half century of continual warfare that has marked the history of the State of Israel. Today a profound ambivalence surrounds this whole question. On the one hand, the Jewish people is very much a part of the modern world; both in Israel and the Diaspora, Jews are highly integrated in the culture of the modern era, and in fact have been cosmopolitans par excellence. Significant portions of world Jewry are assimilating deeply into mainstream society, with many, especially in the United States, losing their Jewish distinctiveness entirely. On the other hand, many Jews retain a natural suspicion of strangers, especially in environments where Jews have suffered murderous assaults and oppression, or are not freely welcomed. Therefore, one will generally find greater openness in places like the United States and more wariness in the former Soviet Union, Germany, or Israel, where Jews have been on the defensive and have developed an understandable cautiousness.

RELIGION OR NATION?

We return in this section to the question of whether Israel (the people, not the modern state) is a religion or a nation, and the answer that many Europeans and Americans may find somewhat obscure. Western definitions of religion and nation derive from of a set of cultural conditions unique to the Western Christian world. The New Testament statement, "Render unto Caesar what is Caesar's, and unto God what is God's,"[1] came to be understood as teaching that religion and state should be separate entities that do not overlap or interfere with one other. Religious identity in the West is based entirely on one's personal faith system, which has no necessary relationship with one's culture, ethnicity, or national identity. The organization and self-definition of Judaism (and, one could argue, also of Islam), however, are on the order of a "national" religious civilization in which belief and

---

[1] Matthew 22:21, Mark 12:17, Luke 20:25.

ritual, moral, and civic rules of behavior are formulated together and respected equally. The people of Israel do not represent a belief or faith system alone, because, as noted above, Judaism does not enforce belief. But Israel is not an ethnic group or a culture either, because although many cultural practices and beliefs are shared in common by Jews throughout the world, there are nonetheless many Jewish cultures, with distinctive foods and customs and languages of their own, in places as diverse as Northern Europe, the Middle East, Southwest Asia, North Africa, the Caucasus, and Eastern Europe. Moreover, Israel certainly does not constitute a race, because Jews may be black or white and exhibit racial features typical of a wide variety of peoples. Neither a religion only, nor merely a culture, ethnicity, or race, but perhaps a combination of all but the latter, the people of Israel might best be described as a religious civilization that has existed, evolved, and developed for more than three thousand years.

We have noted several times that Judaism legislates behavior but not belief. While it is certainly more consistent and easier to observe proper Jewish behavior if one believes in God and the divine nature of the Torah, doing so is not a theological requirement. This reflects an important difference between Judaism and both Christianity and Islam, both of which expect and require certain basic beliefs. Judaism *presumes* basic beliefs but does not require them, and there has never been anything like an Inquisition in Jewish history. The few historical cases of excommunication from Judaism were based ultimately on behavior rather than belief. In these cases it was subversive actions taken at the expense of the community in order to promote ideas, rather than the ideas themselves, that brought about the expulsion.

ISRAEL AND THE NATIONS

Jews have almost always been a minority wherever they have lived. Even in the Land of Israel in ancient times, when Jews certainly made up the overwhelming majority of the population, they saw themselves as a minority and behaved accordingly because the country was small and surrounded by other, often larger national peoples, all of whom were idolatrous. Jews have always tended to see themselves as relatively small and weak, trying to preserve their traditions against pressures from without. This has had a profound effect on Jews' view of themselves and of non-Jews. We must keep in mind that polytheism was the norm and monotheism the exception for centuries and millennia. Before the rise of Christianity and Islam, there may have been individuals who understood the unity of God, but Jews were the only organized monotheists in a world where polytheism was the norm. Not surprisingly, therefore, they felt that free intermingling with non-Jews might be threatening and tended to organize themselves into close-knit communities to protect their religious way of life from outside influences.

While it was absolutely clear that polytheism was forbidden to Jews, one of the questions that Jews debated about non-Jews from early times was whether polytheism was a legitimate form of worship for non-Jews, or whether the worship of other gods was always wrong for everyone. If polytheism was legitimate for others, should Jews simply leave them to their folly or try to bring them around to the correct path? If polytheism was always wrong for everybody, did polytheists engage in their religious practice out of innocent error or perverse wickedness?

The answers to these questions, and the attitude toward non-Jews implicit in them, have not been entirely consistent over the course of Jewish history. Although the Bible does not compromise its insistence that Israel worship the one God alone, some passages, such as Deuteronomy 4:19 and 29:25, suggest that perhaps God does not expect other peoples to be monotheists. We know that some Jews engaged in proselytizing at least as early as Greco-Roman times, and that a great many pagan Greeks and Romans became Jews, but other members of the Jewish community do not seem to have supported such activities. In fact, the attitudes toward other religions held by various Jewish groups in ancient times ranged from neutrality to condemnation.

After the destruction of the Second Temple in 70 C.E., and the subsequent spread of Christianity in the Middle East, Jews were put very much on the defensive. When Christianity became the religion of the Roman Empire in the fourth century, its teachers influenced the emperors to isolate the Jews and restrict their rights by law. Christian thinkers promulgated the idea that Jews should be shunned as a cause of evil in the world, based on the accusation that they had killed God (in the form of Jesus). Such treatment engendered great tension between Jews and Christians, and Jews suffered enormous disadvantages at every level of human interaction as a result.

When Islam became the dominant religious civilization in the Middle East, it too enacted laws restricting the rights of Jews. Unlike Christianity, however, Islam did not develop a theology of inherent Jewish evil. Despite the disadvantages and difficulties imposed on them under Christian and Islamic rule, Jews tended to have mixed views of Christians and Muslims, just as had been the case with pagans in an earlier period. It would not be inaccurate, however, to characterize Jews as polite but certainly not friendly toward the religio-political systems and their adherents who were the cause of their unenviable situation.

Each of the three monotheisms believes that its own form of religion represents the most perfect response to the divine will. This reality is naturally a source of friction among adherents of the different religions. Although Jews, like Christians and Muslims, tend naturally to consider their own religion superior, Judaism does not teach antipathy toward Christianity and Islam or their adherents. The actual attitude of Jews in any given time and place reflects their treatment at the hands of the Christian or Muslim powers that be. When Jews were welcomed, they took a favorable view of their hosts. When they were not, their view became more negative in relation to the treatment they received. The vast library of Jewish literature and law includes material that condemns non-Jews and forbids any kind of interaction with them. It also includes plenty of material that does not discourage close interaction with non-Jews. Upon close inspection, one would discover that, in virtually every case, the Jewish position reflects the historical situation and how Jews were treated by their non-Jewish rulers.

Moses kneeling, receiving the Ten Commandments on Mount Sinai. Standing behind him in a priestly miter is his brother Aaron. The image is from a prayer book made in Germany circa 1320 for the holiday of Shavuot, which commemorates the revelation of the Law on Mount Sinai and the celebration of the wheat festival in ancient times. The male Israelites wear the "Jew's hat" of medieval Europe; the women have animal heads, no doubt to avoid distracting the male worshipers from their devotions. The illustration depicts a momentous event in Jewish history: at Sinai the Jewish people enter into covenantal relationship with God and become God's Chosen People. The Hebrew calligraphy spells *aron*, meaning ark, and refers to the Ark of the Covenant in which the commandments were housed.

ALIZA AUERBACH

A young boy praying at the Western Wall (also called the Wailing Wall) in Jerusalem,
Israel. Judaism's holiest site, it is all that remains of the Second Temple, destroyed by
the Romans after the fall of Jerusalem to the legions of Titus during a mass revolt of the
Jews of Judea in 70 C.E. The Western Wall is traditionally the site of pilgrimage, prayer,
and lamentation. Despite its great spiritual importance to Jews, they were prevented
from praying there from the fall of the Old City to Jordan's Arab Legion during the
Israeli War for Independence (1948-49) until the Israeli victory in the Six-Day War in
1967.

The citadel of Jerusalem originally constructed during the
Hasmonaean period (from 164
B.C.E.) and rebuilt in the reign
of King Herod. The tower,
known as the Tower of David,
dates from Herod's time.
Pictured: Mameluke minaret
on a Crusader foundation.

Mosaic floor of a synagogue of the 6th century C.E. in Beth She'an in northern
Israel. One of the best preserved of the Byzantine period, it is typical of Jewish
mosaic floors of that era. In the middle is a Torah ark with a gabled façade supported by two large columns surrounded by tall menorahs, *shofars* (the ceremonial ram's horn blown on certain holy days) and incense shovels. The geometri-
cal and floral designs are also typical, as is the guilloche border. Byzantine-era
mosaic floors often featured biblical scenes and representations of the zodiac.
The role of the synagogue increased greatly in importance after the destruction
of the Temple in Jerusalem, and the mosaic depicts the façade of a synagogue
while also evoking associations with the destroyed Temple.

The Shrine of the Book in Jerusalem, Israel, built to display the Dead Sea Scrolls. Found in 1947 in the Qumran Caves near the Dead Sea, the scrolls were probably produced by the Essenes, a Jewish sect that sought seclusion in the desert. The scrolls include copies of books of the Hebrew Bible, among them two nearly complete copies of the book of Isaiah. There are also texts of the books now collected in the Old Testament Apocrypha and Pseudepigrapha (e.g. Tobit, 1 Enoch, Jubilees) and documents composed by the Qumran Essenes, including community rules, devotional poetry, and ritual law.

Jewish woman from Yemen wearing traditional costume. According to legend, Jews have lived in Yemen from the reign of King Solomon (circa 950 B.C.E.), and their religious traditions are considered the most ancient that remain in practice within the Jewish world. Many Yemenite Jews came to Israel in response to the call of Zionism in the late 1940s.

Ethiopian Jews on a pilgrimage on Mt. Zion. The origin of their community remains obscure. Calling themselves *Beta Israel* (House of Israel), they believe their community was established by Jews from Jerusalem who migrated to Ethiopia during the reign of Solomon. Some scholars believe they adopted Judaism from Jews from Southern Arabia or Egypt. Isolated from mainstream Judaism for nearly two millennia, they practice a form of Judaism based on the Hebrew Bible and certain apocryphal books. In 1975 the Israeli rabbinate declared them officially Jewish. During the Ethiopian Civil War (1984-1985) about 10,000 were airlifted to Israel, and a second airlift in 1991 brought an additional 14,000. There are currently some 75,000 Jews of Ethiopian extraction living in Israel.

Jews have lived in Bukhara since the time it became a great trading center along the famed Silk Road; the community was established as early as the 10th century.

The medieval Altneushul in Prague built in the Gothic Style in 1290.

A rabbi in the Sorrero Synagogue in Fez, Morocco. Jews settled in the Maghreb in Roman times and many Berber tribes converted to Judaism. When Morocco became independent of the Baghdad Caliphate and King Idris II (791-828) permitted Jews to settle in the capital, Fez, the golden age of Jewish life in Morcco began. Jews also flourished under the Almoravids (1051-1147). Luminaries included Dunash ibn Labrat (c. 920-c. 990) and Judah ben David Hayyuj (c. 940-c.1010), the two earliest Hebrew philologists; and Yitzhaq Alfasi (1013-1103), the first post-Talmudic codifier of Jewish law. Later Jews were persecuted and ghettoized in a special quarter, the *mellah*; still, Morocco attracted Jewish refugees from Christian Spain and Portugal. For much of their history, Moroccan Jews lived apart from their Muslim neighbors and suffered periodic oppression. Many were impoverished. Most eventually left for Israel.

The illuminated medieval Sassoon Spanish Haggadah, circa 1320, is one of twenty that survived the expulsion of the Jews from Spain in 1492. Illuminated Haggadahs are among the finest examples of Jewish religious art. Probably of Catalan origin and written in square Sephardi script, this one combines local artistic conventions (principally the grotesque Spanish gothic style) with foreign ones, such as the elongated figures typical of French manuscripts and the coloring associated with ones from Italy. Produced at a time when Jewish communities were living in harmony with their Christian neighbors, it shows the influence of Christian art on Spanish Jews, another instance of Jewish tradition being enriched by and enriching the culture in which Jews lived.

The entrance to Kazimierz, the medieval Jewish ghetto of Krakow, established in the 14th century and named for Casimir III, "the Great," king of Poland (1333-70), who improved the condition of Jews in his country and made it a beacon for Jews seeking to escape persecution. Roman Vishniac took this famous photo less than two years before the German invasion and occupation of Poland led to the wholesale annihilation of Poland's Jews, once the demographic heart of world Jewry. A premonition of looming catastrophe is captured in the powerful, brooding image.

The ghetto of Florence, founded in the 16th century. Ghettos, neighborhoods in which Jews were segregated, were established in medieval times by decrees of the Lateran Councils of 1179 and 1215. Compulsory ghettoization began in 14th-century Spain and Portugal. Ghettos were walled with gates closing at fixed hours. Inside, Jews had some autonomy; ghettos often had their own legal, social and religious institutions. Napoleon abolished most European ghettos. The last in Europe, Rome's, was abolished in 1870. From the 18th century on, ghettos existed primarily in some Muslim countries. During World War II, the Germans reestablished ghettos in Europe. Jews lived in crowded, squalid conditions where many died of starvation and disease; the remnant was transported to the death camps.

Gideon offering sacrifices to God from a manuscript by a Persian Jewish artist. Executed in classic Persian style, it is written in Judaeo-Persian Shirazi dialect, a combination of Hebrew and Persian written in Hebrew characters. The image and calligraphy are classic instances of Jewish cultural adaptation: the art borrows heavily from local tradition and the language, like other Diaspora languages such as Ladino and Yiddish, uses Hebrew letters and marries the local language with Hebrew and other historical linguistic influences.

אָסוּר לְדַבֵּר
בִּשְׁעַת הַתְּפִלָּה
וּקְרִיאַת הַתּוֹרָה

A photo of the interior of the Rabbi Isaac Aboab Synagogue in Safed, Israel, with the *bema*, the platform from which services are conducted, in the foreground. Sacred to the Jews since antiquity, Safed was a center of Jewish learning and then of trade, especially in the 15th century with the arrival of Jewish refugees from the Spanish Inquisition. It was the home of Rabbi Joseph Caro, the 16th-century author of the *Shulchan Arukh*, a compilation of Jewish law and ritual. It was also the center of Jewish mysticism. Rabbi Isaac Luria, Ha-Ari (the "Lion'), the leading interpreter of Jewish mysticism, the Kabbalah, also lived and taught in Safed in the 16th century.

Dedicated in 1763, the Touro Synagogue in Newport, Rhode Island, is the oldest in North America. The original congregation (1658) was principally Iberian (or Sephardic), which is reflected in the Spanish, Portuguese and Latin inscriptions in the temple's cemetery. Like many other Sephardic synagogues, it was modeled after those in Amsterdam. The synagogue is associated with historic expressions of religious liberty in the early United States. In 1790, George Washington visited Newport and he later wrote a famous letter to the congregation, in which Washington states, "Happily the government of the United States ... gives to bigotry no sanction, to persecution no assistance."

A Torah from 19th-century Afghanistan decorated in a unique Afghani/Persian style. It has an unusual mix of three pairs of finials, the ornamentation topping the wooden rods around which the parchment is wrapped. The silver finials consist of a pair of flat *ketarim* (Hebrew for "crowns") and two rounded pairs resembling fruit and called *rimonim* (from the Hebrew for "pomegranates"). Both kinds are decorated with floral, foliage and geometric patterns with bells attached. The Jews of Meshed in Persia were forced to convert to Islam by militant Shiites in 1839, but they practiced Judaism in secret. Many also fled to Afghanistan to escape religious persecution. The Persian Jews contributed significantly to the cultural life of the local communities and brought the cultural traditions of Persian Jewry to Afghanistan.

From the late middle ages to the Holocaust, Central and Eastern Europe was the demographic center of world Jewry, with especially large Jewish communities in Poland, Russia, the Baltic States, Romania, and Hungary. With the exception of Hungary, the first language of these communities was Yiddish, a fusion of medieval German dialects and secondarily of Hebrew and Aramaic, various Slavic languages, Old French, and Old Italian, written in Hebrew characters. An enormously rich Yiddish-based civilization developed over a 1,000 years, producing both a vibrant religious and popular secular culture as well as a sophisticated literary one. The photograph, from Belorussia in 1913, shows a group of prominent Yiddish writers and a publisher. Standing, from the right, is the publisher Boris Kletskin and the writers Yaakov Dineson, I.L. Peretz, and Mendel Elkin; seated is the writer A.Y. Paperno. Most Yiddish speakers were annihilated during the Holocaust, and most Yiddish writers and intellectuals were murdered either by the Nazis or by the Soviets under Stalin.

Two young Jewish partisans being hanged by the Germans in Minsk, Belarus (then Belorussia) in October 1941. The young woman, aged 17, was named Masha Bruskina. Despite facing impossible odds and though abandoned by the world and often betrayed by their own countrymen, many Jews took up arms to resist the Germans whenever there was an opportunity. There was even an uprising at the Auschwitz-Birkenau death camp.

Prisoners at Buchenwald concentration camp in Germany at time of liberation in 1945. Some six million European Jews, one third of all the Jews in the world, were systematically murdered by the Germans and their allies and collaborators in the Holocaust. Hundreds of thousands died by execution and as a consequence of disease, starvation and the grueling conditions of forced labor in the concentration camps, and millions more perished in the gas chambers of the major Nazi death camps.

Jewish refugees from Transnistria arriving in Palestine from Turkey by rail in 1944. Transnistria was Russian territory awarded by the Nazis to their Romanian allies. The Romanian fascist regime under Marshal Antonescu was one of the most brutal in its treatment of Jews, killing some 260,000; over 100,000 Jews were annihilated in Transnistria alone until Romania surrendered to the Russians in 1944. Here we see young Jews, survivors of the Holocaust, about to start a new life in the land that would soon become Israel.

From the 1880s on, there were five important waves of Jewish immigration to Palestine. The fifth such wave, from 1929 to 1939, brought mainly German Jews. The photo shows a young German Jewish pioneer, part of a mounted Jewish self-defense unit.

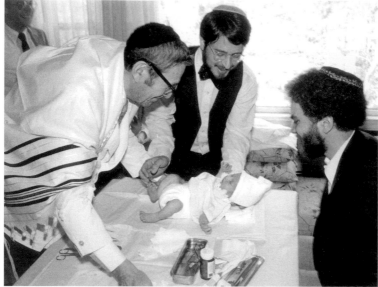

A *brit* (from the Hebrew for "covenant") or ritual circumcision. All Jewish boys are circumcised on the eighth day after birth; male converts to Judaism also undergo circumcision. According to Jewish tradition, Abraham introduced this practice among the Jews. Jews regard circumcision as a symbol of membership in the community and of the covenant between God and human beings. Muslims also circumcise their male children.

A boy recites from the Torah on his bar mitzvah. The bar mitzvah of a boy or bat mitzvah of a girl at age thirteen marks their passage into the world of adult moral and religious responsibility. The ceremony in the synagogue features the bar mitvah or bat mitzvah chanting in Hebrew the weekly portion from the Torah and the *haphtarah*, the selection from the books of the Prophets that follows each lesson from the Torah. The woman in the photograph is a rabbi. Women are ordained as rabbis in several of the principal branches of Judaism: Reform, Conservative and Reconstructionist. While women are not formally ordained in the Orthodox movement, they can become recognized experts in Jewish law within the Orthodox community.

At their wedding, the young American-Jewish bride and groom stand under a wedding canopy or *chupa*, a traditional feature of Jewish weddings. The Jewish population of the United States, numbering some 5,700,000, is the largest in the world. Of all the lands Jews have lived in over the 2,000 years of the Diaspora, none has proved nearly so welcoming as America. Jews are fully integrated into the national life, and they have, as a community and as individuals, exercised enormous influence on American culture and society.

A mother and daughter light the Sabbath candles. The home is an important center of Jewish religious practice, and for many Jews the regular observance of the Sabbath forms a cornerstone to their religious lives. The lighting of the Sabbath candles at sundown on Friday by the women of the home ushers in the Sabbath, a day of rest, worship and peace. Marking the distinction between the sacred and the profane, the Sabbath has often been portrayed as a foretaste of the World to Come. The only day in the Jewish liturgical calendar that is more important is Yom Kippur, the Day of Atonement. When Yom Kippur falls on a Sabbath, the rites of the holiday, including fasting, take precedence over usual Sabbath observance. But even Yom Kippur is called "the Sabbath of Sabbaths."

A family gathers around the table for the celebration of the seder, the ritual feast commemorating the exodus of the Jews from Egyptian bondage; it is celebrated on the first two nights of the Passover holiday. Symbolic foods are served, including matzoh, the flat, brittle unleavened bread, and the Haggadah, containing the story of the Exodus and the ritual of the seder, is read aloud. The holiday also celebrates the strength of Jewish family ties; family members often travel long distances to share the observance.

Today, as in the past, there is no official Jewish teaching that either blesses or condemns Islam or Muslims. As always, the sociopolitical and economic situation influences how peoples think about one other. The current conflict between Israel and the Palestinians and other Middle Eastern nations has had a powerful impact on attitudes and beliefs. Having traveled widely in Israel, Palestinian areas, Jordan, and Egypt, I have witnessed the mutual anger and frustration expressed by Muslims and Jews as a result of the seemingly unending conflict. Angry, frustrated people latch onto negative stereotypes. Muslims have told me that one can never trust a Jew, and Jews have told me that one can never trust a Muslim. I have heard people on each side condemn the other's religion as dishonest, primitive, and violent. But neither view is justified by official religious teachings, despite the fact that both Jews and Muslims tend to feel that their own form of monotheism is superior to all others. In fact, since Islam is closer than Christianity to Judaism because of its foundation in law and its rejection of the trinitarian concept of God, Jews have generally been more comfortable in Islamic religious environments than in Christian. Whereas Orthodox Judaism forbids Jews to enter churches where icons and figures of Jesus and saints adorn the walls, Jews are not forbidden to enter mosques, where there are no representations of the deity or the human form.

THE LAND OF ISRAEL

The question of who owns the land situated between the Jordan River and the Mediterranean Sea was one of the most intractable international problems of the twentieth century, and remains unsolved in the twenty-first. Both Jews and Arab Muslims have marshaled nationalist and religious claims to justify their control of the area. The discussion here is not intended to convince anyone that the Jewish claim to the land is more just or reasonable than the claims put forward by Palestinians, Arabs in general, or Muslims in general. The intent is simply to examine the major Jewish positions on this vexed question.

In the Hebrew Bible, God repeatedly promises the land to Israel, and this, in fact, is the origin of the term "Promised Land." The promise is implied in God's first revelation to Abraham in Genesis 12:1: "Go forth from your native land and from your father's house to the land that I will show you. I will make of you a great nation, and I will bless you; I will make your name great, and you shall be a blessing." The promise is articulated in concise terms in Genesis 15:18–19: "On that day the Lord made a covenant with Abram, saying, 'To your offspring I assign this land, from the river of Egypt[2] to the great river, the river Euphrates.'" These borders are the broadest provided by the Bible and define a piece of land extending from about Gaza in the southwest to the Euphrates River of Iraq in the east. In other biblical passages, however, the land defined by the promise is much smaller. Genesis 17:7, for example, defines the Promised Land as limited to the area of the Canaanite peoples among whom Abraham journeyed: "I will maintain My covenant between Me and you,

---

[2] Biblical scholars are of the opinion that this does not refer to the Nile, but to a small river defining the border with Egypt near Gaza.

and your offspring to come, as an everlasting covenant throughout the ages, to be God to you and to your offspring to come. I assign the land you sojourn in to you and your off-spring to come, all the land of Canaan, as an everlasting hold-ing. I will be their God."

According to the biblical history, Abraham's offspring were unable to enjoy God's promise for centuries because they went down to Egypt during a terrible famine, remained after the famine ended, and eventually were enslaved there. They did not return until four centuries later, when God brought Israel out of Egyptian slavery through the leadership of Moses, who brought them to the eastern border of the land near the Jordan River. His successor, Joshua, then led Israel in conquering the land from the various tribes living there who were known collectively as Canaanites. Around this time the name for the land in the Bible changes from the Land of Canaan to the Land of Israel.

At the root of the biblical view is the notion that the land actually belongs to God and not to any nation or people. According to the Book of Joshua (chap. 23), Israel succeeded in conquering the land only because God willed it. God is the owner of the entire world and assigns portions to whom He wishes, assigning the Land of Israel to the people of Israel. Disobedience to God may result in withdrawal of the divine protection and therefore cause Israel to perish and even lose the land. The land is holy and must not be polluted by har-lotry, bloodshed, and other crimes.[3]

---

[3] Leviticus 19:19, Numbers 29–34, Deuteronomy 21:6–9, 22–23, etc.

In the later prophetic books, the prophets pronounce doom on both Israel and the Land of Israel for the sins of the people. Jeremiah, in particular, takes a positive view of exile and even calls for the people to leave the Land of Israel for Babylon (38:2). Alongside the prophecies of doom, however, are the many promises of restoration, such as this one by Amos (9:14–15):

> I will restore My people Israel. They shall rebuild ruined cities and inhabit them; they shall plant vineyards and drink their wine; they shall till gardens and eat their fruits. And I will plant them upon their soil, nevermore to be uprooted from the soil I have given them, said the Lord your God.[4]

As may be readily understood from the preceding passage, no time frame is given for Israel's return to the land. It can be understood as applying at any time. After the final destruction of the Jerusalem Temple in 70 C.E. and the horrible destruction of the Bar Kokhba rebellion some sixty years later, the survivors still expected a divinely led restoration. This expectation is clear from the legal code known as the Mishnah, completed in 200 C.E., fully one third of which treats laws that are only applicable in the Land of Israel. In the same period the Midrash recorded the words of a famous sage and rabbi:

---

[4] Promises to bring the exiles back to the Land of Israel may also be found in Isaiah 2:1–5, 9:1–16, 24–27; 26:15–20, 29:16–21, 32:15–20; Jeremiah 3:18–19, 11:4–5; and Ezekiel 4:15.

Rabbi Shimon bar Yohai opened a discourse with [a biblical verse from Habakkuk 3:6]: "He rose and measured the earth." The Holy One, blessed be He,[5] considered all the generations and found no generation more fitting to receive the Torah than the generation of the desert; the Holy One, blessed be He, considered all the mountains and found no mountain on which the Torah should be given other than Sinai; the Holy One, blessed be He, considered all the cities, and found no city wherein the Temple might be built, other than Jerusalem; the Holy One, blessed be He, considered all the lands, and found no land suitable to be given to Israel, other than the Land of Israel. This is indicated by what is written [in the biblical passage from Habakkuk]: "He [God] rose and measured the earth—and He released nations."[6]

The rabbis, based on their reading of the Bible, considered the connection between God's Torah, the Land of Israel, and the people of Israel to be intimate and unbreakable. They referred to the Land of Israel simply as *ha-aretz*, meaning "The Land," and all countries outside of it simply as *hutz la-aretz*—"outside The Land." These terms are even today used by speakers of Modern Hebrew in referring to the State of Israel and other countries. It is also written in the Talmud: "The Holy One, blessed be He, gave Israel three precious gifts, and all of them were given only through suffering.

---

[5] This is a common name for God regularly used by the rabbis and sages in the period after the destruction of the Temple.

[6] Leviticus Rabbah 13:2.

These are the Torah, the Land of Israel, and the world-to-come" (Berakhot 5a).

The depth of feeling for the Land of Israel is not simply an emotional issue for observant Jews, but a deeply religious and even a legal one. As just mentioned, one third of the laws in the Mishnah apply directly to living in the Land of Israel. These are mostly agricultural laws and laws concerning Jerusalem and the Temple, none of which apply outside the Land of Israel. For very observant Jews, therefore, living outside the land means that one is unable to fulfill a substantial part of God's commandments. Full Jewish living is only possible through organized Jewish religious life within the borders of the Land of Israel. This reality renders the Land of Israel more holy than any other. According to the Talmud in Mishnah Kelim (1:6–9), "There are ten degrees of holiness. The Land of Israel is holier than any other land. . . . The walled cities [of the Land of Israel] are still more holy. . . . Within the wall [of Jerusalem] is still more holy. . . . The Temple Mount is still more holy."

Many more examples of the deep Jewish connection to the land and to the city of Jerusalem may be cited. The daily prayers entreat God to gather the Jewish people from throughout the world and return them to the Land of Israel, where Jewish sovereignty will be reinstated under God's providence. The final statement of the ritual for Passover and the Day of Atonement, the most sacred day of the Jewish calendar year, calls for a return to Jerusalem in the coming year.

Why, then, it must be asked, did the Jews not attempt to return to the Land of Israel during all those many centuries of exile? Why did the Zionist movement only come into being at the end of the nineteenth century under the influence of modern European nationalism and colonialism? Since Jewish ties to the Land run so deep and are so powerful, why weren't there earlier attempts to reclaim it?

The question is a good one, and the answer is simple: there *were*. We find large and important Jewish movements to reestablish control of the Land of Israel as early as the Roman period. The Great Revolt against Rome in 66 resulted in the destruction of the Temple and the burning of Jerusalem. The Bar Kokhba rebellion in 135 resulted in huge massacres and the "ethnic cleansing" of Jews from the entire land around Jerusalem. Subsequent attempts to bring large numbers of Jews back to the land met with more failures and devastation of Jewish communities. As a result, several great sages of the Talmud concluded that it was forbidden for Jews to attempt to bring about their own restoration to the Land of Israel. It became Jewish custom and even a legal requirement to await the final return prophesied by the biblical prophets. A famous talmudic text became the foundation for this position. In Tractate Ketubbot 110b–111a, Rav Yehudah interprets certain biblical verses to mean that Jews are forbidden to try to reconquer the land by force of arms or even to move back to the land *en masse*. They must wait until God causes the people of Israel to return to the Land of Israel through divine means: "Whoever goes up from Babylon to the Land of Israel transgresses a positive commandment, for it is said in Scripture: 'They shall be carried to Babylon, and there shall they be, until the day that I remember them, says the Lord' (Jeremiah 27:22)." The interpretation of another passage led to the conclusion that God requires three things of the Jewish people in regard to the Land of Israel: (1) mass emigration from the Diaspora to the Land of Israel is forbidden until God brings this about Himself, (2) rebelling against the nations among whom they dwell in exile is also forbidden, and (3) the nations of the world are forbidden to oppress Israel overly much.

The biblical promise of the Land of Israel, therefore, came to be understood as referring, not to continuous possession of the land, but to eventual repossession contingent upon observance. If the Jewish people observed all the commandments properly and according to the divine will, then God would fulfill the promise of redemption and return. Every generation knew that the promise would be fulfilled, eventually, but perhaps not within its own lifetime.

ZIONISM IN RELATION TO JEWISH HISTORY AND TRADITION

Zionism began as a secular national movement that was not based upon the strictures and rules of religious law. On the contrary, it was far more strongly influenced by modern Western ideas of nationhood and the modern, secular nation-state. It developed in the late nineteenth century within the crumbling borders of the Russian Empire, where the Jews were often victims of state-sponsored terrorist massacres known as pogroms and terrible economic and social restrictions. The early Zionists were virtually all secular. Although they were very strongly conscious of their Jewish identity, they did not feel compelled to follow Jewish religious law. Thus the talmudic restrictions against mass immigration to the Land of Israel did not dissuade them. On the contrary, as we noted in chapter 5 above, mass immigration became their major goal as a means of establishing a Jewish homeland in order to solve the overwhelming problem of anti-Semitism in Europe.

Religiously observant Jews did not initially support the Zionist movement. Most Orthodox Jews condemned Zionism because they believed that its goal of establishing a Jewish homeland represented an attempt to "force the hand of God" by attempting to bring political redemption. According to the normative Orthodox position, any attempt to force God's hand would result in disaster, just as in the past. Jews were required to wait patiently until God decided that it was time for the ultimate redemption. The insolent forcing of the hand of God by the secular Zionists would only result in divine anger and bring about another disaster. To this day, some Orthodox Jews continue to condemn Zionism and the State of Israel for this very reason, but most observant Jews now support Zionism and the State of Israel with great enthusiasm.

Why the change? First of all, the Holocaust convinced many that a Jewish state was the only way to ensure that the world's Jews would have a place where they were protected from the depravity of anti-Semitism. Many Orthodox Jews therefore supported Israel and worked toward its establishment and vitality, although they continued to feel uneasy about the seeming contradiction between a Jewish state created through human effort and the traditional prohibition against human attempts to force the hand of God.

This internal conflict among most Orthodox Jews was relieved by the growing belief, especially after the June War of 1967, that God actually willed the successes of Zionism. According to this view, God ensured that Israel would win the 1948 War of Independence as well as the miraculous victory of 1967, and has quietly brought about the ingathering of Jewish exiles from throughout the world, just as the prophets promised. In other words, the establishment and success of the State of Israel are results of the divine will and mark the beginning of the divine process of bringing Israel and the world to the final redemption. Because this is all part of the divine will, the old restrictions against forcing God's hand no longer apply. All Jews are now required by Jewish law to bring Israel to its ultimate success.

Ironically, this means that the Orthodox see the secular Zionists as unknowingly doing God's will by beginning the process of ultimate redemption. God will soon complete the process. In the meantime, however, striving on behalf of the State of Israel is no longer considered the insolent act of forcing God's hand. On the contrary, since the process of the final redemption has now begun, it is incumbent upon all Jews, Orthodox or not, to extend every effort to aid and abet the process. Those who are familiar with the history of Zionism and the State of Israel know that the early pioneers and radical nationalist activists were all secular. This has gradually changed, and today the most radical nationalist activists are religiously motivated and come largely from the ranks of the Orthodox. A parallel may be found in the Palestinian national movement. Originally almost entirely secular in orientation, the more radical activists today tend to identify themselves far more as Islamists than before.

Part III
Practice

9

Prayer

The Hebrew word for "prayer" is *tefillah,* derived from the root *palal,* meaning "to judge," "to intercede," "to plead." Prayer is the human attempt to judge oneself and to plead for forgiveness in divine judgment. It is the human attempt to communicate beyond the bounds of the human self to the Creator of all, in order to bind oneself up with the divine will. Prayer is also an articulation of human reliance on God's mercy for assistance in living a meaningful and happy life. As was explained in chapter 3, Aramaic stands with Hebrew as a language of the Jewish tradition, and the Aramaic word for "prayer," *selota,* which literally means to bow and humble oneself in prayer, is related to the Arabic *salaat.*

Prayer is a core act of Jewish ritual life. The best prayer is the prayer of the heart, and Jewish tradition notes that words are often insufficient to express the deepest emotions. Nevertheless, words are the primary means of human communication, and the Jewish prayer book, or *siddur,* embodies thousands of years of human creativity related to the act of prayer. The prayer book contains the formal affirmation of Jewish prayer, but individuals can add personal prayers and petitions if they wish. Jews may pray in any language, but the sacred Hebrew of the Torah holds special significance. The rabbis teach that we should not allow our prayers to be a matter of routine, but instead should try to inject fresh meaning and understanding, so as to make them a truly personal plea for divine mercy and compassion. The sages often spent an entire hour in meditation before they began their prayers, and the prayer service of today also includes an early section in which one "warms up" to the task of truly pouring forth one's soul before God.

In some ways, the Jewish and Islamic prayer services are quite different. Whereas the Islamic service takes place five times per day, the Jewish prayer occurs three times. What it lacks in number it makes up for in length, for the regular Jewish prayer service is longer than regular Islamic prayer and consists of a complex literature of poetry, prose, and formal blessings. Some of the material comes directly from the Bible; and some of the liturgy was composed by the sages, rabbis, and poets. There is some bowing, but most of the prayers are said either standing or sitting. Only during the High Holy Days, New Year (Rosh Hashanah) and the Day of Atonement (Yom Kippur), do Jews prostrate themselves fully at prayer. Although it is possible that the ancient Israelites removed their shoes before entering a sacred place, this custom no longer obtains. On the other hand, Jews customarily cover their heads in prayer as a sign of piety and respect before God. Some Jews wear a head covering at all times, but this is a matter of custom and not religious law.

In addition to the three daily prayer services, there is an additional service on the Sabbath and holidays. Although prayers may be said individually or in a group of any size, certain parts of the service may be recited only with a quorum of ten, called a *minyan*. Communal prayer is therefore considered preferable to individual prayer. The biblical verses known as Shema Yisra'el, acknowledging the unity of God and the requirement to love and obey God with one's entire being (Deuteronomy 6:4–9), are recited twice each day. All prayer services also contain the basic core called the *amidah*, or "standing prayer," so called because the worshipers stand during this part of the service.[1] The *amidah* is a series of benedictions that praise God, identify with the history of the Jewish people in ancient times, seek God's forgiveness, ask that the community be granted sustenance, good health, peace, and final redemption, and thank God for the gifts of life that have been received. All these prayers are articulated in the plural "we" rather than the singular "I," which places the individual worshiper entirely within the community. In Jewish prayer, the individual prays on behalf of the community and the community prays on behalf of each individual. When the communal prayers have been completed, those who wish may add individual prayers.

READING OF THE TORAH

On the Sabbath and festivals, fixed lections from the Torah, the first five books of the Bible, are read publicly in the synagogue, and shorter ones are also read at the services on

---

[1] It is customary to stand for certain important sections of the service. The *Amidah* is also called the *Shemoneh Esreh*, meaning "eighteen," because it originally consisted of eighteen benedictions.

Monday and Thursday mornings. The Torah lections are read in sequence on every Sabbath so that the entire Torah is recited publicly during each calendar year. On Sabbaths and festivals the Torah lection is followed by the reading of a related selection from the Prophets or the Writings.

The formal recitation of the Torah is chanted aloud from a handwritten scroll using a formal style of musical recitation that is similar to the *tajwid* of the public readings of the Qur'an. The handwritten Torah scroll has no inscribed vowels or punctuation, so the reciter must be very carefully trained in the meaning of the words, the grammar, and the music. In addition to owning a few precious Torah scrolls, every synagogue will have many copies of the Torah in printed form, so that members of the congregation can read along with the reciter. These books often contain translations and commentaries as well, so that the worshipers can study the Torah and its interpretation individually whenever it is recited publicly. There are also many copies of the prayer book containing the order of prayers and citations from the Bible that are recited, sung, and chanted in the course of a prayer service. Most synagogues provide a prayer book and a printed Torah in book form for every worshiper.

The Torah readings are not only a ritual recitation of the divine word, they are opportunities for learning. On Sabbaths a rabbi or a learned member of the community will often deliver a sermon or a lesson associated with the Torah reading. This practice parallels the Islamic custom of the *khutba* sermon or public address on Fridays.

SYMBOLS AND ACCOUTERMENTS

Head Covering

In Jewish tradition, covering the head is a sign of humility before God, but the practice was not required by most early authorities, and the Talmud considers it optional. Over the generations, however, it has become customary to wear a head covering in prayer, and many men wear one at all times. The small cap worn by most is called a *kippah* in Hebrew and is sometimes referred to as a *yarmulka*.

In biblical and talmudic times, women covered their hair for the sake of modesty, and this has become customary among Orthodox Jews. Girls generally do not cover their hair until married. Some Orthodox women cover their hair with a wig. Today, Jewish women who are not Orthodox do not usually cover their hair, but many women wear hats in the synagogue. Women in the liberal movements have begun to adopt the custom of wearing a *kippah* at worship services.

Tallit and Tefillin

Jewish prayer requires no intermediary, no special equipment, and no special time or location. It can be done anywhere, anytime, and by anyone. However, the three daily prayers are recited within certain allotted time frames: one in the morning, one in the afternoon, and one in the evening. Traditionally, the various prayers that comprise the official prayer services are recited in a specified order, so it is helpful to have a prayer book, or *siddur*, which means "order" of

prayers. The more liberal branches of Judaism are less exacting about following the tradition as laid out in the Talmud,
but daily prayer is an expectation of all Jewish movements.

Traditionally, Jewish men wear a fringed shawl-like garment for morning prayers called a *tallit* or *tallis*, based on the
biblical verses commanding Jews to place fringes on the four
corners of their garments as a reminder to follow God's laws
as set out in the Torah (Numbers 15:36–41). Many men also
wear *tefillin* (phylacteries), small leather boxes bound with
straps to their foreheads and upper arms. This custom is
linked to the scriptural texts that call upon Israel to take
God's words and "bind them as a sign on your arm and let
them serve as a symbol on your forehead [literally: 'between
your eyes']."[2] This command is understood both figuratively
and literally. Figuratively, we take God's words and commands seriously in our efforts to live up to the divine will.
Literally, the verses calling on us to bind God's words into
our very being are written on tiny handwritten parchment
scrolls and inserted into the boxes that are placed on the forehead and the upper arm opposite the heart. In this way, the
tefillin symbolize the binding nature of the covenant.
Traditionally, only men have worn *tallit* and *tefillin*, but more
and more women are beginning to take up this custom.

The Torah Scroll

The only ritual object in the synagogue that is highly adorned
is the Torah scroll, which is wrapped in a precious mantle of

---

[2] Deuteronomy 6:8, 11:18; Exodus 13:9, 13:16.

silk or velvet, or kept in an intricately carved and decorated wooden box. In either case, the poles upon which the leather parchment is rolled are often adorned with silver crowns. The Torah scroll is stored in a beautifully decorated vault or cabinet built into the wall of the synagogue that faces Jerusalem. All Torah scrolls are hand calligraphed by highly trained scribes who follow precise guidelines to ensure that the text is accurate and beautiful. Some letters are written with special "crowns" on them while others are not; the letters of certain words are larger than the identical letter in others; and lines are carefully constructed according to special patterns established thousands of years ago to ensure the accuracy and beauty of the text. When a scribe sets to work, he recites his spiritual intent to engage in the copying of God's word: "I am writing with the holy intent of writing a Torah." This, it will be noted by any Muslim, is exactly the same as the *niyya* that is recited before making the *rak`as* or engaging in certain other religious acts. It takes up to a year for a scribe to write one Torah scroll. In order to protect the text when it is read publicly, the reader uses a special silver or ivory pointer known as a *yad* (meaning "hand," Arabic *'id*) to keep the place. This protects the scroll from being soiled by the natural oils and grime on human fingers and hands. Many of the Torah scrolls in use today are hundreds of years old and are zealously cared for.

Mezuzah

The Torah twice instructs Israel to take God's words and "inscribe them on the doorposts of your house and upon your gates" (Deuteronomy 6:9, 11:20). This injunction has been taken literally for centuries by affixing a small box with these two passages handwritten on parchment onto the doorpost of the home. The doorpost is called *mezuzah* in Hebrew, and this word has also come to designate the small container with the two passages.

10

Synagogue and Home

Before the synagogue emerged as an institution, people prayed only at sites considered sacred because they were believed to be places where the gods lived or revealed themselves or where great miracles had taken place. In the ancient world—and this was as true of Israelite monotheists as of polytheists of any stripe—it was inconceivable to worship a deity except in a place where that deity could "hear" the prayer or "taste" the sacrifice. The synagogue, in contrast, was the first place of worship to derive its sanctity not from its physical location but from the activity that occurred within it. Underlying this change in the essence of sacred place was the notion that the one God of monotheism is the God of the universe and can respond to human prayer anywhere and at anytime. Thus the emergence of the synagogue was revolutionary in that it was a concrete demonstration of the unity and universality of God in Judaism.

The origin of the synagogue as a place of prayer is lost in the mists of antiquity. By the first century C.E., it was a well-established institution. In all probability, the Jews exiled in Babylon after the destruction of the First Temple in 586 B.C.E. established places of prayer where they could gather on Sabbaths and holidays for worship. Since they could not offer sacrifices, because this was allowed only in the Jerusalem Temple, they experimented with substitute activities through which they could express their love for God and obedience to Him. After the exiles were allowed to return to Jerusalem and rebuild the Temple, synagogues and Temple existed side by side until the final destruction of the Temple in 70 C.E.

The Temple represented the presence of God among Israel. Like the Ka`ba, which is referred to in the Qur'an as *al-bayt*, "The House [of God]," the Jerusalem Temple was referred to as God's house even though the Torah makes it clear that God is not limited in space. The Temple was seen as the center of the world, and the Temple Mount was the gateway to heaven. When the Temple ceased to exist, synagogues were built facing the holy city so that prayers would be directed toward it. As in Islam, the leader of the Jewish prayer service need not be a priest or religious official; the leader is simply a pious and knowledgeable member of the community who knows the service well enough to lead the congregation in prayer.

There are no ordinances regulating the style of the synagogue, so Jewish houses of worship have typically mirrored the styles of their locale and period. During the nineteenth and early twentieth centuries in the West, many synagogues were built in "Moorish" style to set them apart from Christian churches while retaining the feel of a great house of prayer. Today, synagogue buildings often exhibit daring modern architectural styles.

Every synagogue has a reader's table from which the representative of the community leads the service. Sometimes this stands in the middle of the room, and sometimes it is at the front. Every synagogue also has an *aron kodesh* or "holy ark," a cabinet or niche in which one or more Torah scrolls are stored. Even these two minimal requirements are not necessary, for prayers may be conducted in any clean, respectable room, so long as it contains no idolatrous images, and they may also be held out of doors.

Synagogue decor and decorations vary considerably. One rarely finds human portraits and never sculptures in synagogues, but some have adopted the use of stained-glass windows that include depictions of biblical characters. This trend has largely ended, however, with modern synagogues returning to the custom of excluding all human portrayals from the sanctuary.

While the synagogue eventually replaced the Temple as the locus for communal worship, the home of the individual Jew is also a kind of replacement for the Temple. This change is sometimes pointed to as an example of the democratization of Judaism that followed upon the destruction of the last Jerusalem Temple. When the Temple was standing, only members of the priestly class were allowed to offer the sacrifices and even to clean the Temple grounds. After the destruction, every home became a symbolic temple, every dining room table an altar, and every Jew its high priest. The very act of eating a meal was given a new meaning by analogy to the ancient Temple worship. The bread on the home table is taken to represent the ancient sacrifice. A prayer acknowledging God as provider of all sustenance is recited before eating any food or even drinking water, and a blessing of thanks to God for having provided it is recited afterward.

On Sabbaths and festivals, a special bread called *hallah*, the same name used for the breads offered in the ancient Temple, is blessed and then eaten in a ritual reminiscent of the Temple sacrifices. There are no longer any priests officiating at services in the Temple, nor are priests or rabbis required to lead the ritual in the home or the synagogue. Any knowledgeable adult Jew is able to do so, although in Orthodox communities women are generally excluded from officiating in most religious rituals.

The home has become a *mikdash me'at*, a "small sanctuary," through which daily life is brought to a higher spiritual level by acknowledging God's bounty for virtually every human activity. Even using the toilet is acknowledged by the observant Jew, who thanks God for granting that our internal bodily systems are in order, allowing us to function and carry out the divine will.

MEN, WOMEN, AND CLERGY

In terms of communal structure, Judaism and Islam are more alike than either is to Christianity. Judaism and Islam have no church hierarchy; there are no popes, and no formal organizational structure as found in Catholicism and Eastern Orthodoxy, or even in most Protestant denominations. There are, rather, rabbis and imams who lead as educated laymen, not as ordained priests who alone may offer a sacrament to God. Unlike Christianity, neither Judaism nor Islam possesses an intercessory clergy; every believer may approach God individually and without clerical mediation.

Judaism still maintains the distinction between the three ancient biblical classes, the priests, Levites, and the rest of Israel; but since biblical times, priests and Levites have been considered equal to the laity except in one or two minor ceremonial rituals that recall the grandeur of the ancient Temple. Although certain families retain their status as *kohanim*, meaning "priests," or Levites, a lesser status in the priestly class, any knowledgeable, emotionally stable, and reasonably pious adult Jew may lead any religious ritual. The major division in ritual observance and leadership still revolves around gender.

Traditionally, men and women were separated in prayer, but nowadays this practice is limited to Orthodox congregations, which form a relatively small proportion of the Jewish community. This historical practice has been explained as intended to encourage worshipers to concentrate on their relationship with God rather than their relationship with the opposite sex. Traditionally, women have not been required to perform the full range of rituals, as a concession to their responsibilities in the home and in rearing children. Since this arrangement effectively reduces the number of divinely ordained ritual activities expected of women, it is considered problematic to most non-Orthodox Jews because it is perceived as assigning women a considerably lower status than men. Because Judaism assigns great status to observing as many of the divine commandments as possible, the exemption of women in effect gives them a lesser status. And because they need not know the intricacies of tradition and law if they need not perform as many commandments as men, women have tended to be less knowledgeable of Jewish tradition. Education has always been a marker of status in Judaism, so this has further eroded the status of women in relation to men. Most Orthodox Jews do not see the role division this way, but a significant and growing minority on the modern and liberal end of Orthodoxy have also become uncomfortable with the traditional system.

Traditionally, only men became rabbis, but the tradition is fast disappearing. Rabbis attain their status by virtue of their learning, and women were traditionally not expected to learn Torah and tradition in great depth. There have always been notable exceptions, of course, known from the Bible, the Talmud, and in medieval times. This has changed greatly in recent years. Every Jewish movement, aside from the strictly Orthodox, currently trains women as well as men to serve as rabbis. Some very modern Orthodox groups are currently training a few women with the same expertise as men, but they do not call them rabbis, and have not allowed them to take leadership roles beyond women's groups. Some on the liberal end of the Orthodox movement believe that within a few years there will be women rabbis among the liberal Orthodox groups.

As this brief discussion of gender and hierarchy demonstrates, modern ideas and trends in Western thought have profoundly affected the worldview of Jews and Judaism. Traditional Jewish values and ideas are constantly being challenged and reinterpreted in light of modernity. The varied Jewish responses to modernity have not caused a significant change in the basic nature of Judaism, but they have encouraged ways for it to remain relevant while retaining its core values. The results differ, depending on which Jewish group one examines, but no branch of Judaism has been immune to the challenge of the modern world.

THE DIETARY LAWS

The system of dietary laws in Judaism is called *kashrut*, meaning "fit" or "proper." An acceptable food item is referred to as *kasher*, sometimes pronounced *kosher*, which has the same basic sense as the Arabic *halal*. The basic dietary restrictions are laid out in the Torah in Leviticus 11 and Deuteronomy 14, although a few other verses add further restrictions. One will immediately notice the similarities to the dietary laws established by the Qur'an (Al-Baqara 2:172–73; Al-Ma'ida 5:3–5; Al-An`am 6:141–45).

There are no prohibitions against vegetables. Wine and other forms of alcohol are likewise permissible. According to Leviticus 11:3 and Deuteronomy 14:4–5, any land animal may be eaten that "has true hoofs, with clefts through the hoofs, and that chews the cud." These criteria allow many domesticated animals, including cattle, sheep, goats, and also deer or gazelles. It excludes the pig, which does not chew its cud, rabbits, horses and donkeys, and camels, which have a split foot but not a true hoof.

The same biblical chapters require that water animals must have fins and scales in order to be *kasher*. This excludes all shellfish as well as eel and sturgeon. The Bible does not establish criteria for birds but provides a list of forbidden species.

The forbidden types are mostly birds of prey and those that eat carrion, allowing most domesticated fowl, such as chickens, ducks, geese, pigeons, and turkeys. All "swarming things" are prohibited, which in the biblical list includes animals ranging from mice to crocodiles and most insects. Finally, animals of the permitted categories that die or are killed without being properly slaughtered are forbidden. All blood is forbidden (Leviticus 7:26). This refers not only to "flowing blood" taken from a living animal, but also to the blood in properly slaughtered animals. Kosher meat must therefore be salted before cooking in order to draw out the blood, or it must be broiled over an open fire that allows the blood to flow out freely. Salting means soaking the meat in water for about a half-hour, then covering it with heavy salt on all sides to absorb the blood, leaving it in the salt for about an hour, and then washing off the salt.

Only a person who has been trained in Jewish law can perform kosher slaughter. Using a very sharp knife without any nicks in it, he must cut the animal's throat by slitting arteries, veins, and windpipe in one continuous stroke without exerting downward pressure. This quickly drains the blood from both the brain and the meat, and immediately renders the animal unconscious. After the slaughter, the animal is carefully examined for disease or damaged organs. If there is disease, damage, or discoloration, the animal may not be eaten.

Three different passages in the Torah state: "You must not cook a kid in its mother's milk" (Exodus 23:19, 34:25; Deuteronomy 14:2). This injunction was understood by the rabbis to teach three prohibitions: against eating meat and milk products together, against cooking them together, and against using any mixture of them. A person who has eaten a meat meal is expected to wait a set number of hours before eating dairy products. In addition, different utensils must be used for meat and for dairy, so that a kosher home has two complete sets of dishes, silverware, and cooking utensils.

Exactly why the Torah provides such a complex set of dietary laws is not articulated in Scripture, and a number of explanations have been proposed. Some suggest that the careful slaughtering procedures and choice of animal foods were hygienic and reduced the possibility of spoilage and disease. Others note that this complex set of rules made it virtually impossible for Jews to eat with other peoples in ancient days, thereby keeping them from mingling freely with idolaters. Whether or not the dietary system is inherently rational, it clearly forces Jews to be very conscious of what they eat. At every level of this system, the Jew is cognizant that sustenance comes from God. Since every category of food has its own specific blessing, Jews who observe the kosher food laws acknowledge God's gifts both before and after eating.[1]

The patterns of observance of these laws vary among Jews today. Many follow them to the letter, while others honor the basic principles but not the minute details. Still others

---

[1] It should be observed that prophetic Hadiths add strictures to the qur'anic prohibition against eating the meat of unslaughtered animals, blood, pigs, and anything sacrificed in the name of anything other than God. The Hadith restricts the eating of monkeys and most carnivorous animals and birds. Some jurists also forbade eating donkeys. Still other animals, although technically *halal*, are considered *makruh* and therefore discouraged. For an overview, see Yusuf al-Qaradawi, *The Lawful and the Prohibited in Islam*, pp. 39–79.

observe the laws in their homes but feel free to disregard
them when eating out. Some simply refrain from the most
basic restrictions, such as the eating of pork, and others do
not feel bound by them in any way. The range of observance
corresponds to the spectrum of Jewish observance and identity in general, from extremely pious believers to secularists.

11

The Calendar

The years on the traditional Jewish calendar are numbered from the date of creation as calculated according to the chronology of the Hebrew Bible. This is done by adding together the ages of all the people listed in the biblical genealogies from Adam onward. The resulting figure for the age of the world is, of course, vastly smaller than the one projected by modern science, but for traditional religious purposes this is of no moment. There is also a significant difference between the Jewish year and the year on the Gregorian calendar, used for secular purposes throughout the world. The Gregorian year 2001, for instance, is 5761 on the Jewish calendar.

Like the Islamic calendar, the Jewish calendar is based on the cycle of the moon. Each month begins and ends with the new moon. In ancient times, the new moon was determined on the basis of testimony by witnesses in Jerusalem, but today its exact date is calculated mathematically. The lunar year is 354 days, about eleven days shorter than the solar year. In order to synchronize it with the solar calendar so as to ensure that the annual festivals occur in the same season every year, the Jewish calendar, unlike the Islamic, is regularly adjusted by a process called intercalation. This is done by adding an additional month of thirty days called Second Adar (*Adar sheni*) seven times in every cycle of nineteen years. Thanks to the intercalation, Jewish holidays move back and forth within a span of about twenty days each solar year,[1] but they always fall in the same season.

Days on the Jewish calendar are reckoned as beginning at sunset. This may be based on the wording of the biblical account of Creation, which says, "It was evening and it was morning, the first day," and so on. On the other hand, the reason may derive from the fact that biblical Israel was basically an agricultural society. Since the workday of the farmer or craftsman ended with the setting sun, that may have been the natural time to begin arrangements for the following day and thus to think of that day as having begun.

In ancient times, when the new moon was determined by the testimony of witnesses in Jerusalem, messengers were sent to all the communities in the Land of Israel to announce the beginning of the new month. Eventually, as Jewish communities were established outside the Land of Israel at ever greater distances from Jerusalem, and it took longer for the messengers to get there, there was concern that Jews in the Diaspora would begin the new month late and as a result celebrate certain festivals on the wrong date. Thus it became the custom in the Diaspora to observe festivals for two days in order to be sure that one of them was on the exact date required by the Torah. In Israel the same festivals were

---

[1] The years when a new thirty-day month is added total 348 days, so the number of days difference between identical dates in relation to the sun is twenty rather than thirty.

observed only on one day because all the communities were close enough to Jerusalem to receive the messengers in time. The custom of observing the festivals for two days outside the Land of Israel has endured even to this day, despite the fact that the exact date of the new moon (and therefore of the festivals) is determined by mathematical calculations.

The Jewish calendar evolved over a very long time and came under the influence of many civilizations. The present names of the months came into Judaism during the Babylonian exile, but other names were used earlier. Most of the festivals and holidays have several different names that reflect different eras and different aspects of the holidays. One result of the calendar changes is that there is more than one New Year on the Jewish calendar. Some civilizations mark the beginning of the yearly cycle of the sun in the spring, while others mark it in the fall. Although the spring month of Nisan is the first month on the Jewish calendar, Rosh Hashanah (New Year's Day) falls on the first day of the seventh month, Tishri, in the autumn. This may appear odd at first sight, but we have a similar situation in many Western countries where fiscal years or academic years are often calculated to begin in July or September, quite in contrast with the New Year's Day in January.

THE SABBATH

The Sabbath day occurs fifty-one times in every Jewish year. Despite its frequent occurrence, however, it is considered holier than all but one of the other festivals. The Sabbath is truly the core holiday of Judaism. Jewish life revolves around the Sabbath day, which serves as the central organizing principle of Jewish life and is linked by the Bible to the very act of creation (Genesis 2:1–4):

> The heaven and the earth were finished, and all their array. On the seventh day God finished the work that He had been doing, and He ceased on the seventh day from all the work that He had done. And God blessed the seventh day and declared it holy, because on it God ceased from all the work of creation that He had done.

This text is linked by the Ten Commandments with the human requirement to cease on the Sabbath day from all manner of creative work (Exodus 20:8–11):

> Remember the Sabbath day and keep it holy. Six days you shall labor and do all your work, but the seventh day is a sabbath of the Lord your God: you shall not do any work—you, your son or daughter, your male or female slave, or your cattle, or the stranger who is within your settlements. For in six days the Lord made heaven and earth and sea, and all that is in them, and He ceased on the seventh day; therefore the Lord blessed the Sabbath day and hallowed it.

The logic of the requirement to rest on the Sabbath derives from the expectation that we humans, created in the image of God (Genesis 5:1–2), must live up to that aspect of our nature by emulating what we can of God's moral-ethical essence. Because God is the ultimate good of the universe, we must attempt to be good. Because God is just but also merciful and compassionate, we strive to be so. Because God ceased from the labor of creation on the seventh day, we too cease from our labor on that day and insist that our employees and even our animals also enjoy a day of rest.

To Jews, the Sabbath has become much more than a day of rest. It is a day of spiritual, social, and intellectual as well as physical revival for the task of living out God's will—a day when Jews spend extra time and effort in prayer, in family meals and social activities, and in learning and study. The Sabbath has been called a sanctuary in time, an opportunity for the individual and the community to "recharge." Historians and theologians suggest that Sabbath observance was instrumental in preserving the Jews over the centuries despite the many difficulties they faced. Observing the Sabbath is itself a sign of the covenant between God and Israel (Exodus 31:16–17).

As with all Jewish holy days, the Sabbath begins in the evening at sunset. The festive meals of the day are cooked beforehand, and everyone bathes and dresses in their finest, most comfortable clothes. Candles are lit at home prior to the setting sun with a prayer that acknowledges the sanctity of the day. Evening prayers are held in synagogue, after which there is a festive meal in the home to which extended family and guests are invited. The meal includes wine, a sign of God's bounty and blessing, and a special prayer is said over it that acknowledges the sanctity of the Sabbath. Two loaves of special rich bread called *hallah* are placed on the table to serve as a reminder of God's bounty in the desert, and a special blessing is recited over them as well. All present traditionally engage in a ritual ablution or washing before this blessing, which, along with the other rituals just mentioned, is a home version of the ritual followed by the priests in the Jerusalem Temple for the formal sacrifices.

The next morning, the family again attends communal worship in the synagogue. The Sabbath prayer service is longer than the daily service because there is more time for prayer and study. The weekly reading is publicly recited from the traditional Torah scrolls and discussed, and an additional service in honor of the Sabbath is appended to the morning worship. The family then returns home for another festive meal and a relaxing afternoon. A late-afternoon service includes another brief Torah reading—this time the beginning of the portion of the Torah that will be read the following Sabbath, thus building a bridge from one Sabbath to the next. Afterward comes another meal, often accompanied by much singing, praise, and fellowship. The evening prayers begin after three stars appear in the sky, designating the beginning of a new day.

The combination of wine and bread is found in association with every Jewish festival; it symbolizes the partnership between God and humanity in that God provides the raw materials, but they must be processed by human hands in order for the final product to be produced. The wine is consumed in acknowledgment of the special day. This is called Kiddush and comes from the same root as the Arabic *qaddasa,* "to sanctify" or "make holy." Judaism uses this word consistently in order to allow, but at the same time place limits on, certain human activities. Kiddush acknowledges the sacred day through drinking wine, a potential intoxicant. According to Judaism, wine is not only allowed, it is also expected because it gladdens the heart on a festive occasion. However, sanctifying the act of drinking wine places limits, so as to avoid the potential negative effects and preserve its sacred character.

So too, marriage is called *kiddushin*. The sexual act is beautiful and holy in Judaism and should be a moment of intense relationship, love, and pleasure. It is not considered dirty, nor should it be embarrassing. But sex, like wine, is potentially an intoxicant and can be terribly damaging if its limits are not acknowledged. *Kiddushin*, the sanctification of sexual union through marriage, places the necessary limitations so that it will indeed be a sacred and special act. The act of sanctification (kiddush, *kiddushin*) encourages while it also sets limits. Whether of wine, sexual relations, or other similar activities, the act of sanctification calls attention to both the gift and the danger that the gift represents, therefore setting limits and providing a reasonable means of engaging in it.

FESTIVALS AND HOLY DAYS

Judaism is a religion of memory, and the yearly cycle of festivals and holy days provides occasions to acknowledge its long history as well as the Jew's relationship with God, nature, and humanity. In the early biblical period, Israel was a farming people. Some of the festivals celebrated to this day thank God for the bounties of farming. Others mark certain occasions in the history of Israel, both triumphs and tragedies. Still others have no historical or economic basis, but concentrate entirely on the relationship between God and humanity.

THE DAYS OF AWE

The beginning of the year is a time for both celebration and contemplation. On the one hand, we celebrate our existence and our success in making a livelihood to meet our own needs and those of our families. At the deepest level, we celebrate our survival through the past year and into the year that is beginning. But this realization should bring us to a point of trepidation as we contemplate the deep nature and meaning of our lives. The Days of Awe is a period during which Jews experience both celebration and trepidation. It begins with Rosh Hashanah (the New Year) on the first of the month of Tishri and ends ten days later with Yom Kippur (the Day of Atonement), the most sacred day on the Jewish calendar.

Rosh Hashanah

Rosh Hashanah is referred to in the Torah both as *Yom Teru`ah*, the Day of Sounding the Ram's Horn, and *Yom ha-Zikkaron*, the Day of Remembering. Jewish tradition considers it the birthday of the world, a commemoration of creation. Although it is a happy time, it is not an occasion for parties, for it also marks the beginning of a very difficult period of personal introspection devoted to careful self-examination. We seek to become aware of the ways we failed in the past year—failed others, failed ourselves, and failed God. The purpose of our intense self-examination is to help us to feel remorse for the harm we have done and to lead us back to the path of the upright so that we will better ourselves and act differently in the coming year. This period of self-examination continues for ten days and culminates in the Day of Atonement on the tenth of the month.

Most of the customs and rituals of Rosh Hashanah occur in the synagogue. However, there is a festive home meal the first evening with special symbolic foods. The most common is honey to symbolize the hope for a sweet year to come. Apples are dipped in honey and eaten, as is the special holiday bread called *hallah*. Most of the day is spent in the synagogue, where the regular daily prayer service is extended considerably with added poems, songs, readings, and rituals. The most distinctive ritual act on Rosh Hashanah is the blowing of the shofar (ram's horn) during the service. This custom is commanded in the Torah. and in some synagogues the shofar is blown one hundred times. The primitive, throaty sound of the shofar is both exciting and disturbing. It can help arouse our slumbering souls or serve as a call to war against the worst part of our natures. On the most basic level, it is a wordless prayer and emotional cry that rises from the community toward God.

The special prayers for the day reflect three important principles of Judaism:

- acceptance of God as king of the universe
- acknowledgment that God punishes the wicked and rewards the good
- recognition that God revealed the Torah at Sinai and will bring about a final redemption

The prayers for the day include the image of a heavenly book in which is written our life's deeds, both evil and good. If our righteous acts outweigh our sinful acts, we will be written into the Book of Life for the coming year, but if our sins outweigh our good deeds, we will be inscribed in the Book of Death. We therefore pray that God will remember us for good, be merciful, and inscribe us in the Book of Life.

Yom Kippur

Yom Kippur, the Day of Atonement, falls on the tenth of the month of Tishri, but the days leading up to it have a special significance. They are the Ten Days of Repentance. According to the tradition, the completely righteous are inscribed in the Book of Life on Rosh Hashanah, while the completely wicked are inscribed in the Book of Death. But the overwhelming majority of humanity are neither wholly righteous nor wholly wicked. During the Ten Days of Repentance, they can still demonstrate honest repentance and be sealed into the Book of Life. The Talmud teaches that we should always consider ourselves half guilty and half meritorious, so that every single one of our acts may be the one that seals our fate for life or for death (Kiddushin 40a–b). Such consciousness will inevitably lead to good and ethical behavior.

The most distinctive aspect of Yom Kippur is the fast, which begins before sunset and ends after sunset the following day. The Yom Kippur fast is probably the same fast as the evening-to-evening `Ashura fast on the tenth of the Islamic month of Muharram, introduced by Muhammad to the community of Medina in 622. In fact, the Arabic name `Ashura may well derive from the Aramaic name for Yom Kippur, `Asora de Tishri*, meaning " tenth of Tishri" (Leviticus 16:29). The Islamic `Ashura is no longer an obligatory fast, but Yom Kippur is quite obligatory in Judaism. It is, in fact, the most sacred day on the Jewish calendar.

In the ancient Jerusalem Temple, elaborate rituals took place on Yom Kippur, the holiest day of the calendar year, to expiate or atone for the sins of the community of Israel. One of these included the formal pronunciation of the ineffable name of God by the holiest person in the community, the high priest, in the most sacred place on earth, the inner sanctum of the Temple. While he was doing so, the assembled masses of Israelites prostrated themselves on their faces in the Temple courtyard and grounds. Many other rituals, including many sacrifices, were also enacted on Yom Kippur in the Temple.

For the past two thousand years, the Yom Kippur ritual has taken place in the synagogue. There is very little reason to be home on this day, since eating and drinking, bathing, sexual relations, and most other activities are forbidden. There is also a prohibition against the wearing of leather shoes. One immediately notes the similarity between these Yom Kippur customs and the *ihram* taken on by Muslim pilgrims for the *Hajj* pilgrimage, with the exception of fasting, of course. The Torah commands Jews to "afflict themselves" (Leviticus 16:31, 23:27, 32; Numbers 29:7) by withdrawing from the regular pleasures of daily life. The purpose of the self-affliction on this day is to become more conscious of God's gifts by depriving oneself of them, and to concentrate on the deeper issues of life without distractions. Jewish tradition depicts the angels as not eating, not sleeping, and, of course, refraining from having sexual relations. On this day, we are like angels contemplating God and the true meaning of our lives.

There are five prayer services on Yom Kippur, and full attendance requires spending most of the day in the synagogue. Each service includes confessionals, some private and others communal. The Torah is chanted with a special melody for the Days of Awe. The biblical Book of Jonah is also chanted in synagogue, as is a prayer service for the dead, another section that describes the ancient Temple ritual for Yom Kippur, and another that recalls the martyrdom of Jews throughout the ages. The haunting melodies, the long periods of prayer in community, the lack of physical sustenance, and the challenging scriptural and poetic readings and prayers deeply enhance the spiritual meaning of the day, enabling one to concentrate on personal repentance, the meaning of life, and relationships with God and family. The purpose of the day is not only to atone but to reset one's personal priorities and get back on track, so that the new year will be a time of good acts and good thoughts.

THE PILGRIMAGE HOLIDAYS

The Torah prescribed that the men of Israel were to make a pilgrimage to Jerusalem three times a year on the three pilgrimage festivals of Sukkot, Pesach, and Shavuot (Deuteronomy 16:16–17). In addition to being occasions for giving thanks to God, these festivals gave testimony to the unity of the Jewish people, as many thousands made their way on foot to the central shrine and capital of the people of Israel in Jerusalem. The three pilgrimage festivals are called *shalosh regalim*, the "three times of going by foot" (Arabic: *thalathe rujlan*). They are also referred to as *hag*, which is exactly equivalent to the Arabic term for pilgrimage, *hajj*. The base meaning of this root is "to jump and dance" or "to move in a circle," both of which activities were part of ancient religious festivals. To this day, Muslims continue to encircle the sacred Ka'ba in Mecca (*tawaf*), and Jews encircle the worshipers in synagogue with the Torah scrolls on the Sabbath and especially during the festival of Sukkot (*hakkafot*).

The three biblical pilgrimage festivals are still primary holidays two thousand years after the destruction of the Temple. When Jews were prohibited from entering Jerusalem after the Bar Kokhba rebellion (132–135 C.E.), they no longer were able to make the pilgrimage. Instead the festivals were transformed into synagogue and home celebrations. During these festivals, the same work prohibition applies as on the Sabbath, but with one exception: the preparation of food and all that pertains to it is permitted (Exodus 12:16).[2]

---

[2] This also applies to Rosh Hashanah and Yom Kippur, although food is not prepared on Yom Kippur except for children and the sick, the infirm, and pregnant women.

Sukkot

Five days after Yom Kippur is Sukkot, the name of the holiday coming from the Hebrew word for "huts" or temporary
shelters. As with all the major Jewish holidays, the celebration of Sukkot is commanded in the Torah (Exodus 23:14–16,
Leviticus 23:33–44, Deuteronomy 16:13–17). Like the other
pilgrimage festivals, Sukkot is an agricultural holiday and is
called the "*Hag* of the Ingathering" (i.e., of the harvest; in
Hebrew: *hag ha-'asif*). It occurs at the end of the fall harvest
and is an opportunity to give thanks for the divine bounty.
But as with all Jewish festivals, its essential meaning transcends the mere opportunity to give thanks, though it offers
that opportunity as well (Leviticus 23:41–43): "You shall
rejoice before the Lord your God seven days. . . . Seven days
you shall dwell in *sukkot*; every citizen in Israel shall dwell in
sukkot, so that your generations will know that I made Israel
live in *sukkot* when I brought them out of the Land of Egypt."
The rejoicing of Sukkot also serves, therefore, as a reminder of
God's redemption of Israel from Egyptian slavery.

While most Jews do not actually live in their *sukkah* for the
week, they do eat as many meals as possible in them, and
some do indeed sleep in them occasionally. The meals taken
in the *sukkah* are usually festive occasions where relatives and
friends dine together. There are also special prayer services in
synagogue during this time, with special holiday readings
from the Torah scroll and a unique ritual of shaking a bundle
of four types of vegetation in the four cardinal directions and
up and down. After the difficult soul-searching of the Ten
Days of Penitence, Sukkot is indeed a joyous time.

At the end of Sukkot comes the holiday called Simhat Torah, meaning "rejoicing of Torah," which celebrates the completion of the annual cycle of weekly Torah readings in synagogue. On this day the closing verses of Deuteronomy (the last of the five books of the Torah) are read, followed by the first few verses of Genesis. Everyone in the community is invited up to say blessings and "read" from the scrolls, including young children and others who generally do not do so. There is also a ritual encircling of the community with the Torah scrolls, during which people typically dance and sing while holding the scrolls. It should be stressed here that the adoration of the Torah is not worship, but an expression of love for the divine words of revelation. Dancing, sometimes quite wildly, with the scrolls offers people the opportunity to act out their love for God and Judaism as represented by God's revelation.

Pesach

Pesach (Passover) is the spring pilgrimage festival, and like the other pilgrimage festivals, it became home- and synagogue-based after the destruction of the Temple. This is the period of both the lambing season and the early spring harvest of grains sustained by the winter rains in Palestine, and both nomadic and agricultural aspects of the festival may still be found in the current ritual. The primary significance of the festival, however, relates to God's redemption of Israel from Egyptian slavery, as summarized in Deuteronomy 16:1–4:

Observe the month of Aviv and offer a *pesach* sacrifice to the Lord your God, for it was in the month of Aviv, at night, that the Lord your God freed you from Egypt. You shall slaughter the *pesach* sacrifice for the Lord your God, from the flock and the herd, in the place where the Lord will choose to establish His name. You shall not eat anything leavened with it; for seven days thereafter you shall eat unleavened bread [*matzah*], the bread of affliction—for you departed from the land of Egypt hurriedly—so that you may remember the day of your departure from the land of Egypt as long as you live. For seven days no leaven shall be found with you in all your territory.

Because the festival of Pesach commemorates Israel's redemption from hundreds of years of slavery in Egypt, it is considered by many today to be a festival celebrating human freedom from slavery. This is indeed an important part of its meaning, but the religious essence of the holiday is not freedom but loyalty—even servitude—to God rather than to human masters. It is God who redeemed Israel from Egyptian bondage, not human freedom fighters. It is therefore to God that Jews must be absolutely loyal. They must not blindly follow the whims of any human leader.

This is an honorable position, but it can lead to excess, violence, and bloodshed. How one understands the demands of God in relation to the demands of the social order may vary considerably, and extremists may commit acts of violence against society in the name of a peculiar and biased interpretation of God's demands. The Talmud, therefore, made it clear that a balance must always be made between the laws of society and the demands of God. This is encapsulated in the Aramaic phrase *dina de-malkhuta dina,* which means: "the law of the kingdom remains the law" (Nedarim 28a, Baba Kama 113a–b). The reader will note again the parallel between Hebrew and Arabic. The root meaning of the Hebrew *din* is "judgment." The Arabic has this meaning as well in such words as *daynuna* ("judgment") and al-Dayyan ("the Judge," an attribute of God), though its main Arabic meaning is either "to loan or borrow," or "to profess a religion."

The celebration of Pesach symbolizes the balance between the demands of God and the demands of humankind, for its stringent but joyous ritual requirements have forced Jews throughout history to find a way to celebrate the divinely commanded holiday while living as good citizens in every land. Like Sukkot, Pesach lasts a full week, but the festival cessation from all work is not required for the entire period. It applies only to the beginning and end of the festival period. The middle days include most of the ritual and celebration of the festivals but also allow people to work and engage in the daily responsibilities to sustain themselves and their families.

The most obvious aspect of the Pesach week is the requirement to remove all leaven from one's household. Leaven, called *hametz* in Hebrew (Arabic: *hamid*), is the sour yeast or any catalyst that promotes the fermentation of grain. Not only leavened breads and pastries are forbidden, but so are grain alcohol and virtually every kind of grain product aside from the large, dry flat crackers known as *matzah*. Matzah is made of wheat flour, but it is baked under strict supervision without yeast and very quickly to ensure that the natural fermentation that occurs after water is added to flour does not take place before baking. Matzah is the staple food for the Pesach week, and many recipes include various forms of matzah. One's entire household and belongings must be carefully inspected and cleaned of any crumbs and even dust, for tiny bits of yeast may still remain. Pesach becomes a time for a thorough spring cleaning. Special dishes and cooking utensils are used for the festival. They are put in storage throughout the remainder of the year in order to avoid contact with any leavening agent or grain.

The Torah does not explain why Jews are commanded to avoid leaven for the week of Pesach. At the heart of the practice is the requirement to submit oneself to God's commands. Sages and rabbis of later generations, however, suggest a number of reasons. One very popular explanation is that just as leaven puffs up bakery products, so do we humans tend to get puffed up and forget the requirement of humility. During Pesach week we try to rid ourselves not only of the physical leaven but of our personal leaven, so that we can be more humble and caring for others. *Hametz* is also symbolic of the human inclination to do evil. Removing all leaven is a metaphor for the personal process of purging and freeing oneself of impurity—the *hametz* that lies within us.

Although the giving of resources to the poor is a requirement throughout the year, Pesach is a special time for collecting money to help the needy. This *ma`ot hittin* ("wheat money") is intended to help them buy matzah—and by extension all their other needs—so that they can celebrate the holiday joyously.

The most popular Jewish ritual of the year is the *seder* of Pesach, which takes place in the home. In the Torah it is written, after the commands to celebrate Pesach (Exodus 13:14): "When, in time to come, your child asks, 'What does this mean?' you shall say: 'It was with a mighty hand that the Lord brought us out from Egypt, the house of slavery.'" The requirement to tell of God's redemption has been formalized in a long and joyous ritual meal during which the story of the Exodus from Egypt is retold with riddles, games, singing, and commentary, and much food. The evening's activities are centered on the children, who participate fully.

The seder ritual and meal are replete with symbolic objects. The Haggadah, a book recounting the story and the ritual activities, provides the outline. Four glasses of wine are drunk to commemorate the four different ways in which God promised to redeem Israel. An additional cup of wine awaits the prophet Elijah, who, according to tradition, will come and drink of it when the time arrives for him to announce the advent of the redemptive messiah. The eating of matzah is required at the seder meal, and a ceremonial plate placed prominently on the table holds a number of symbolic foods. A roasted shankbone is a reminder of the Pesach offering in the ancient Temple. An egg is placed next to it, symbolizing the awakening of spring as well as the Temple sacrifices. A dish of green vegetables is symbolic of nature and spring, but they are dipped in saltwater reminiscent of the tears of slaves; the bitter herbs (*maror*, Arabic: *murr*), too, are symbolic of the bitterness of slavery. And a dish of a brownish-colored mixture of nuts and fruit (*haroset*) is symbolic of the mortar used in the slave construction of ancient Egypt's cities.

At the beginning of the evening the head of the household lifts a piece of matzah and proclaims in Aramaic:

> This is the bread of poverty and affliction that our ancestors ate in the land of Egypt. Let all who are hungry come and eat. Let all who are in need, come and share in the Pesach meal. This year we are still here—next year in the Land of Israel. This year we are still slaves—next year, free people.

This declaration is complex and multilayered. It articulates a deep yearning for redemption when the poor and hungry will no longer be in want, and when oppressed peoples will be free.

The Jewish hope for redemption has always been intimately connected with the expectation to return to the Land of Israel. But for many centuries this was only a dream that would take place in some vague future time. Personal piety and good deeds would hasten the day, but the horrible aftermath of so many failed messianic movements taught the bitter lesson that political or military action would not bring redemption. As discussed above in chapter 5, it was only when the new ideas of modernity developed in the West that Jews again began organizing to control their own destiny. Nonetheless, even during the quietist centuries when they waited passively for the redemption, an intimate spiritual and, indeed, ethnic or national tie with Jerusalem and the Land of Israel was always an integral part of the Jewish ethos and self-concept.

The youngest child at the seder then asks, "Why is this night different from all other nights?" The answer to this question takes up the remainder of the evening through the telling of stories, recitations of biblical and rabbinic texts, singing, the eating of symbolic foods, and discussions. Many other customs and practices fill up the remainder of the week, including special prayer services in synagogue and special readings from the Bible. Starting on the second day of Pesach, fifty days are counted (Leviticus 23:15–21) that lead to the third and last of the annual pilgrimage festivals.

Shavuot

Shavuot, also called Pentecost in English, marks the early summer agricultural harvest that the Torah calls the "Pilgrimage Festival of Harvesting the First Fruits" (*hag ha-katzir bikkurei ma`asekha*; Exodus 23:16). As with all the pilgrimage festivals, a historical association is combined with the obligation to give thanks for God's bounty. The biblical requirement to count fifty days from Pesach to Shavuot links the two holidays, and those fifty days correspond to the period between the Exodus from Egypt and the giving of the Torah at Mount Sinai (see Exodus 19:1). Shavuot, therefore, marks the Sinai revelation that followed freedom from Egyptian bondage. Freedom is meaningless without law, and God's freeing Israel from slavery would have been incomplete without a means of ongoing divine guidance. Thus the redemption from Egypt culminated with the mass dedication of the entire people of Israel to God's covenant of Torah.

Shavuot is the only pilgrimage festival that does not last a full week. It also has the fewest ritual activities. It is customary to eat dairy foods on the holiday and to decorate the synagogue and home with green plants and branches. The origin of these customs is unclear. It is also customary to stay up the whole night of Shavuot studying Torah. This custom was begun by the medieval mystics as a way of preparing for the momentous revelation that was said to have occurred the following morning. Today most synagogues have a study program on the night of Shavuot that may include Bible, Talmud, commentaries, Midrash, or modern topics related to Judaism and religious life. The prayer services in the synagogue include readings from the Bible and a special series of psalms called *hallel* ("praise") sung on all the festivals. The Torah reading describes the revelation at Sinai. It is customary for the congregants to stand when the Ten Commandments are read aloud, as a symbolic way of identifying with the original Sinai experience, when all of Israel stood to receive God's revelation.

Lesser Holidays

The major festivals and holidays of the Jewish calendar are the Days of Awe (Rosh Hashanah and Yom Kippur) and the three pilgrimage festivals of Sukkot, Pesach, and Shavuot. There are many other holidays on the calendar, however. The three most important are Hanukkah, Purim, and the ninth day of the month of Av. All of them are of historical significance only and do not have agricultural or pastoral roots. Their lesser status derives from the fact that they evolved after the biblical period or commemorate events that occurred outside the Land of Israel.

Hanukkah

Hanukkah, which means "dedication," commemorates the rededication of the Jerusalem Temple after its defilement by the Greeks. In the year 167 B.C.E., Antiochus IV, the Greek overlord of Syria, desecrated the Temple by introducing idolatrous worship there and prohibited the free practice of Judaism. The Jews rebelled and managed to defeat the Greek armies that tried to regain control of the region. The story is complicated by the fact that there was a significant faction of Jews who, influenced by the appealing aspects of Greek culture, actually fought on behalf of the Greeks. The Jewish traditionalists persevered and eventually were victorious.

Although the rebels achieved their goals fighting and winning a war, the rabbis of the Talmud downplayed this fact by telling a story that deflected the significance of Hanukkah from military valor to something more spiritual. There was a sacred lamp in the Temple that was always lit, but the Greeks had snuffed it out. When the Jews rededicated the Temple, the priests went to rekindle the hallowed lamp but found that there was only one small container of sanctified oil bearing the seal of the high priest—just enough to keep the lamp burning for one day. It would take eight days to prepare a new batch of suitable oil, as was required by biblical injunction (Leviticus 24:1–2). Miraculously, the single container of oil burned for eight days until the new supply had been prepared (Talmud, Shabbat 21b). In memory of this, it was decided that every home should burn a light for eight days to commemorate God's miracle.

Hanukkah is actually a very minor holiday. It has assumed grand proportions in some Jewish communities in the West because it occurs around the same time as Christmas. As a tiny non-Christian minority in the Christian West, many Jews felt that their children would be attracted to the tremendous publicity of the national celebrations of Christmas and be tempted away from Judaism. Largely in response to this threat, the celebration of Hanukkah was enhanced in order to satisfy the needs of Jewish children.

Purim

Purim is a biblical holiday, but it remains a minor holiday because it commemorates an incident that occurred outside the Land of Israel. Purim occurs in the spring month of Adar exactly one month before Pesach. It commemorates the salvation of the Jewish community of Persia from the evil plans of the king's vizier, Haman.[3] The entire story is found in the Scroll of Esther, one of five short books or scrolls included in

---

[3] In the biblical Book of Esther, Haman is the vizier of the Persian king Ahashverosh. In the Qur'an, he is the vizier of Pharaoh (Al-Qasas 28:6, 8, 38; Al-`Anqabut 29:39; Al-Mu'mun 24, 36).

the Writings, the third and last section of the Hebrew Bible. Scholars suspect that the story is fictional but that it was greatly meaningful to Jews because it epitomized the precariousness of minority life in foreign lands. According to the story, the two Jewish heroes, Esther and Mordecai, turned the tables on the evil vizier and saved the Jews of Persia from certain destruction. Surprisingly, God is not mentioned anywhere in the book; despite this, it was included in the canon of the Hebrew Bible because the tale was so beloved.

On Purim, as on Hanukkah, Jews are not required to refrain from labor, as they must during the pilgrimage festivals and on Rosh Hashanah, Yom Kippur, and Shabbat. Like Hanukkah, Purim is an especially joyous holiday. Children dress in costumes, and gifts of sweets are given away. The entire Scroll of Esther is read aloud in the synagogue. It is obligatory to hear every word of the chanting of the scroll, yet the worshipers are also required to stamp their feet and otherwise make noise whenever the name of the evil vizier is mentioned, so as to blot out his name from history. The requirement to hear yet not hear is a source of entertainment for the children and a lesson for the adults. Purim is also a time to give charity to the unfortunate.

The Ninth of Av

The Ninth of Av (*Tishah be-Av*), which occurs in midsummer, is a collective day of mourning. It commemorates the day on which both the First Temple and the Second Temple were destroyed. The Book of Lamentations is read aloud in synagogue, and the observant fast for the entire twenty-four hours. In addition to the two Temple destructions, tradition dates many other calamities and disasters to the ninth of Av, including the massacre of several Jewish communities in Europe by the Crusaders. The ninth of Av in the year 1492 was the date on which the great and glorious Jewish community of Spain was officially expelled by the united Christian monarchy.

MODERN HOLIDAYS

The story of the Jewish people continues to unfold, and the twentieth century was marked both by mourning and by celebration. The Holocaust brought the Jewish people closer to annihilation than ever before (one-third of world Jewry was murdered), while the founding of the State of Israel gave Jews the first opportunity for self-government in nearly two thousand years. Both of these occasions are commemorated in Jewish communities throughout the world.

Yom ha-Sho'ah

Yom ha-Sho'ah (Holocaust Day), sometimes called Yom ha-Sho'ah ve-ha-Gevurah (Holocaust and Resistance Day), is observed in the late spring after Pesach. It commemorates the attempted genocide of the Jews by the Nazis and their many willing collaborators throughout Europe, and it also commemorates the resistance by Jews who, without hope for victory, nevertheless refused to allow themselves to be led like sheep to the slaughter. Jewish resistance occurred in many ways besides conventional military means. Some Jewish slave-laborers who manufactured Nazi ammunition, for example, put in small flaws or defects that would render it unusable. Others resisted in other ways.

Yom ha-Atzma'ut

Yom ha-Atzma'ut (Independence Day) occurs a week after Yom ha-Sho'ah and marks the establishment of the State of Israel. It is an especially important holiday in Israel, but most Jews around the world observe it as well. As with Yom ha-Sho'ah, no authoritative rituals are universally observed because of the newness of the holiday.

12

The Jewish Life Cycle

Like all religions and world cultures, Jewish tradition marks the most important occasions of life with special rituals, ceremonies, and prayers. Every religion or culture expresses its "personality" in the particular way it marks these occasions, and Judaism is no exception. At the core of the life-cycle rituals is the belief that humanity is in a partnership with God in the history of the world. While God is the creator, we too contribute to the world, and our acts may be negative as well as positive. Our place in life, then, is to act out the divine will to the best of our ability.

Birth and Berit

It is a divine commandment to bring children into the world, although those who are incapable of doing so are not punished or excluded. It is also incumbent upon parents to educate their children, provide them with a trade or profession, and even teach them how to swim, so that they will have the necessary skills to lead safe, healthy, and productive lives. Judaism is a this-worldly religion that always emphasizes living in the world for its own sake, and not merely in order to enter into the world-to-come. The birth of a child is a happy affair, for a child is brought into the world pure and neutral, neither sinner nor saint. It is up to the parents, family, and community to ensure that the child realizes its potential and contributes positively and happily to the world.

A child born of a Jewish mother is considered Jewish by the tradition. The Torah commands that all males are to be circumcised at the age of eight days (Genesis 17:10–14, Leviticus 12:3), but even the rare uncircumcised son of a Jewish mother is still considered Jewish. The Hebrew name for the circumcision ceremony is *berit milah*, meaning "covenant of circumcision." Ever since the Genesis story of Abraham, circumcision has been understood to be one of the "signs" of the covenantal relationship between God and Israel. The obligation to circumcise a male child falls upon the father, but he typically designates a professional called a *mohel* (circumciser) to do it. The ceremony takes place on the eighth day after birth unless the newborn's physical condition makes this unwise.[1] Even the requirement to "rest" on the Sabbath is superseded by the commandment of circumcision, and thus the ceremony may take place even on a Sabbath or a holiday.

The circumcision ceremony is a joyous occasion, and it often draws large crowds of family and friends to the home of the boy's parents. Since it is an honor to participate in the ritual, very close relatives are appointed to bring in the child and hold it during the ceremony. The ritual consists of read-

---

[1] Note the similarity to the old Islamic custom of the `aqiqa sacrifice and naming, which customarily take place seven days after birth.

ings and prayers in addition to the medical procedure, after which the family and guests engage in a happy feast.

The *berit* ceremony, sometimes pronounced *bris*, is the occasion when the name of the newborn is revealed. Any name may be chosen, but it is customary to name children after others in the immediate family. In the Ashkenazi tradition, one names a child only after a relative who has died, so that the departed's life may be a guide and inspiration for the new child. In the Sephardi tradition, children are often named after forebears who are still living, in order that the child may look upon a living grandparent as a special guide and counselor in life.

Why circumcision is a sign of the covenant in Judaism is unknown beyond the example and commandment found in relation to Abraham in the Book of Genesis. It is applied to the male child only. Judaism knows of no female circumcision or genital mutilation of any form. This does not mean, however, that females are excluded from the covenant. On the contrary, the divine covenant is understood to apply to all Jews. The special ceremony and feast, however, occur in relation to males only. Traditionally, the birth of a girl is announced in the synagogue, but with far less fanfare and excitement. Since the late 1970s however, a movement has developed to conduct a ritual for welcoming baby girls into the community that would parallel the *berit milah* ceremony and feast for boys. The ritual has taken many forms and has not yet been standardized, but it has become quite popular in many communities.

The prayers and blessings for both genders ask God to ensure that they grow in Torah, marry and carry on the tradition, and never cease from engaging in acts of loving-kindness. At the *berit* ceremony, the father recites the prayer: "Blessed are You, O God . . . who has commanded us to enter him [the newborn] into the covenant of our father Abraham." The people who have joined to celebrate with the family then respond all together: "As he has entered the covenant, so may he enter into [the study and performance of] Torah, into marriage, and [the performance of] good deeds."

BAR/BAT MITZVAH

Children start school at an early age and are expected to learn Torah and grow into the fulfillment of Jewish life. Teenagers, not quite adults but no longer children, are beginning to mature intellectually as well as physically. At this point in their development, they are expected to take responsibility for their acts and contribute to the well-being of the larger community. At the age of thirteen, a boy becomes *bar mitzvah*, or "obligated by commandment." This means that he has attained his religious majority and is now required to fulfill the religious duties of an adult. He may now be counted in the minyan, the quorum required for public worship. The bar mitzvah is expected to fast on Yom Kippur and to perform all the other ritual and ethical commandments.

A boy is officially recognized as a bar mitzvah by being called to the Torah on a Sabbath shortly after his thirteenth birthday. He demonstrates his competence by reciting the requisite blessings before the congregation and by chanting from the Torah and from the reading from the Prophets. He is expected to teach Torah to the community by analyzing and discussing the scriptural section he read, and he may also lead part of the communal prayers. Thereafter, he may participate or lead any Jewish ritual for which he can demonstrate competence. Although the marking of this milestone in the life of the Jew has traditionally been limited to the prayer service in synagogue, it has become customary in many places to celebrate afterward with a festive meal and sometimes with music and dancing.

Until recently, the acknowledgment of attaining one's religious majority applied only to boys. In the second half of the twentieth century, however, more and more girls have been recognized by their communities as *bat mitzvah* (sometimes pronounced *bas mitzvah*). As we learned in chapter 10, Judaism has traditionally excluded women from participation in most ritual acts, though this has changed greatly in the past few generations. Women in the liberal branches of Judaism are now obligated equally with men and are expected to engage in the same ritual and leadership activities. Orthodox Judaism maintains the separation between the genders in terms of both obligation and ritual acts, but even in Orthodoxy a form of recognition of bat mitzvah girls has developed. While they are not permitted to read publicly from the Torah scroll, they demonstrate their learning and knowledge in other ways. Because girls typically mature earlier than boys, both physically and intellectually, they become bat mitzvah after their twelfth birthday.

MARRIAGE

As was mentioned earlier, the Hebrew word for marriage is *kiddushin*, meaning "holiness." The marital relationship is sacred. It is not only for procreation or companionship, although both of these are essential aspects of marriage. According to the Talmud, "He who has no wife is not a proper man." An unmarried man lives "without joy, blessing, goodness. . . Torah, protection . . . and peace" (Yevamot 62b–63a). Sexual desire is not evil or shameful, but it can be dangerous, and so must be regulated through the institution of marriage. According to the tradition, the sexual urge is beneficial and good for the individual and for society as long as it is properly regulated: "Were it not for the sexual urge [*yetzer ha-ra`*], no man would build a house, marry a wife, or beget children" (Genesis Rabbah 9:7). Anyone who fails to produce children because he denies his sexual urge "is as if he shed blood, diminished the essence of God, and made the divine presence depart from Israel" (*Shulhan Arukh*, Even ha-Ezer 1:1).

Polygamy is allowed in Judaism, and the Bible depicts prophets and patriarchs with more than one wife. Despite the legality of polygamy, however, monogamy seems to have been the norm in both the Bible and the Talmud. Many biblical texts presume only one wife,[2] and polygamy was almost unknown among the rabbis of the Talmud. In the Islamic world, Jews were far more likely to have more than one wife due to the permissibility of polygamy in Islam. In the

---

[2] See Psalm 128; Proverbs 12:4, 18:22, 19:14, 31:10–31; Ecclesiastes 25:1, 26.

Christian world, where polygamy is forbidden, the rabbis forbade it also in order to avoid condemnation and possible reprisals by Christians.

In Jewish law, the husband is obligated to supply the wife with food, clothing, and sexual satisfaction (Exodus 21:10). He must deny his own material needs if necessary in order to provide properly for his wife and children (Talmud, Hullin 84b). Divorce is allowed but not encouraged. Officially, only the husband may grant a divorce, but the wife may appeal to a court of law to pressure a recalcitrant husband into doing so through sanctions. Although divorce is allowable in Judaism, there is no evidence of temporary marriage (*mut`a*) as has occurred in Islam.

Traditionally, the husband gives his bride a *ketubbah* (Arabic parallel, *kitab*), a marriage contract that guarantees her economic security in the event of his untimely death or divorce. This practice derives from the biblical *mohar* (Exodus 22:15, Arabic: *mahr*), the price the groom paid the family of the bride, but in postbiblical Judaism (as in Islam) the *mohar* "gift" became the legal property of the bride, as guaranteed in the ketubbah. The wife is entitled to own and manage property. In modern marriages among non-Orthodox Jews, the ketubbah tends to dwell on the emotional and spiritual, rather than economic, obligations of husband and wife toward each other.

The marriage ceremony is simple. Held under a canopy (*huppah*) that symbolizes the couple's new home, it is often held outdoors rather than in a synagogue, and may take place in any reasonable location. Any Jew who has reached the age of majority can officiate at a wedding ceremony, although it is customary today for a rabbi to do so. In order for the ceremony to be binding, however, the ketubbah must be signed by two witnesses who have no blood relationship to either bride or groom.

The actual ceremony consists of two parts. The first is called *erusin* (betrothal). In ancient days, a young man and woman were obligated to each other at this public ritual, after which they returned to their parental homes and waited months or years until the marriage ceremony was completed. The second part, *kiddushin* (sanctification), completes the ritual process of marriage. Today, the two originally separate ritual parts are joined into one ceremony.

The betrothal section (`erusin*, related to the Arabic word for "wedding," `urs*) consists of two blessings praising God and thanking Him for the institution of marriage. As in many Jewish rituals, the blessings are "sealed" or confirmed by the act of sipping from a glass of wine. At this point begins the *kiddushin* section, during which the groom places a ring on the bride's finger and recites the following statement in Hebrew: "With this ring you are consecrated unto me in accordance with the laws and teachings of Moses and the people of Israel." In ancient days, the ceremony confirmed publicly that the bride was forbidden to all others for the duration of the marriage. In modern times, when polygamy is almost nonexistent among Jews, it has become customary for the woman to give the man a ring as well, making the relationship mutual.

The public reading of the marriage document (ketubbah)

follows the brief ring ceremony. This, in turn, is followed by the singing of seven blessings that praise God for the creation of man and woman. The blessings are intended to perpetuate the couple's life together in love and happiness. These blessing are "confirmed" by the groom and bride sipping from a new cup of wine, and the ceremony is ended by the groom (or both) stepping on a glass and shattering it. Even at their moment of greatest joy, the married couple thus recalls the destruction of the ancient Temple in Jerusalem. The ceremony ends here and the couple are married. Then follow feasting and celebration, the exact details varying from place to place and from community to community.

The Torah commands that humans are to be fruitful and multiply (Genesis 1:27–28), and the married couple is required to have children if they are physically able to do so. In ancient times, inability to bear children was grounds for divorce. Contraception is permissible in traditional Judaism under certain circumstances and after a family has already been established. Abortion for convenience is forbidden by Jewish tradition. However, in a problematic pregnancy, when the mother's life is in danger, abortion is mandatory. The mother's life takes absolute precedence over the potential life of the unborn child, even in the very latest stages of development—even as late as the birth itself (Mishnah, Ohalot 7:6). The fetus is regarded as potential life but not full life until very late in the birthing process.

The practice known as family purity has a powerful impact mainly on the Orthodox. During the wandering in the desert after the revelation of the Torah at Sinai but before entering the Land of Israel, the Israelite camp was considered sacred. Bodily functions had to occur outside it, and both men and women were required to remain outside the camp if they fell into the state of ritual impurity called *tum'ah*. They were readmitted to the camp after taking part in a ceremony of purification called *taharah*. One of the causes of defilement was the inadvertent emission of bodily fluids. Therefore, men who had a nocturnal emission and women having their menses were considered ritually unclean (Leviticus 15). The Torah states further that sexual relations with a woman having her menses is forbidden because it transmits ritual uncleanness (Leviticus 15:24, 20:18).

Most of the ancient rules regarding ritual purity were dropped from Jewish practice after the destruction of the Temple, but the rules regarding the menstrual period have been retained. It is forbidden to engage in sexual relations with a woman while she is menstruating and for a time immediately thereafter. When she is ready, the postmenstrual woman enters a specially constructed pool called a *mikveh* (but she can also use a stream or the ocean) where she immerses herself completely, after which she is permitted to her husband. Orthodox Jews strictly observe this custom, but the liberal streams of Judaism are less stringent. It is interesting to note the parallels with Islam regarding purity (*taharah*) and defilement (*najasa*), where bodily emissions render a person ritually unclean and restrictions also apply to women during their menses (*al-ha'id*). In addition to these categories of defilement and purity, it is still customary for Jews to ritually wash their hands before reciting the blessing over bread.

This custom derives from the ancient practice of priests attaining ritual purity before offering the sacrifices in the Temple.

GROWING OLD

There is a famous saying in the Talmud attributed to Rabbi Yehudah ben Tema:

> At five [the child is ready for study of] Torah.
> At ten for Mishnah.
> At thirteen for [the responsibility to fulfill] the commandments.
> At fifteen for Talmud.
> At eighteen for marriage.
> At twenty for pursuing a livelihood.
> At thirty for [reaching fullness of] strength.
> At forty for (reaching) understanding.
> At fifty for [giving proper] counsel.
> At sixty for [entering] old age.
> At seventy for [entering the highly respected age of] elderhood.
> At eighty [one's survival reflects] strength.
> At ninety for being bent [from the weight of old age].
> At one hundred, it is as if one were dead and past, withdrawn from this world.

This passage reflects the Jewish view of the life cycle: that growing old is a time of maturity and understanding, a time for giving counsel, but also a time when a person begins to let go of day-to-day leadership. A psalm notes that the righteous "still bring forth fruit in old age; they are full of sap and freshness, attesting that the Lord is upright, my rock in whom there is no wrong" (Psalm 92:15–16). Judaism considers old age to be a time for respect and distinction. The Torah commands: "You shall rise before the aged and show deference to the old; you shall fear your God" (Leviticus 19:32). The Hebrew word for an elder is *zaqen,* derived from the word for "beard" (*zaqan*; Arabic *dhaqan*). The Talmud defines a *zaqen* as a person who has acquired Torah (Kiddushin 32b). It is a period of life that garners respect.

In the modern world, youth is regarded as beauty and strength, while the aged often suffer the rejection of being outdated and irrelevant. Judaism, like Islam, does not accept this. The elderly are supported by the community and encouraged to participate and contribute their counsel. Both the family and the community assume responsibility for the elderly and work to keep their contributions meaningful and their lives comfortable both physically and socially.

DEATH AND MOURNING

Death is naturally a fearful thing, but Judaism acknowledges that it is a part of life and of God's world. The daily prayers refer to God as "the One who causes death and life" (*memit u-mehayeh*), a concept and idiom found in the Qur'an as well (*yuhiy wayumit;* e.g., 3:156, 15:23, 50:43). There is no demiurge or evil power with which God is in battle. On the contrary,

God is the source of life and the source of death. There is hope, however, that someday God will put an end to death: "He will destroy death forever. My Lord God will wipe the tears away from all faces" (Isaiah 15:8).

The belief in resurrection and a world-to-come is a basic element of Judaism. Although these concepts are not explicit in the Bible, they are very much a part of the Talmud. Judaism does not emphasize heaven and hell, however, for one should follow God's commandments out of love of God, and not because of the enticement of reward or the fear of punishment. Hell, for example, is not very well imagined in Judaism, but it is considered a place where one may atone for one's sins. According to Jewish tradition, those who are evil and go to hell will atone there and, after a year of suffering, will leave.

The sages of the Talmud differed over such questions as the nature of heaven and hell, the resurrection, and the world-to-come. They decided that since these matters could never be understood, it was better not to invest great time and energy in analyzing their essence and meaning. Better to devote oneself to improving this world and one's behavior in it. The Talmud nevertheless offers some consolation in the moment of transition from this life to the world-to-come. Commenting on the verse "O God, my Lord, the strength of my deliverance, You protected my head on the day of *neshek*" (Psalm 140:8), it asks, what is the day of *neshek*? One of the answers teaches the following: "It is the day when two worlds kiss each other (*noshkin*). This world is departing, the world-to-come is entering" (Yerushalmi, Yevamot 15:2).

Judaism holds that every effort must be made to heal the sick, and nothing may be done to hasten death. On the other hand, it is acceptable to remove obstacles to death. There is a story in the Talmud about a dying sage who was prevented from expiring because of the great power in the prayers of his colleagues, who were praying without pause. The rabbi's maid is praised for dropping a jar with a crash that startled the colleagues and interrupted their prayer long enough for the rabbi's soul to enter its final rest (Ketubbot 104a). According to some authorities on Jewish law, this means that it is permitted to disconnect a life-sustaining mechanical device under certain circumstances when a patient is dying, but the issues are very complex. Each situation merits its own decision.

When a person approaches death and begins to expire, those in attendance help him or her to utter *shema yisrael*, the Hebrew statement affirming the unity of God, parallel to the Islamic practice of facing Mecca and reciting the *shahada* while expiring. The Muslim reader will note many similarities between Jewish and Islamic burial practices, from the washing of the body to the obligation to accompany the dead and the simplicity of burial. The mourning practices also find a number of parallels.

It is customary upon hearing of a death to recite the words *barukh dayyan ha-emet*, "Blessed is the True Judge." The mourner then makes a small tear in his or her clothes as a sign. The body of the deceased is never left alone until burial. It is "watched," even in the mortuary, both as a sign of respect and to protect it from possible desecration.

A dead body is ritually impure and renders those who touch it unclean. The body must be cleansed and dressed in a simple white shroud before it is buried. This process is called *taharah* ("purification"). Embalming is not approved of because it delays the natural process of decomposition.

In some areas, the body, wrapped in the shroud, is interred directly into the earth. In most places, it is put in a plain wooden coffin that is shut, for Judaism does not approve of open caskets. Death is the great equalizer, and fancy coffins are considered impious. An ostentatious funeral violates the spirit of Judaism. The coffin should be made of wood, with no metal or fiberglass parts, so that it will decompose along with the body. These requirements are based on the verse "For dust you are, and to dust you shall return" (Genesis 3:19; and see Qur'an 20:55). The body is buried within twenty-four hours whenever possible. Because the body is expected to return to the dust, cremation is not accepted in traditional Judaism, although liberal Jews may choose to cremate.

Accompanying the dead to the burial site is so important a commandment that sages and rabbis are required to interrupt their study of Torah in order to do so (Ketubbot 17a). The funeral service, which often takes place in the cemetery, is quite simple. It consists of one prayer for the dead (*el male`*
rahamim) and one prayer praising God (Kaddish). Additional psalms from the Bible have been added through the centuries, and a eulogy is often delivered as well.

The casket is then carried to the grave site and lowered into it. Sometimes relatives tear their garments at this point and recite "Blessed are You . . . the True Judge." The survivors and relatives of the deceased spread earth on the casket, each person taking a handful or shovelful. Kaddish is again recited, after which the assembly forms two rows of comforters; the mourners walk through the aisle thus formed while the assembly says to them: "May God comfort you amid those who mourn Zion and Jerusalem." When leaving the cemetery, mourners and friends pour water over their hands as a form of *taharah*. The procession then proceeds to the house of mourning, the home of a close relative of the deceased that has been chosen as the center for the following seven days of mourning, known as *shivah*.

Mourning is a process. Healthy mourning allows those who suffer deep losses to grieve deeply, but not alone, and encourages them to pass through their darkest moments and eventually reenter society, acknowledging their loss but ready to move on in life. Judaism recognizes that this process has several stages. The first stage, called *aninut*, is the period between learning of the loved one's death and the burial. During this brief period, the mourner is not expected to follow any of the commandments aside from arranging for the burial. At this moment of existential shock, the mourner is incapable of accepting consolation. No one is expected to try to comfort him or her. Tradition teaches, "Do not console your friend at a time when his dead lies before him" (Avot 4:23). The funeral and burial serve as a catharsis as the mourners observe their loved one being lowered into the grave.

The stage that follows is a seven-day period called *shivah*. This is the time of deepest mourning. A candle burns in honor of the departed in the home, and all the mirrors are covered. The mourners are not permitted to engage in marital relations, or to shave or cut their hair, work at their occupations, or even study Torah, except for passages treating woe and sadness. It is expected that their thoughts will be taken up entirely with their loss and grief and in remembering the departed loved one. The mourners are not alone during this period, for the community comes to them, bringing meals and consoling them in the traditional manner. The mourners do not greet the visitors, nor do they greet the mourners. The visitors simply enter the home with their food and prepare meals for the mourners and other guests. Then they sit quietly in order to allow the mourners to talk about the deceased and express grief or any other feeling. The visitors encourage the mourners to express their feelings and to eat. Daily prayers are held in the house of morning to ensure that the mourners can recite the Kaddish, the prayer of praise to God that is recited in association with the dead.

The next stage, *sheloshim*, ends thirty days after the day of burial (and thus twenty-three days after the end of *shivah*). During this period, the home is no longer filled with visitors bringing food. The mourners return to work and synagogue, and resume a mostly normal life. However, they still do not cut their hair or beard, nor may they go out for entertainment, parties, or be married. This is an interim stage between the time of deepest grief and the time when life returns to normal. During this period, close friends and family continue to visit and console the mourner.

Completion of *sheloshim* ends the mourning except for children mourning their parents, which continues for a year. Some refrain from shaving for this entire time, but it is not required. Mourners may attend festivities and entertainment, but they recite the Kaddish prayer daily in a minyan or communal prayer service. This "year" period actually consists of only eleven months because according to tradition, after eleven months even terrible sinners are irrevocably admitted to their reward in the world-to-come. With the setting of the headstone for the grave at the end of this period, the time of mourning is officially ended. Children will observe the death anniversary of their parents by reciting Kaddish and lighting a twenty-four-hour candle, and will also attend *Yizkor*, a special memorial service for the dead observed on the last day of pilgrimage festivals and on Yom Kippur.

13

Personal Observance

Jewish tradition teaches that the Torah contains 613 divine commandments; 248 are positive commandments (what one is required to do), and 365 are negative commandments (what one is forbidden to do). Thus the Ten Commandments are only a small part of the total body of Jewish law, and have no greater or lesser worth than the other commandments. Judaism tends not to emphasize the Ten Commandments for this reason, and also because Christianity, historically critical of Judaism's emphasis on the law, has traditionally taught that the Ten Commandments represent the only divine commandments in the Torah that humans are required to observe.

As discussed in chapter 6, Judaism does not separate the commandments into categories familiar to the modern West, such as civil law, rules of religious ritual, criminal law, moral-ethical precepts, and social mores. The divine commandments were not separated into categories in the Torah, nor are they categorized in the Jewish legal codes and commentaries. A great many of the commandments in the Torah can no longer be fulfilled because they relate to the Temple sacrifices or other ancient practices. Many other commandments, however, were added in the Oral Torah, the rabbinic literature of the Talmud and Midrash, and the medieval codes and commentaries.

Prior to modern times, Jews led a traditional life defined even more by culture than by religious law. It was natural to lead a fully Jewish life because Jews tended to live largely separately from non-Jews and therefore functioned as a corporate community. Observance of the dietary laws, for example, was simply a part of life in the Jewish community. The possibility of eating nonkosher foods was virtually unthinkable, and because nonkosher food was not easily available to Jews, individuals did not have to think much about how kosher their eating habits might be. Eating kosher was simply a natural part of life. The situation today is radically different. In most parts of the world, Jews are deeply integrated into modern society, living and working and socializing among non-Jews. Jews shop in the same supermarkets as everyone else rather than in the small Jewish shops that were the only places to procure food in the ghetto. Today, in fact, it is usually more of an effort to find and prepare kosher foods than nonkosher foods. Jews today, therefore, are confronted with the challenge of deciding how to observe the dietary laws. Will they observe the traditional rules strictly, or not strictly, or not at all? Nowadays there is a broad range of kosher food habits.

The question, however, is not merely whether one is willing to observe *all* the rules. Some Jews observe *more* than is expected by the tradition. Some, for example, in an attempt to shield themselves from the temptations of the modern world, have added dietary restrictions that were never considered

before the modern period. One can observe today, both in the
State of Israel and in every significant Diaspora Jewish community, that dietary habits vary from the lax to the super-
strict that add new restrictions to the tradition. This observation may be applied to other Jewish behaviors as well. Many
Jews do not observe the tradition to the letter, whereas others
are radically observant in order to shield themselves from the
challenges of modernity and protect themselves from the
remote possibility of inadvertently neglecting some aspect of
the law. Simply put, before modernity most Jews practiced a
moderate form of Judaism. Today, Jewish practice ranges
from those with no religious practice to those who are far
more rigorous than necessary to fulfill the requirements of
the divine law.

Jews are highly integrated into the surrounding cultures
and are not expected to live in segregated ghettos. Even in the
State of Israel, the values of the secular, modern Western
world have had a profound influence on behavior. The laws
and national culture of the State of Israel strongly promote
Jewish life, but they are not Jewish laws as defined by the
halakhah of Jewish tradition. On the contrary, they are enacted by the Knesset, or parliament, and often contradict Jewish
legal teachings. One immediately notes a parallel in the
Islamic world, where many modern nation-states with an
overwhelming majority of Muslims would not be classified as
Islamic states in which *shari`a* is the law of the land.

As a result of the influence of modernity, there is a wide
range of Jewish practice today, from the ultra-Orthodox to the

completely secular. Particularly on the margins of the scale, there is a tendency to be critical of what other Jews do. Such criticisms may be vociferous, but they very rarely lead to violence.

TZEDAKAH

Judaism, like Islam, does not rely on the largesse of charitable giving but instead requires giving as part of the divine law. Charity is not a favor to the poor but something to which they have a right. Moreover, the donor is obligated to give. In biblical times, when almost all Israelites were farmers, the corners of the fields were not reaped so as to leave something for the poor to reap, and in addition all produce that dropped during the reaping of the main part of the fields was also left for the poor (Leviticus 19:9–10, 23:22). The Hebrew Bible stresses the requirement to feed the hungry, clothe the naked, and care for the orphan, the widow, and the poor. The Book of Deuteronomy describes the giving of charity as a divine attribute (10:17–18):

> For the Lord your God is God supreme and Lord supreme, the great, the mighty, and the awesome God, who shows no favor and takes no bribe, but upholds the cause of the fatherless and the widow, and befriends the stranger, providing him with food and clothing. You too must befriend the stranger, for you were strangers in the land of Egypt.

Jews are taught to emulate God's goodness in their own limited human ways. In an interesting biblical verse that finds a parallel in the Qur'an, emulation of God's goodness is taken to a metaphorical extreme (Proverbs 19:17): "He who is generous to the poor makes a loan to the Lord; He will repay him his due" (compare especially Al-Taghabun 64:17: "If you lend unto God a goodly loan, He will double it for you and will forgive you; God is responsive, compassionate.").[1]

The term for the required charitable giving is *tzedakah* (Arabic: *sadaqa*), and it is used in the Qur'an in the same way as *zakat* (Al-Baqara: 196, 263–264; Al-Nissan' 4:114; Al-Tawba 9:103). In Hebrew the word means "righteousness" or "justice," and it is required of everyone. Those who receive *tzedakah* are required to give to others less fortunate (Gittin 7a). The laws of giving are complex, but a tenth of one's wealth is expected. Giving a twentieth or less is regarded as mean. However, one is not expected to give more than a fifth, lest in doing so one become impoverished and dependent on charity. The importance of giving *tzedakah* cannot be overstated. A great talmudic sage, Rabbi Assi, stated that *tzedakah* is as important as all the other commandments put together (Bava Batra 9a).

Judaism also recognizes several other forms of assistance to the needy. These include deeds of loving-kindness (*gemilut hasadim*), caring for and burying the dead, providing jobs for the unemployed, and so on. The following passage from the

---

[1] See also Al-Ma'ida 5:12, Al-Hadid 57:18, etc.

Talmud (Shabbat 27a) is recited every day in the morning prayers:

> These are some of the deeds that yield fruit in this world and for which merit is acquired for the world-to-come: honoring parents, doing deeds of loving-kindness; attending the house of study morning and evening, providing hospitality, visiting the sick, providing for a needy bride, attending the dead, deep devotion in prayer, making peace between one person and another; and the study of Torah is equivalent to them all [because it leads to all such deeds].

HUMAN VIRTUES

Like most religions, Judaism stresses the importance of living up to the highest virtues. These include humility, respect for others, modesty, personal honesty and honest business practices, and of course much more. The purpose of life is not merely to exist, procreate, and pass on, but to live life to its fullest with both passion and compassion, and to bring the world a little closer toward perfection. The Bible and the Talmud, as well as the many other Jewish writings on religion, teach a great deal about human virtue and how to live life fully and in keeping with God's expectations. These lessons are found as proverbs, moral aphorisms, and stories. Only a few examples from this very large literature can be provided here. Here is one from the Midrash (Leviticus Rabbah 33:1):

Rabbi Shimon ben Gamliel once said to Tabbai, his servant: "Go and buy me some good food in the market." Tabbai went and bought him a tongue. He [later] said to him: "Go and buy me some bad food in the market." So Tabbai went and bought him another tongue. He said to him: "What is this? When I told you to get good food, you bought me tongue, and when I told you to get bad food, you also bought me tongue!" Tabbai replied: "Good comes from it and bad comes from it. When the tongue is good there is nothing better, and when it is bad there is nothing worse."

This story is interesting, not only for its direct message, but also for its indirect message that the great rabbi and sage, Shimon ben Gamliel, learns a lesson from his humble servant. The danger of evil speech is an issue of great concern because its effect can be extremely damaging. Rabbi Hama ben Hanina taught in the Talmud that just as a hand can kill, so can the tongue (Arakhin 15b). A discussion in the same section of the Talmud concludes that evil speech destroys three people: the person who tells the slander, the person who listens to it, and the person about whom it is said.

On another topic, the responsibility of the individual both to himself and to the community, the great sage Hillel of the Mishnah is quoted as saying: "If I am not for myself, who will be for me? And if I am only for myself, what am I? And if not now, when?" (Avot 1:14). Many lessons are given in forms that find close parallels in Islamic tradition and ancient Arabian wisdom. One example is the clever mnemonic or alliterative statement of Rabbi Ilay in the Talmud (Eruvin 65b): "A person's character may be judged from three things: *be-koso, be-kiso,* and *be-ka`aso*: by his cup, by his pocket, and by his anger."

In the Jewish world, studying Torah has been the most honorable occupation for thousands of years, and the learned and wise have always been held in high esteem. Nonetheless, note this famous saying by one of the most sagacious sages of the academy in Yavneh, as recorded in the Talmud (Shabbat 17a):

> I am God's creature, and my [ignorant] comrade is God's creature. My work is in the town [i.e., the academy], and his work is in the country [i.e., on a farm]. I rise early for my work, and he rises early for his work. Just as he cannot excel in my work, I cannot excel in his work. Will you say that I do great [work] and he does insignificant work? We have learned that it does not matter whether great or little, as long as he directs his heart to [God who is in] heaven.

Judaism, like Islam, has had various schools of legal interpretation. A tale is told in the Talmud (Eruvin 13b) about an ongoing dispute between the school of Shammai and the school of Hillel:

> The former said: "The law agrees with our views." The latter said: "The law agrees with our views." Then a heavenly voice announced: "Both are the words of the

living God, but the law agrees with the rulings of the
school of Hillel." But since "both are the words of the
living God," why was the law determined according to
the rulings of the school of Hillel? Because those in the
school of Hillel were kindly and modest. They studied
their own rulings and those of the school of Shammai,
and were so humble that they mentioned the rulings of
Shammai before their own. . . . This teaches that whoever humbles himself, the Holy One raises up, and whoever exalts himself, the Holy One humbles. From the
person who seeks greatness, greatness flees. But the person who flees from greatness, greatness follows.[2]

Judaism teaches modest dress, modest eating habits, and a
modest life-style. Moderation is to be practiced in all pursuits
and activities. Business practices must be fair, even to the
extent that if a visitor to a shop has no intention of purchas-
ing an item, he should not ask its price, for such an act will
unfairly raise the expectations of the shopkeeper. These values are, of course, not restricted to Judaism, for most religious
civilizations extol the same ethical and moral virtues. It is not
the intent here to try to prove any moral or ethical superiori-
ty of Judaism. It is, rather, to demonstrate that Jews, like
Muslims and the adherents of most religions, are taught an
excellent moral code by which to live. Too often, prejudice or
the natural human tendency to raise up one's own kind at the

---

[2] As in Islam, both schools are respected to this day, and certain rulings are credited
to each, although neither exists any longer as a separate school of law and interpretation.

expense of the "other" gets in the way of promoting brother-hood and harmony between peoples and religions. Rather than presume that the other is inferior, logic would suggest that the other's thousands of years of religious experience and hundreds of millions of religious adherents should garner one's serious respect. As with all human groups, one can find the exceptionally bad as well as the exceptionally good; most people fit somewhere in the middle.

Part IV
Human Destiny

Judaism, like Christianity and Islam, assumes that existence continues in some way after death. As mentioned in the preceding chapter, Judaism has generally not invested a great deal in trying to uncover the details of the afterlife, and the tradition encompasses a range of views. Two general areas of concern emerge in the discussion. One is the question of what happens immediately after death, a concern generally referred to as the afterlife. A second and related question pertains to what will happen at the future time when the dead are resurrected for judgment.

14

Prospects and Purpose

The Afterlife

The Bible does not mention the afterworlds of heaven for the righteous and hell for sinners. Reward and punishment, according to such biblical sources as Deuteronomy 13 and Jeremiah 3:10 ff., occur only in this world and not in a hereafter. According to the Hebrew Bible, therefore, all of the dead, whether righteous or wicked, enter into a shadowy world located under the earth and referred to as *She'ol*.[1] Even the great prophet and priest Samuel enters this underground domain (1 Samuel 28:8 ff.). There are only two possible exceptions to this rule in the entire Hebrew Bible. The first is Enoch, who, according to Genesis 5:24, "walked with God; then he was no more, for God took him." The second is the prophet Elijah, who is carried heavenward in a chariot of fire (2 Kings 2:11). What might seem to be a discrepancy in these two depictions does not seem to have been considered a problem in the biblical period, but later the rabbis of the Talmud attempted to make sense of it.

---

[1] See Genesis 37:35, 52:38; 1 Samuel 2:6; 1 Kings 2:6; Isaiah 14:15; Psalm 30:4, etc. The root of the word *she'ol* is uncertain. Some suggest that it is *sha'al,* meaning "to ask or question" (Arabic: *sa'alah*); if so, *She'ol* is the "place of question" after the end of life as we know it in our world.

Many human observers note the apparent inconsistency between God's justice in reward and punishment and the daily perception that the righteous often seem to suffer while the wicked prosper. This problem became an issue of great importance only toward the end of the biblical period. It was resolved by the belief that the individual's reward and punishment would be fully meted out in this world *and* in the afterlife. This occurred during the earliest period of the Mishnah and Talmud, and these sacred texts contain ideas and opinions about the afterlife in a heaven (*gan `eden*) and a hell (*gehinnom*; Eng. Gehenna).

The Bible makes reference to a valley outside the gates of Jerusalem called *Gey Hinnom*, the Valley of Hinnom, where it had been customary for Canaanites to practice human sacrifice to the idol Molech. The Bible states that some Israelites also offered their children in fire to idols there and condemns them harshly (2 Kings 23:10, Jeremiah 19:5–6; 2). In the Bible, therefore, the Hinnom Valley, where this practice was carried out, was considered a place of immoral and mistaken religious practice, but there is no sense of an afterlife in hell. The association of *Gey Hinnom* with fire and death (Jeremiah 19:6), however, later provided a name for hell in Judaism, and the word became a part of Arabic as well as European languages (Arabic: *jahannum*). The association between this location and fire and death is biblical, but the concept of hell and heaven in an afterlife seems to have entered Jewish tradition only toward the very end of the biblical period or after.

In the view of the afterlife promulgated in the Talmud and

Midrash, the soul leaves the body after death, but retains a temporary relationship with it for about a year until the body is fully decomposed. Opinions differ among the sages about exactly what occurs during this period and after. Some see this year as a purgatorial period for the soul; others hold that it is purgatorial only for the souls of the wicked. Some maintain that the souls of the righteous enter heaven immediately, whereas the souls of the sinful either suffer in Gehenna or are unable to free themselves from the decomposing body until the year has passed. It is during this period, therefore, that children say the Kaddish prayer for their deceased parents, for the righteous acts of children will help the souls of the parents to enter the Garden. After one year, the headstone is set and the mourner's recitation of Kaddish ceases except on the anniversary of the death.

As noted above, the Bible is almost completely silent about the afterlife. The sages of the Talmud were not all of the same opinion about the condition of the soul after death. Some felt the soul is fully conscious, others that it is quiescent; and there are many discussions about such subjects as how much the dead know of the world they have left behind, whether the dead can communicate with the living, and so on. Although the rabbis believed that there was an afterlife of some kind, they were not much troubled about the details of what was expected to occur there. They did not mind a broad range of speculation, relying ultimately on the statement of Psalm 64:3: "No eye has seen, O God, but You."

RESURRECTION

The idea of resurrection, meaning the belief that the dead will be revived in their bodies and live again, is quite different from the idea of a spiritual life in heaven or hell and also from the idea of the immortality of the soul. While logically separate and distinct, these three concepts are interrelated in that they all deal with what occurs after death, and religious discussions of the afterlife often combine them. The Bible does not have much to say about any of these concepts. However, God is depicted unambiguously as having the power to revive the dead (e.g., Deuteronomy 32:39, 1 Samuel 2:6, Ezekiel 37:1–14). A clear articulation of the mass resurrection of the dead in a future time is only found in one of the latest books of the Bible, Daniel (12:2): "Many of those that sleep in the dust of the earth will awake, some to eternal life, others to reproaches, to everlasting abhorrence."[2] The expectation of a future resurrection, however, is quite common in the Talmud, Midrash, and later Jewish literature. The resurrection revives the dead for judgment. Those who merit it will enter the world-to-come (`olam ha-ba').

Judaism has few theological dogmas, but the concept of resurrection became a very important way to distinguish true believers from those who believed in falsehood. Mishnah Sanhedrin 10:1 gives a sense of the idea's relative importance.

---

[2] Other biblical passages, such as Isaiah 26:19 and Ezekiel 37, are probably metaphorical statements that do not reflect a belief in the resurrection.

All of Israel have a portion in the world-to-come, as it is said: "And your people, all of them righteous, shall possess the land for all time; they are the shoot that I planted, My handiwork in which I glory" (Isaiah 60:21). But these are those [among Israel] who have no share in the world-to-come: those who say that there is no resurrection of the dead.

The resurrection joins body and soul together for the final judgment, for neither may be judged separately, as is explained in a discussion between Rabbi Judah the Prince, known as Rabbi, and a Roman officer in the Talmud:

Antoninus said to Rabbi: "The body and the soul can both free themselves from judgment. The body can plead: 'The soul has sinned, [the proof being] that from the day it left me I lie like a dumb stone in the grave [powerless to do anything].' The soul can say: 'The body has sinned, [the proof being] that from the day I departed from it I fly about in the air like a bird [and commit no sin].'" Rabbi replied: "I will tell you a parable. To what may this situation be compared? To a human king who owned a beautiful orchard which contained splendid figs. The king appointed two watchmen to guard the fruit, one lame and the other blind. One day, the lame man said to the blind: 'I see beautiful figs in the orchard. Come and take me on your shoulder so we can get them and eat them.' So the lame rode the blind, and they took and ate them. Sometime later the owner of the

orchard came and asked them, 'Where are my beautiful
figs!?' The lame man replied: 'Have I feet to walk with?'
The blind man replied: 'Have I eyes to see with?' What
did the king do? He placed the lame upon the blind and
judged them together. So will the Holy One bring the
soul, place it in the body, and judge them together, as it
is written: 'He shall call to the heavens above and to the
earth, that He may judge His people' (Psalm 50:4). 'He
shall call to the heavens above'—this refers to the soul;
'and to the earth, that He may judge His people'—to the
body."

Who will be resurrected for judgment? The sources are not
consistent about this. Some indicate that only Israel will be
resurrected and judged, but most are of the opinion that it
applies to all of humanity. Who will merit the world-to-
come? The Mishnah text quoted above states that all Israel
merits the world-to-come, except for those who commit certain specific sins. The passage continues by including non-
Israelites in the discussion. According to Rabbi Joshua b.
Hananiah, righteous non-Jews have a place in the world-to-
come (Tosefta Sanhedrin 3:2). Opinions vary and are not considered of great importance, because the rabbis recognized
that they are only speculations and do not determine religious law; all would admit the likelihood that all humanity
will be judged, and that the righteous of all faiths and peoples
may merit the world-to-come. Psalm 64:3 ("No eye has seen,
O God, but You") is cited to support the ultimate conclusion
that only God knows the answers to speculative questions of

this kind. The Jewish discussions end much the same way as parallel discussions in Islam on subjects where no final answer may be known for sure: *Allahu a`lam* ("God knows best").

THE REDEMPTION OF THE WORLD

In order to understand the Jewish view of redemption, one must remember the biblical view of world history. Humankind is created with a unique ability to transcend the bonds of instinct, to act creatively, and even to influence nature. Its creativity and willfulness may be dangerous, however, for they can lead as easily to disaster as to excellence. Because of its unique nature, humankind can realize its potential as a blessing only when guided and shaped by God's commandments. The Torah provides the guidance and foundation for the type of human behavior that will lead to blessing and, potentially, to ultimate redemption.

In the Jewish view, the ultimate redemption that will bring blessing to the entire world will be led by those loyal to God's will as formulated in the Torah. Because Jewish thinkers and sages write primarily for their fellow religionists and rarely for non-Jews, their perspective tends to be particularistic rather than universalistic. Although they understand the final redemption as a universal phenomenon, their texts often couch it in terms of its impact on the Jews. This was especially the case in periods when Jews were oppressed. In these eras, Jewish tradition often described the final redemption as bringing succor and consolation to a suffering people, some-

times at the expense of the nations and peoples that were
Israel's oppressors.

In the Bible, God redeemed Israel from the misery of Egypt
in ancient times (Deuteronomy 7:8, 13:6), and will bring ultimate redemption to His people at the End of Days (Isaiah
1:27, 35:10). "[God] shall come as a redeemer to Zion [a poetic reference to Jerusalem], to those in Jacob who turn back
from sin—declares the Lord" (Isaiah 59:20). While the preceding verse implies that redemption is conditional upon
repentance, other passages state that God's forgiveness and
love transcend human sin. "In slight anger, for a moment, I
hid My face from you; but with kindness everlasting I will
take you back in love—said the Lord your Redeemer" (Isaiah
54:8).

Many of the biblical passages treating Israel's redemption
are products of an age in which the Jewish people yearned to
return to their land and reestablish their ancient political and
religious system. Thus the prophecies of redemption often
stress that God will restore Israel to its ancient homeland
under God's protection. The "nationalist" character of some
of these prophecies is clearly discernible in the following
example (Jeremiah 32:37–41):

> See, I will gather them from all the lands to which I
> have banished them in My anger and wrath, and in
> great rage; and I will bring them back to this place and
> let them dwell secure. They shall be My people, and I
> will be their God. I will give them a single heart and a
> single nature to revere Me for all time, and it shall be

well with them and their children after them. And I will make an everlasting covenant with them that I will not turn away from them, and that I will treat them graciously; and I will put into their hearts reverence for Me, so that they do not turn away from Me. I will delight in treating them graciously, and I will plant them in this land faithfully, with all My heart and soul.

One of the biblical terms that conveys this sense of divine redemption is *pada*, equivalent to the Arabic word *fada*, "to redeem." A second biblical term with much the same meaning is *ga'al*, which has no parallel in Arabic, but in the post-biblical period was very widely used in Jewish texts. The term *ge'ullah* ("redemption") almost always refers to the national redemption of the people of Israel and has come to connote national freedom in the modern Hebrew spoken in the State of Israel. In the Talmud, national redemption is dependent upon repentance and good deeds (e.g., Shabbat 118b, Yoma 86b).

The Jewish view of redemption was more thoroughly universalized under the influence of Islam. In the tenth century, Sa`d Ibn Yusuf al-Fayumi (Sa`dia Ga'on), the great sage who headed the most important Jewish academy of the era, situated in Baghdad, wrote that although Jews are the chosen of God, salvation is attained by the righteous of all peoples. From this period onward, writings about the final redemption take on a decidedly more universalistic tone, but one cannot deny that the concept continued to have a strongly nationalist aspect. As was noted in chapter 5 above, it was the idea of national redemption so deeply embedded in Jewish tradition that enabled the modern Zionist movement to have such a powerful impact on Jews throughout the world.

MESSIANISMS

As with many complex religious ideas in Judaism, the concept of messianism has evolved over the ages. The Hebrew word *mashiah* (Arabic: *masih*) means "anointed one" and originally referred to a king or priest who had been officially inducted into office by anointing his head with oil (1 Samuel 10:1).[3] When David became king of Israel and created a great and powerful people and country, he was adored as the great king and called "the anointed one" (*mashiah*). It was assumed that the reign of his dynasty would last forever. After his great empire collapsed, there arose a belief that the House of David would someday be restored by a powerful Davidic king, another *mashiah* like David himself. The yearning for the restored House of David soon took on a sense that the future king would be distinguished by his zeal for justice, and would be intuitively endowed with the ability to judge all cases rightly. Thus the expected "anointed one" was not only a great military and political leader, but a righteous judge who would rule with dignity and justice. After the end of the biblical period, this idea continued to develop. In Roman

---

[3] The meaning of the Arabic root is "to wipe or stroke" or "to measure." The sense of *messiah* is derived from the Aramaic *meshiha*, as confirmed by al-Zamakhshari and al-Baydawi in their Qur'an commentaries.

times Jews believed that God would raise up a great king from the House of David to break the yoke of the infidel empire and reign over a restored kingdom to which the Jews living in exile in the Diaspora would return.

By the time of the Talmud, the messianic redemption had been removed from any immediate historical context. The *mashiah* was now conceived as a king who would redeem and rule Israel at the climax of human history. He would be the agent who established the righteous kingdom of God on earth at the End of Days. He would restore an era of both physical and spiritual happiness. It should be stressed here that all Jewish visions of the Messiah understand that he is only an agent of God, not a savior or redeemer as in Christianity. In Judaism, God is always the savior and redeemer. The Messiah is merely God's agent. Thus the Jewish concept of the Messiah, which preceded the Christian idea of a divine savior, is quite similar to the Islamic concept that came to be associated with the *mahdi*, the rightly guided one, who will restore religion and just rule to the world.

TIKKUN OLAM

All responsible religions are faithful responses to what their adherents believe to be God's expectations. Of course the different religions do not agree with one another about God's expectations, nor do they usually agree internally about how to carry out God's expectations in real life. Nevertheless, one of the primary goals of all responsible religions is to bring individuals, communities, and the world at large to a better place.

Judaism, like all honest religious systems, is concerned with the right and the good, not only for its own adherents but for the world at large. Like all responsible religions, it must balance the needs and requirements of the individual with those of the larger religious community and of the entire world. Judaism therefore has a particularist component of concern for its own adherents and a universalist component of concern for the health and welfare of the whole world, whether Jewish or not. Since this book treats Judaism as a religious civilization, it has centered almost entirely on the particularist aspect; and quite obviously Judaism, like most religions, favors its own believers above the believers of other faith traditions. Moreover, as was explained above, the Jewish people's long history of being a vulnerable and largely powerless minority tended to encourage self-preservation and looking inward rather than looking outward toward others. Nonetheless, Judaism has an important universalist component.

Judaism's sense of dual responsibility for both the particular and the universal is clearly expressed in the following passage from the Talmud (Shabbat 54b): "Whoever can protest and prevent his household from committing a sin and does not, is accountable for the sins of his household; if he could protest and prevent his fellow citizens from sinning and does not, he is accountable for his fellow citizens; if the whole world, he is accountable for the whole world." Similarly, the criteria for deciding whether a person is fit to be a legal witness or judge include that the candidate "be concerned with the welfare of the world" (`oskin bi-yshuvo shel `olam; Sanhedrin 24b).

Universalist concern of this kind is called *tikkun olam*, which literally means "repairing the world" or "setting the world right." It has always been a basic part of Judaism, but the emphasis has been stronger in some periods and weaker in others. As a vulnerable minority religion living in a state of exile for many centuries, Judaism tended to be introspective, stressing the particularist aspects of the tradition in an effort to preserve itself against outside pressures ranging from persecution to conversion.

In the past century in the West, as Jews have been emancipated from the status of persecuted minority and have entered mainstream life, they have often been at the forefront of social and ethical movements working to bring justice and morality to modern society. Not all of these efforts have been successful, but they reflect Judaism's central concern for making the world a better place. For example, Jews make up only a tiny fraction of the population of the United States, but they were a majority of the white activists who participated in the civil rights movement to bring equal rights to African-Americans. Jews were primary organizers of labor unions in the United States in the early twentieth century, and comprised an inordinate part of the leadership and rank-and-file of the socialist and communist movements in Europe, including the revolutionaries who overthrew the czarist regime in Russia. Although communism and socialism did not live up to their utopian ideals—and communism became overtly hostile, indeed murderous, to Judaism and to Jews—their founders and pioneer activists were impelled by a vision of improving the condition of the disadvantaged. The humanitarian impulse so fundamental to Jewish life continues to be expressed in many ways and in many places. Among other things, Jews were deeply involved in the movement to save and aid Bosnia, sent relief to the victims of the devastating earthquake in Turkey, and support charitable work in the United States at levels of participation beyond that of any other group.

Concern for the poor, the hungry, the orphan, and the widow is the legacy of the great prophets of Israel:

> If you banish lawlessness from your midst, the menacing hand and evil speech, and you offer your compassion to the hungry and satisfy the famished creature—then shall your light shine in darkness, and your gloom shall be like noonday. The Lord will guide you always; He will slack your thirst in parched places and give strength to your bones (Isaiah 58:10–11).

But responsibility for those in need was established in law as well as prophetic inspiration. Jewish law requires that one care for the sick, orphans, poor, widows, and others in need. Many of these laws apply to non-Jews as well as to Jews:

> You shall not wrong a stranger or oppress him, for you were strangers in the land of Egypt. You shall not ill-treat any widow or orphan. If you do mistreat them, I will heed their outcry as soon as they cry out to Me (Exodus 22:20–22).

Hear out your fellow men, and decide justly between any man and fellow Israelite or stranger. You shall not be partial in judgment: hear out low and high alike. Fear no man, for judgment is God's (Deuteronomy 1:16–17).

King Solomon even asks God to accept the prayers of non-Israelites at the Jerusalem Temple:

If a foreigner who is not of Your people Israel comes from a distant land for the sake of Your name . . . when he comes to pray toward this House [*bayit*], oh, hear in Your heavenly abode and grant all that the foreigner asks for you. Thus all the peoples of the earth will know Your name and revere You, as does Your people Israel (1 Kings 8:41–43).

Like all religions, Judaism has had to balance its concerns. Over the two thousand years following upon the destruction of the Temple, it tended toward the particularist side of the tradition in order to maintain itself as a small minority in a world overwhelmingly Christian and Muslim. Today, in a world that has shrunk due to incredible advances in communication and transportation technology, and in a much more dangerous world due to the development of weapons of mass destruction, Judaism must reevaluate how it positions itself between the poles of particularism and universalism. All religions today must retreat from inwardness and reach out to nonbelievers in fellowship. Geography no longer insulates us from the other, as we are forced to live among those who will not agree with our religious beliefs. How we are able to succeed in this new, diverse, and crowded world will determine our ability to carry out our own understanding of God's will. Indeed, it will determine our ability to survive.

15

Conclusion

God, in His wisdom, created a diverse world with many different species of plants and animals, and humans with a vast range of external and internal characteristics. The Bible and the Qur'an both acknowledge human diversity. Should it be so surprising, given the tendency for people to disagree about nearly everything, that humanity does not agree about God's designs for us?

Jews, Muslims, and Christians agree that God is one, living, merciful, omnipotent, Creator of the universe. We disagree on the nuances imbedded and derived from our mortal attempts to understand an immortal Power that is beyond human understanding. Even within the three great monotheistic traditions there are major divisions over the meaning of God's designs, as may be so clearly discerned from the variety of religious movements within each tradition.

Historically, the three religious traditions and the institutions that represent them have viewed their sister religions with suspicion and mistrust. If God is one, good, merciful, and all-knowing, why would God give three separate revelations—with much in common, of course, but also with much that seems to be quite contradictory? The nearly universal response to this problem has been to assume that only one

revelation is true or accurate—the others false, no longer
valid, or falsified. Which revelation could represent God's
truth? The answer has always been simple: *my* revelation. The
reader will note how this argument cancels itself out when
voiced by all parties to the debate.

There is a more reasonable response to the impasse, however. Over the course of so many centuries, millions of believers adhered to their separate faiths. And so much wisdom
originated in these faiths, so much compassion flowed from
them, and so much beauty was created to honor them, that it
is logical to believe that the divine will is associated with all
of them. It is logical to assume, given these observations, that
the religious claims of every great civilization should at least
be given the benefit of a doubt. On the other hand, evil and
hatred, sinfulness, and even massacres and other horrible
crimes have been perpetrated in the name of each of these
religions. But sinful acts do not prove that the religions are
false. They simply prove that human weakness is capable of
misunderstanding and distorting God's message. The divine
message is God's. The religious institutions that interpret and
carry out the message are human and therefore prone to
error. The fact of human weakness does not cancel out the
likelihood of divine truth investing all three systems.

The Qur'an teaches that God willed the creation of humanity into multiple communities (Hud 11:118): "If your Lord
had so pleased, He would have made humanity one community; but they continue to disagree."[1] While it is true that the

---

[1] See also Al-Ma'ida 5:48, Al-Nahl 16:93, and Al-Shura 42:48.

following verse suggests that this diversity is a way to test individuals to take the right path, it does not condemn all paths that are not Islam. "Those who believe, and the Jews, Christians, and Sabaeans—whoever believes in God and the Last Day and acts uprightly—they have their reward with their Lord; no fear shall come upon them, neither shall they grieve" (Al-Baqara 2:62). Ultimately, the individual is responsible for his own journey (Al-Nahl 16:93, Al-Shura 42:8).

We would all agree from our own experience that when a number of different witnesses observe an event, each views it from a particular physical and personal angle. When asked in separate interviews to describe the event, they invariably describe it differently and attach a different meaning or sense to it. While all agree that the event truly occurred, they will not agree about its details and meaning. No two human witnesses can possibly understand any event in exactly the same way, though they may agree on certain aspects and may find that their views fall within certain parameters that are shared by a larger group. God, too, is seen by every individual from a different physical and personal angle. But groups agree about certain aspects of their witnessing of God, and these groups represent religious communities.

The Qur'an suggests this very phenomenon in Surat al-Baqara (2:147–148): "The truth is from your Lord, so do not be one of the doubters. Each [community²] has a direction to

---

² The second member of this construct phrase is not given and may refer to verse 146, in which Jews and Christians are mentioned. This is Muhammad b. Jarir al-Tabari's view in his great commentary that relies on the views of the earliest Muslim scholars: *likulli sahib millatin* ("every member of a religious community")" (s.v.

which it turns, so strive [or, compete] with one another in doing good works. Wherever you may be, God will bring you all together, for God has power over all things." According to traditional Muslim commentators, this verse refers to the direction of prayer. Each community has its own *qibla*, or direction, in which it turns toward God in prayer. Each religion sees God from a different angle.

God, who is everywhere, may be experienced everywhere, and different communities will observe God differently, as the Qur'an acknowledges. The essential purpose is to strive, even compete, in doing the good (*al-khayr*). This is healthy competition. Wherever we may be, from whatever angle we observe God, when we strive to do right, God brings us all together, for God, indeed, has power over all things.

2:128, vol. 2, p. 28). For a full examination of this qur'anic theme, see Isa Boullata, "A Qur'anic Principle of Interfaith Relations," in *Christian-Muslim Encounters*, ed. Yvone Yazbeck Haddad and Wadi Zaidan Haddad (Gainesville: University Press of Florida, 1995), pp. 43–53.

Chronology[1]

B.C.E.

Circa 1700   Beginning of the "patriarchal period" during which live Abraham, Sarah, and Hagar in the first generation; Ishmael, Isaac, and Rebecca in the second generation, and Jacob, Rachel, Leah, and Esau in the third generation. At the end of this period, according to the biblical chronology, Joseph brings his father and brothers to live in Egypt with the blessing of Pharaoh (Genesis).

Circa 1250   The approximate period of the biblical Exodus or escape from Egypt into the Sinai Desert, where, according to the biblical chronology, the Israelites lived for forty years (Exodus and Numbers).

Circa 1210   The approximate date for Israel's "conquest" of the Land of Canaan (Joshua).

1210-1010   The Tribal Period, also called the period of the Judges, when Israel is comprised of a loose confederation of twelve tribes living in separate tribal areas within the Land of

---

[1] This chronology is a much expanded version of the work of Judah Gribetz et al., *The Timetables of Jewish History* (New York: Touchstone, 1993). I thank Dr. Stephen Steinlight for his assistance.

Israel (Judges). The tribes worship at a variety of shrines, each headed by a priestly family.

1020 Saul is acclaimed king and anointed by the prophet Samuel (1 Samuel).

1010 David, the youngest son of Jesse from the tribal area of Judah, joins Saul against the Philistine enemy (1 Samuel).

1005 Saul and his son Jonathan fall in battle, and David begins his rule as king from his capital, Hebron (2 Samuel).

1000 or 990 David conquers Jerusalem from the Jebusites (a Canaanite tribe), and Jerusalem becomes the capital of the united tribes of Israel. David captures large areas of land reaching from Sinai to the Upper Euphrates.

967 David dies and Solomon becomes king of the united Israel. Solomon makes alliances with many neighboring nations, but some peoples of the areas captured by David break away and form independent states. Solomon builds a port and fleet on the Gulf of Aqaba and conducts trade to distant lands (1 Kings)

950 Solomon builds the First Temple in Jerusalem and the sacrificial system is unified under the Temple priesthood.

928 Solomon dies and the northern tribes of Israel refuse to recognize his son, Rehoboam. They break away and form a

separate kingdom called Israel, with its capital in Samaria or Shechem (today's Nablus). Independent temple shrines are built also in the north, although many continue to feel allegiance to the Jerusalem Temple. The southern kingdom with its capital still in Jerusalem is called Judah after the name of its most powerful tribe.

928-722 The period of the divided kingdom. The northern and southern kingdoms are sometimes in alliance and sometimes at war. The prophets Elijah, Elisha, Hosea, Amos, and Isaiah are active during this period (1 and 2 Kings, Isaiah, Hosea, Amos, Micah, and Psalms).

721 The northern kingdom of Israel falls to the Assyrian army, and many of its inhabitants are deported to foreign lands. The deported peoples, the so-called Ten Lost Tribes, assimilate to their new homes and lose their identity as Israel. The southern kingdom of Judah survives under King Hezekiah.

715 King Hezekiah helps to consolidate the religious system and unify the surviving kingdom of Judah.

609 The Assyrians are defeated by the Babylonians, who now become the most powerful empire in the Middle East.

721-586 Judah survives as an independent kingdom, occasionally paying tribute to the empires of Mesopotamia and Egypt. The prophets Isaiah, Jeremiah, Zephaniah, Nahum are active during this period (2 Kings, Isaiah, Zephanaiah, Nahum, Ruth, Proverbs).

587-6   Babylonia conquers Jerusalem and destroys the Temple. Judean officials are executed or exiled to Babylonia with thousands of others, and Judah is made a province of Babylonia (2 Kings, Ezekiel, Jeremiah, and Lamentations).

539 King Cyrus of Persia defeats Babylonia.

538   King Cyrus allows the Judean exiles living in Babylonia to return to their native land in Judea and rebuild the Temple (Ezra, ch. 1).

515 The Second Jerusalem Temple is completed and rededicated, but Judah is weak. The prophets Haggai and Zechariah serve during this period (Haggai. Zechariah), and the last biblical prophet, Malakhi, serves around 450 (Malakhi).

445-370   The approximate period during which Nehemiah and Ezra came from Persia to Judah to help rebuild Jerusalem's fortifications, administer the community and instruct the Jews in the laws of the Torah after a long period of religious and social decline. There is great consolidation of the Jewish community in Judah, although very large populations of Jews continue to live in many areas of the Middle East (Nehemiah, Ezra).

333-323 Alexander the Great conquers most of the Middle East from Egypt to India, including Judah, which will prosper for a time under benevolent Greek rule.

323 Alexander dies and his empire is divided among his top generals. Judah with its capital, Jerusalem, passes between Ptolemaic Egypt and Seleucid Mesopotamia during the next century and a half. The last books of the Bible, Ecclesiastes and Daniel, are written during this period.

260 Around this time, the Septuagint translation of the Torah (the first five books of the Hebrew Bible) is made into Greek. Jerusalem is growing into a Hellenistic commercial center with increasing importance for both the Jewish and Greek populations of Judea under the Ptolemaic Greeks centered in Egypt. The Judean population is growing at an unprecedented rate.

175 Antiochus IV succeeds his brother to become the ruler of the Mesopotamian Greek Seleucid Empire, which has taken Judah from the Egyptian Greek Ptolemaic Empire. He is a strong Hellenizer whose program attracts many Jewish Judeans. The Jewish population of Judea divides into factions that support or oppose increasing Hellenization, and even the high priest of the Temple begins to introduce Greek religious ideas, rituals, and symbols into the Temple worship.

165 A rebellion begins against the Hellenizing Jews of Jerusalem led by a family of priests from Modi'in (near

today's Lod). The revolt becomes a large uprising against Hellenizing trends among Jews and their supporters, the Seleucid Empire. The family and their followers, known as the Maccabees, repel repeated attempts by the Seleucid Greeks to regain control of Judah.

164   The Maccabees purify and rededicate the Temple in Jerusalem, an event commemorated in the holiday of Hanukkah, but the battles with the Seleucids continue for twenty years. Jews are living throughout the Mediterranean by this time, including Rome, Southern France and Spain, and all of North Africa. The Maccabees establish a dynasty of kings deriving from their priestly family known as the Hasmonean dynasty, and rule Judah for more than 150 years. Despite their platform of anti-Hellenism, the Hasmoneans themselves become very strongly influenced by Hellenism.

Circa 100   Two groups of Jews, known as Pharisees and Saducees, emerge out of the Jewish population of Judea and begin to have influence over religious issues and practice.

Circa 75   The Dead Sea community, perhaps the same community known as the Essenes, moves into its desert abode and separates from the rest of the Jewish community in Judea.

63 The Roman general Pompey conquers Judea, enters the sacred enclosure of the Temple and violates its sanctity. Judea becomes a vassal state of Rome.

50 The Jewish population of Rome has reached well over 10,000. Many of the so-called Dead Sea Scrolls discovered in caves near the Dead Sea are composed around this time.

40 The Roman Senate appoints Herod king of Judea. He later marries Mariamne of the Hasmonean royal house to gain popular support.

22 Herod begins a huge construction program throughout Judea, including the port of Caesarea on the Mediterranean, and builds fortresses and cities throughout the land. These include Herodiom and the palace-fortress of Massada, and a huge reconstruction of the Jerusalem Temple.

4 Death of Herod

C.E.

10 The great rabbis Hillel and Shammai live during this period. Jews make up some 10 percent of the population of the Roman Empire and 20 percent of the eastern provinces in the Middle East.

33 Pontius Pilate, the Roman governor of Judea, has a Jewish preacher named Jesus of Nazareth crucified in April. Jesus' followers (virtually all of them Jews), calling themselves Nazarenes, regard him as the anointed descendant of King David, the Messiah.

36   Pilate is dismissed as governor after the Samaritans protest his cruelty.

38   In Alexandria, Egypt, Jews are attacked and many are killed because they refuse to worship the Roman emperor Caligula. The following year, the Jews in Yavneh (in Judea) destroy an altar set up by Caligula to himself. In retribution, Caligula orders a gold statue of himself to be placed in the Jerusalem Temple. The order is canceled after great Jewish protests. The tension between Jews and their Roman overlords grows worse through the following three decades, with occasional violence and much disruption.

50   The Jewish community of Egypt reaches hundreds of thousands, and Jews are spread throughout the Mediterranean in large numbers. Many Greco-Romans convert to Judaism or begin Jewish practices without formal conversion.

66   Large numbers of Jews throughout Judea revolt against Rome, beginning in Caesarea and Jerusalem. The Roman Empire responds by sending General Vespasian and 60,000 Roman soldiers. He captures most Judean cities over the next three years and arrives at the walls of Jerusalem. Called back to Rome and declared emperor, Vespasian is replaced in the field by Titus.

70 Jerusalem falls in mid-summer and the Temple is burned. In the meantime, Rabbi Yohanan ben Zakkai establishes an

academy in the small town of Yavneh and continues to teach the traditions of Judaism under Roman occupation. In so doing, he establishes the new Pharisaic strategy for Jewish national survival: no longer political sovereignty but religious autonomy. The Romans impose a punitive tax on the Jews and seriously restrict their rights.

73   The last Judean fortress, Massada, falls to the Roman army.

79   The great Jewish historian, Flavius Josephus, completes his detailed histories, *The Jewish War* and *Antiquities of the Jews*, which provide invaluable historical information about Jewish life and politics in Judea.

80   Rabbi Gamaliel II takes over the Yavneh academy and begins to strengthen and reorganize the Jewish communities of the land that had been disrupted so badly by the war against Rome. The rabbis mentioned in the Mishnah continue to learn and teach the traditions, organizing their material into oral literature that would spread throughout the region in rabbinic study circles. Students seek knowledge at the feet of master rabbis.

100   The followers of Jesus and his teaching have increased significantly by this time, with a great many Greco-Romans as well as Jews now considering him the Messiah and carrying a sense of divinity. The organized Jewish community of Judea rejects this idea and tries to keep the Jewish believers in Jesus

apart from the remainder of the Jewish community. Tension and friction increase between Jews and Christians.

100-132 Tension between the Roman occupiers and the Jews of the land continue, with a number of open revolts in Judea and in Roman cities such as Alexandria and Cyrenaica (west of Egypt in North Africa), and in Mesopotamia. Jews are punished severely and plan a rebellion, carrying out occasional guerrilla attacks against occupying Roman troops.

132 An open rebellion against Rome is led by Simon bar Kosiba, also called Bar Kokhba (son of a star). The Jews defeat the combined standing armies in Syria, Egypt and Arabia and take Jerusalem. They mint their own currency and declare their independence from Rome. Rome then counterattacks with legions from as far away as England, destroying the resistance.

135 The last stronghold of the Jewish rebels at Betar falls to Rome. The Roman historian Dio Cassius counts over 600,000 dead, such large numbers supported by the descriptions in Jewish sources (Eikhah Rabbah and Jerusalem Talmud). Hadrian punishes the Judeans by turning Jerusalem into a pagan city, Aelia Capitolina, forbidding Jews even to enter it, and wreaking destruction in Judea. The Jewish religious leadership moves to the Galilee in the north. Some groups of survivors flee to the huge Jewish community in Babylonia (Mesopotamia), where they establish schools.

200 The Jewish community of Babylonia is very large and organized under the *resh galuta*, the "Head of the Exile," who reports to the Persian king.

215 Judah Ha Nasi ("Judah the Prince") edits the large compendium of Jewish lore and law retained mostly in oral form and commits it to writing as the Mishnah. The Mishnah contains the laws by which the rabbis govern the Jewish community. More academies are established in Babylon in which the Mishnah is taught, expanding rabbinic knowledge into the large Jewish communities outside the Land of Israel.

220 Roman persecution of Jews begins to subside as it increases its persecution of Christians. The Jews no longer rebel against Rome, but develop a response to living in Diaspora that strengthens Judaism as a religious civilization without boundaries. Intense study of the Mishnah results in continued expansion of Jewish oral law and lore that will eventuate many years later in a composition called the Talmud. The Jerusalem Talmud is used to govern the Jews in Israel; the parallel Babylonian Talmud is ministered by the *resh galuta*.

250 Jewish interpretive literature known as Midrash begins to emerge in the Land of Israel, along with Hebrew poetry known as *piyyutim*. A form of Jewish mysticism also evolves, called *ma`aseh merkava*, that attempts to unite practitioners with the divine through a mystic journey. The Jewish community of Babylon continues to grow stronger as it establishes highly successful academies of learning.

312 Emperor Constantine takes control of Italy and promotes
Christianity in his domains. As a result, the organized
Christian Church, which has been in competition with
Judaism since its inception and rejection by the Jewish com-
munity, begins aggressively to proselytize and humiliate
Jews. Constantine begins to pass legal edicts oppressive to
Judaism. His support for Christianity eventuates in that reli-
gion becoming the official religion of the empire. Thus the
Roman Empire henceforth is referred to as the (Christian)
Byzantine Empire.

337 Constantius succeeds his father as Byzantine emperor
and extends his father's anti-Jewish laws. Succeeding emperors will continue to pass extensive anti-Jewish legislation that
will establish the degradation of Judaism in Byzantine law
and in the consciousness of Christians everywhere. The situation will become so difficult for the Jews of the Land of Israel
that within a few decades they will not be able to continue
their ambitious program of intense religious study of rabbinic
lore.

400 The lore of the Land of Israel, called the Jerusalem
Talmud, is edited, encompassing two centuries of rabbinic
wisdom and lore. This marks the end of productive rabbinic
study in the Land of Israel under intense and official
Christian pressure. The program of rabbinic study will continue with great success in Babylon for many more centuries

under the rule of the Sassanian Persians and then the Muslims. Jewish communities are well established in Arabia, both in the Hijaz and the Yemen.

400-638 The Jewish communities of the Byzantine Empire continue to decline as the anti-Jewish legislation and persecution increase. Synagogues are occasionally destroyed, communities are pressured and occasionally forced to convert to Christianity, and violence is intermittently perpetrated against Jewish individuals and communities. The balance of Jewish strength and creativity shifts definitively to Babylon (today's Iraq).

456-502 Waves of anti-Jewish acts are ordered by the Persian monarchy, resulting in the closing of Jewish academies, the assassination of Jewish rabbinic leadership, and the migration of Jewish communities.

517 The Jew Yusuf Dhu Nuwas becomes king of the Arabian Himyar tribal kingdom in what is today Yemen and leads a powerful movement that is eventually overpowered by the Christian forces of Abyssinia.

Circa 600 The Talmud of Babylonia is edited and published.

613 The Visigothic Christian king of Spain, Sisebut, orders all Jews to convert or leave. Some leave, some convert, and some remain Jews in secret.

614 The Persian army captures Jerusalem from the Byzantines and places Jews in charge. Jews exact revenge against their Christian oppressors with violence and by banning Christians from the city. When the Byzantines regain control of the city three years later, the Jews are violently punished.

622 Year of the Hijra. Muhammad and his community move to Medina where they come into contact with its well-organized Jewish community.

624 Battle of Badr, followed by the banishment of the Jewish tribe of Medina, the Qaynuqa'.

625 Battle of Uhud, followed by the banishment of the Jewish tribe of Medina, the Nadir.

627 Battle of the Trench (al-Khandaq), followed by the destruction of the Jewish tribe of Medina, the Qurayza.

628 Capture of Khaybar with favorable terms given to the Jews.

632 Death of the Prophet Muhammad.

638 Muslims conquer Jerusalem from the Byzantines, establish a more tolerant policy regarding the Jews, and allow a Jewish community to be established in Jerusalem permanently for the first time since the second century.

639 Babylonian Jews assist in the Arab conquest of Persia, hoping for (and enjoying) a more tolerant Jewish policy than that of the Sassanian Persians.

711 Jews or, more likely, crypto-Jews (Jews practicing outwardly as Christians as a result of Christian persecution and forced conversions) assist Tarik bin Ziyad to conquer Spain, serving in military outposts and helping to supply them. Many Jewish refugees in North Africa return to Spain.

717 The caliph Umar II begins to enforce laws discriminating against religious minorities in Babylonia, excluding Jews and others from government appointments and compelling them to wear distinctive dress.

732 At the Battle of Tours, Charles Martel defeats the Arabs and stops their further incursion into Europe.

755 The Umayyad kingdom in Spain with its capital in Cordoba welcomes Jews and allows them to enter all professions. The tolerance of Islamic Spain attracts many Jews from other countries.

762-765 The Abbasid caliph al-Mansur builds the new capital of Baghdad, which will become a center for Jewish as well as Islamic learning and civilization.

765 Anan ben David, a Babylonian Jew, emerges as the head of a Jewish group eventually to be called the Kara'ites that

opposes the Rabbinic system and reliance on the Talmud. It is generally believed that the Kara'ites were influenced by the Islamic political as well as religious environment.

786 After a period of relative tolerance in the east, Jews suffer from heavy taxes and restrictions under the caliph Harun al-Rashid.

853 Natronai, the gaon of the academy of Sura in Babylonia, is the first Jewish leader to write religious legal letters in Arabic. Previously, all were written only in Hebrew or Jewish Aramaic.

873 Byzantine emperor Basil forces many Jews to convert to Christianity.

900 Bought off the land and forbidden further land ownership in Islamic lands, Jews emerge as a potent force in international commerce, in both the Christian and Islamic worlds, traveling easily across international borders and trading from as far as Spain and France to China. Wealthy Jews assist both Christian kings and Muslim caliphs and sultans to finance their projects.

940 The Jew Hasdai ibn Shaprut becomes the personal physician and minister of finance for the Cordovan caliph, Abd al-Rahman III. He, like other prominent Jews, supports Jewish scholars, poets, scientists, and philosophers, helping to develop one of the highest periods of Jewish civilization in Spanish cities and in the urban centers of other parts of the Islamic

world. Hasdai supports the great lexicographer Menahem ibn Shaprut and the poet and linguist Dunash ibn Labrat. The Jewish "Golden Age of Spain" begins under the caliph Abd al-Rahman III and will continue for some two hundred years.

940-1146 The Jewish "Golden Age of Muslim Spain."

942 Saadia ben Yosef (whose Arabic name is Sa`d Ibn Yusuf al-Fayumi), gaon of the Babylonian academy in Pumbedita, dies. Philosopher, linguist, poet, and legal scholar, he translated the Bible into Arabic and wrote an Arabic commentary (in Hebrew letters) which, although not entirely extant, is used to this day.

1000 Gershom ben Yehudah, rabbi and recognized head of the Jewish communities of Rhineland Germany, begins to develop the German (or Ashkenazi) school of Jewish learning. One of his most important decrees was to place a ban on bigamy among Ashkenazi Jews, a practice that continues among the Jews living in the Islamic world.

1024-1038 Shmuel HaNagid (Isma1`il ibn Naghrela) is the vizier of the Muslim king of Granada, Habbus. He continues as vizier under Habbus's successor, Badis. He is also the general of the king's army, a poet, scholar, and head of the Jewish community.

1030 Abdul-Walid Marwan ibn Janah (known also as Rabbenu Yonah), a Spanish Jewish physician and linguist, writes a book using the discovery of his predecessor Yehudah ibn Hayyuj that as in Arabic, all Hebrew words derive from roots made up of three consonants. His lexicon of Hebrew written in Arabic, *The Book of Roots*, is so original that Hebrew linguists consult it even today.

1020-1057 Solomon ibn Gabirol, exceptional Hebrew poet from Malaga, Spain, writes a famous metaphysical work translated into Latin and read throughout Christian Europe as *Fons Vitae*, "The Fountain of Life."

1066 Muslims riot against Jews in Granada, and many Jews are killed, including Yosef HaNagid, the son and successor of Shmuel HaNagid.

1080 Rashi (Rabbi Shlomo ben Yitzhak) of Troyes, France, writes an extensive commentary on most of the Bible that is still read by most Jews today. He will later write the most important commentary on the Babylonian Talmud. Rashi will be one of the few Jewish survivors of the First Crusade.

1096 In May, people gathering in the German Rhineland for the First Crusade attack and slaughter Jews in all the cities in the region, and they continue to massacre Jews on their way to the Middle East. In Hungary, locals who do not tolerate the Crusaders' violent behavior finally put a stop to these attacks on Jews.

1099 Crusaders under Godfrey of Bouillon capture Jerusalem and indiscriminately massacre Jews and Muslims. They also kill many local Christians who are mistaken for Muslims or Jews because of their eastern-style dress.

1144 Jews in Norwich, England, are accused of murdering a Christian child for alleged ritual use of his blood. This is the first in a series of vilifying and false accusations that spread through much of Europe in the following decades and centuries, resulting in violence against Jews.

1148 The Almohad Muslims (*al-muwahhidun*) conquer Spain from the more tolerant Muslim rulers, close Jewish schools of learning and synagogues, and force conversion to Islam. Many Jews emigrate to the Christian part of Spain or elsewhere. This marks the end of the "Golden Age of Muslim Spain."

1140-1350 The Jewish "Golden Age of Spain" continues in the Christian north as Jews, extremely worldly and well educated in the advanced environment of Muslim Spain, are welcomed for their learning and talents. They serve the Christian kings who welcome them, advancing the technology and civilization of northern Spain at the expense of the southern, Muslim areas. Jewish linguists translate many Arabic works of philosophy and science into Spanish, thereby introducing them to the Christian world for the first time. Great Jewish poets, philosophers, linguists, and religious scholars of Christian Spain include Abraham ibn Daud, Yehudah HaLevi, Abraham ibn Ezra, and many others. Many of the great Jewish works of Muslim Spain written originally in Arabic are translated into Hebrew.

1165 Moses Maimonides arrives in Egypt with his family after escaping the persecutions of Almohades. Serving as the personal physician of the Muslim vizier, al-Fadil, he writes some of the most important and brilliant works of Jewish philosophy, law, and religion since the Talmud.

1190   Following his conquest of Jerusalem from the Crusaders, Salah al-Din (Saladin) allows the Jews to resettle in the city.

1200s Position of Jews in Christian Europe declines greatly, leading to their eventual expulsion from virtually every state in Central and Western Europe.

1240s The Talmud is publicly burned in Paris.

1290 The Jews are expelled from England.

1298 Rindfleisch massacres in Central Europe cover a much larger geographical area than that of the first Crusade, with some 3,400 Jews killed.

1306 The Jews are expelled from France.

1315 The Jews are invited to return to France.

1322 The Jews are again expelled from France.

1329 Jews are invited by Peking to assist in outfitting the imperial army.

1333 Casimir the Great comes to power in Poland, bringing with him a favorable attitude toward Jews. Jews begin to move from Western Europe to a growing and united Poland, which welcomes them for their skills and in order to offset the power and influence of the ethnic Germans. The Jewish community of Poland will become the largest in the world.

1348 The Black Death reaches Europe from central Asia. Although the Jews die in the plague along with everyone else, they are accused of causing it by poisoning wells. The church authorities attempt but fail to protect them against the mobs in many parts of Europe, and thousands are killed.

1354 Under Sultan al-Malik al-Salih, Jews and Christians in Egypt-Syria must wear special clothes to distinguish them from Muslims, along with other restrictions.

1391 Anti-Jewish riots, fomented by Ferrant Martinez, a Jew-hater who held high church office in Seville, spread throughout Christian Spain and result in the deaths of thousands and the burning of many synagogues. Many Jewish refugees settle in Algeria, which becomes a new Jewish center. Jews will continue to flee to North Africa and other Muslim countries as Christian Spain further restricts their freedoms.

1438 The first *mellah* or Jewish quarter is established by the government in Fez, Morocco, in order to protect Jews from mob violence in the city. Such Jewish quarters initially spread in order to benefit the Jews, but by the sixteenth and seven-

teenth centuries they become ghettos to which Jews are ostra-
cized.

1453 The Ottoman Turks capture Constantinople. Because
the Ottoman Empire adopts an open and liberal policy
toward Jews, many flee Western and Central Europe for the
Ottoman Empire.

1478 Pope Sixtus IV authorizes Ferdinand and Isabella, the
rulers of Spain, to organize an Inquisition in order to extirpate
false Christians, mostly former Jews who converted to
Christianity.

1492 The Jews are expelled from Spain. Most flee to Portugal,
where they will be expelled a few years later. Others flee to
the Ottoman Empire which welcomes them; some flee to
North Africa, Western Europe and the New World of the
Americas. The Inquisition eventually arrives in the Americas.

1516 Palestine becomes part of the Ottoman Empire, facili-
tating the movement of Jews to the Land of Israel. Safed
becomes an important commercial and cultural center, and
the Jewish community there greatly increases.

The first ghetto is established in Western Europe in Venice;
the name probably derives from a cannon foundry in the
vicinity.

1536 Suleiman the Magnificent, the Sultan of the Ottoman
Empire, begins construction of the wall surrounding

Jerusalem. It will be completed six years later, offering protection to the city and thereby attracting Jews as well as others to settle there.

1580 The Council of the Four Lands emerges in Poland, offering a limited amount of autonomy to the Jewish communities there. Jewish life in Poland attracts many emigrants that will swell the Jewish population there to be the largest in the world.

1602 A community of Jews begins to live openly in Amsterdam, which will become another haven for Jews fleeing persecution in other parts of Christian Europe. The Jewish community of Amsterdam will become highly influential and will attempt to help troubled Jews throughout the world. It will also become a Jewish intellectual center as well as a center for free thinkers.

1622 The Jews of Mashshad, Iran are forced to convert to Islam. Known as "New Muslims" (*Jadid al-Islam*), most continue to practice their Judaism in secret.

1648 Led by Bogdan Chmielnicki, Ukrainian peasants and Dnieper Cossacks revolt against their Polish landlords by sacking their Jewish agents and their families, and slaughtering tens of thousands of Jewish victims in over 300 communities. This leads to a large-scale Jewish migration back toward Western Europe. With the exception of the Holocaust in the twentieth century, the Chmielnicki pogroms result in

the greatest loss of Jewish life in all of Jewish history in
Christian Europe.

1654 The first Jews arrive in New Amsterdam (later to be
called New York) after being expelled from the Dutch
colonies in Brazil when the Portuguese capture them.

1656 Barukh Spinoza is excommunicated from the Jewish
community of Amsterdam for denying the divine origin of
the Torah. He will become an outstanding figure in world
philosophy.

1665 Shabbetai Zevi, a Jewish false messiah, mesmerizes
huge numbers of Jews who believe him to be the Awaited
One. Many Jews abandon their property and livelihoods in
order to follow him. The following year he is summoned to
Constantinople by the sultan and given the choice of conversion to Islam or death for his messianic claims. He converts to
Islam.

1676 The leader of Yemen destroys all the synagogues and
attempts to exile all non-Muslims, though they will be
allowed back four years later.

1740 Israel Ba'al Shem Tov, the founder of Hasidism, establishes himself at Medzibezh in Podolia. His emphasis on
inner fervor and joy over cold attempts at intellectualism
attract many followers that will build an extremely influential
Jewish movement.

1777 The Jews of New York are granted equality under the law as the New York State constitution abolishes religious discrimination.

1789 The French General Assembly grants civil and political rights to Protestants, but the deputies from Alsace and Lorraine refuse to agree to the emancipation of Jews.

1791 The French General Assembly admits all Jews, as individuals, to full emancipation. The offer requires the dismantling of the organized Jewish community.

1795 The Third Partition of Poland brings almost a million Jews under Russian rule. Although Jews have been prohibited by Russian law from living in Russia for hundreds of year, czarist Russia now has the largest Jewish population in the world. By the early 1800s, the Jews of Russia will become among the most impoverished and destitute of the world.

1800 Population census. Among a world population of 720 million, the Jews number 2.5 million.

1802-1816 Napoleon Bonaparte becomes first consul, thus undisputed master of France, and later emperor (1804-1814). As a result of French victories during the Napoleonic Wars many of the remaining shackles of medieval life are broken throughout mid-Europe, and the principle of equality is introduced into many countries. The effect of Napoleon's domination of Europe is to do more to promote Jewish emancipation than had been accomplished in the previous three hundred years. German Jews in particular regard Napoleon as one of principal forerunners of their emancipation in Germany.

1808-1810   Israel Jacobson, German financier, gathers like-minded Jews together to pioneer the introduction of reforms in order to "modernize" Judaism. He will open a Reform synagogue in his Berlin home in 1815.

1818   The New Israelite Temple Association of Hamburg institutes the first systematic Reform synagogue prayer services.

1824 Karl Marx is baptized at the age of six. His father could not practice as a lawyer in Prussia, so he baptizes his family into Christianity.

1832   Rabbi Abraham Geiger becomes rabbi in Weisbaden, Germany, where he institutes his first efforts to introduce reform into synagogue services.

1835 Czar Nicholas I issues new laws further restricting the economic, civil, and social rights of Jews in Russia.

1836 Tzvi Hirsch Kalischer, Orthodox rabbi and early proto-Zionist thinker, asks the wealthy Rothschild family in Frankfurt for funds to purchase land in Palestine for colonization by Jews.

1844 The Russian government abolishes the last vestige of Jewish self-government and transfers Jewish communal supervision to the municipalities and the police.

1845 Rabbi Zacharias Frankel, chief rabbi of Dresden, withdraws from the Reform Rabbinical Conference because of its extreme liberalization. He forms a middle-way between Reform and tradition that will become the movement known as Conservative Judaism.

1875 Hebrew Union College, the first Jewish seminary in the United States, is founded in Cincinnati, Ohio, by Isaac M. Wise.

1878 Petah Tikvah, a Jewish farming community, is established in Palestine. Meanwhile, the situation of the Jews in Russia and Poland is deteriorating significantly, and Jewish leaders throughout Europe are attempting to find a solution for the terrible situation of their brethren. Some suggest funding communities for them in Ottoman Palestine.

1879 The German historian Heinrich von Treitschke justifies racially based German anti-Semitism and attacks the Jewish desire to establish a "mongrel" German-Jewish culture. His scholarly reputation provides anti-Semitism with a cloak of respectability.

1881 After the assassination of Czar Alexander II, a wave of massacres (pogroms) against Jews occurs in more than 100

Russian communities, condoned if not inspired by the minister of the interior, Ignatiev. In response to these pogroms and increasing government persecution, Jews begin a mass-migration from Eastern Europe to the Americas, Western Europe, and Palestine.

1882 Czar Alexander III promulgates the May Laws, further restricting Jewish life and causing an intensification of Jewish flight from Russia.

1882 Rishon Le-Zion is the first Jewish settlement in Palestine established by Jews from outside the country.

1884 The first conference of the Hovevei Zion (Lovers of Zion) groups is held in Kattowitz in Germany. It calls for European Jews to return to agriculture in Palestine.

1890 The Hovevei Zion found Haderah, a village on the coastal plain in Palestine.

1891 The Russian government orders the expulsion of Jews from Moscow.

1894 Captain Alfred Dreyfus, a Jewish officer in the French army, is accused of passing military secrets to the Germans and is arrested. He will be court-martialed, degraded, and sentenced to solitary confinement on Devil's Island off the coast of French Guiana. It will later be discovered that he was framed. Theodor Herzl, then Paris correspondent of a

Viennese newspaper who covered the case, comes to the conclusion that Europe will never accept the Jews as equal citizens. He becomes instrumental in forming an international Zionist organization.

1897   The First Zionist Congress convenes in Basel, Switzerland, under the leadership of Theodor Herzl. It advocates large-scale migration and settlement of Palestine. In the same year, the Bund, the social-democratic league of Jewish workers in Russia, Poland, and Lithuania, is founded one year before the Russian social-democratic party. It works on behalf of the Russian and Jewish proletariat and fights against anti-Jewish discriminatory laws.

1900 The world Jewish population is about 10.5 million out of a world population of 1.8 billion), having increased fourfold from the 2.5 million in 1800. Jews in Prussia and Vilna are still being falsely accused of ritual murder, but they are vindicated in public trials.

1903 Kishinev pogrom (massacre), organized by the Russian Interior Ministry and local officials, results in hundreds of Jewish dead and injured, and thousands of shops and homes plundered or destroyed. This event strongly influences many Jews to find their way to Palestine and to begin the formation of Jewish defense groups to try to protect themselves from the mob. It also stimulates a worldwide outcry against Russia by organized Jewry.

1904 Forty-three pogroms throughout Russia are recorded.

1905 Government-inspired pogroms take place in 660 Russian Jewish communities during one week, resulting in thousands of dead and wounded and widespread damage of property. This, too, spurred tens of thousands of Jews to flee Russia for the West and Palestine.

Albert Einstein publishes *The Special Theory of Relativity*, which includes his famous $E = mc^2$. Sigmund Freud writes *Three Essays on the Theory of Sexuality*.

1906 In the wake of and to protest the pogroms in Russia and Moldavia (now Moldova), the American Jewish Committee, the first of the historic American Jewish defense agencies, is founded to secure and defend Jewish rights and interests around the world and in the United States. Its history of advocacy regarding Jewish causes internationally and particularly on behalf of democratic pluralism, civil rights, religious liberty, and interreligious understanding in America is symbolic of the acculturation and inclusion of America's Jews and the ascent of the Jewish community to power and influence in the United States.

1909 The first kibbutz, Degania, is founded in Palestine. The city of Tel Aviv is founded.

1913 Leo Frank is falsely convicted of murdering a white Christian female in the state of Georgia and is lynched when his death sentence is commuted. His murder by a mob inflamed by anti-Semitic and racist populist politicians, and the general political exploitation of his case by anti-Semites, marks a particularly virulent moment in the history of American anti-Semitism and leads to the founding of the Anti-Defamation League of B'nai B'rith.

1914 Archduke Franz Ferdinand is assassinated at Sarajevo, leading to the outbreak of WWI.

1917 The Bolsheviks, led by Vladimir Lenin and Leon Trotsky, seize power in Russia. British forces attack Jerusalem and the Turks withdraw. The British government issues the Balfour Declaration, viewing "with favor the establishment in Palestine of a national home for the Jewish people, and will use their best endeavors to facilitate the achievement of this object, it being clearly understood that nothing shall be done which may prejudice the civil and religious rights of existing non-Jewish communities."

1918 On November 11, WWI ends.

1919 Great social trauma and dislocation throughout Europe in the aftermath of the war is often blamed on the Jews. Ukrainian soldiers and peasants in a number of locations kill nearly 3,000 Jews. The new Soviet Union dissolves all Jewish religious communities and bans Zionist movements. During the Russian Civil War that follows the Revolution, the counterrevolutionary Russian White Army and their Ukrainian nationalist allies under General Petliura conduct numerous

pogroms, killing over 1,500 Jews. A Ukrainian band of peasants conducts pogroms in forty communities killing about
6,000 Jews. Altogether, some 685 pogroms and 249 lesser riots
against Jews occur in the Ukraine in 1919.

1920 Palestine Mandate granted by the League of Nations to
Great Britain. Arabs riot in Jerusalem in response to the open
British policy on Jewish immigration to Palestine. Seven Jews
are killed. Jewish defense forces are organized, and the armed
conflict between Jews and Arabs in Palestine begins.

1922 British government forbids Jewish land purchase and
immigration in Palestine Mandate east of the Jordan River.

1924   Calvin Coolidge signs the Immigration Act of 1924
which ends unrestricted immigration, including mass Jewish
immigration, to the U.S.

1929 Widespread Arab riots throughout Palestine result in
130 Jewish deaths. The British respond with a policy to limit
Jewish immigration, which in turn increases political pressure by all parties. Further outbreaks of violence will occur
for the next two decades until the withdrawal of the mandate
and the partition of Palestine in 1948.

1933 Hitler becomes chancellor of Germany and the Nazi-
controlled government immediately begins to implement a
long series of anti-Jewish laws, boycotts of Jewish businesses,
book-burnings, dismissals of Jews from government, the mil-

itary and academic posts, beatings and, eventually, mass-murder. Jews begin to flee Germany, many of them immigrating to Palestine.

The Nazis establish their first concentration camp: Dachau.

1935 The Nazis enact the Nuremberg Laws. Among other harsh measures against Germany's Jews, they deprive them of the right to vote and hold public office, and they outlaw marriages between Jews and non-Jews.

1936 The Arab Higher Committee is established in Palestine, demanding cessation of Jewish immigration and the establishment of a democratic Palestinian government. The "Arab Revolt" begins, which lasts for three years during which violent acts and reprisals are undertaken by both sides. In the meantime, German persecution of Jews increases and influences anti-Semitic acts in other countries, putting more pressure on Jews to escape Europe. The Jews of Palestine will begin to facilitate illegal Jewish entry in order to rescue Jews from Europe.

1938 President Roosevelt convenes the Evian Conference in France where delegates from thirty-two countries discuss the refugee problem. The meeting accomplishes little except to underscore the refusal of most Western countries to accept Jewish refugees.

On *Kristallnacht*, November 9-10, the Nazis destroy Jewish property throughout Germany and Austria, burning many synagogues, murdering many Jews in the streets, and deporting some 30,000 Jews to concentration camps.

1939 WWII begins with the German invasion of Poland. Russia then invades Poland from the east and the country, with its millions of Jews, is divided between them. Thousands of Jews are murdered within the first few weeks of the German occupation.

1940 The Warsaw ghetto is created and sealed; the *Judenrat* is established in Lublin; and the Lodz ghetto is sealed.

1941 The Germans construct the Auschwitz II-Birkenau concentration camp, the largest of the five principal Nazi death camps. In the course of the war, close to one million Jews are murdered at Auschwitz, along with thousands of Poles, Gypsies, and others before it is liberated in 1945. Most Jews are killed in gas chambers and their bodies are burned in massive crematoria.

The Germans invade the Soviet Union and the Einsatzgruppen, mobile killing squads of the regular German army, German police units and Waffen SS, begin carrying out systematic mass murders of Jews in Ukraine, Bessarabia, White Russia, and the Baltic States. Hundreds of thousands of Jews are massacred in such places as Babi Yar, Bogdanovka, Brest-Litovsk, Kamenets-Podolsk, Kovno, Lvov, Minsk, Odessa, Pinsk, Ponary, Riga, and Vitebsk.

1500 Jews are murdered by Romanian fascists in Iassi. Before the war ends, the Romanian fascists and their German allies kill 270,000 Romanian Jews.

Ghettos are established, sealed and then liquidated with thousands of Jews shot in such places as Lublin, Minsk, Vilna, Bialystock, Kishinev, Zhitomir, Vitebsk.

Additional death camps begin operation: Majdanek and Chelmno.

1942 The Nazi leadership holds the Wannsee Conference, during which they detail their plan to kill 11 million Jews in Europe.

Concentration and expulsion of Dutch Jewry begins.

First transport of French Jews to Auschwitz

The first mass killing takes place in the Sobibor extermination camp, the construction of the Belzec and Treblinka death camps is completed, and the first Jews are deported to the Theresienstadt concentration camp.

Deportations from Lvov to Belzec begin; 50,000 gassed, and more than 600,000 are eventually murdered there.

The BBC reports that 700,000 Jews have been murdered in Poland, and Himmler informs the Nazi leadership that all of the Jews in the Genereralgouvernement (Poland) have been "eliminated."

The Jewish Fighting Organization (ZOB) is founded in Warsaw and Jewish partisans engage the Germans in Belarus and in the environs of Krakow.

News of the Nazi plan to murder the Jews of Europe reaches Gerhart Riegner, who informs the U.S. State Department, which later confirms the report. Rabbi Stephen Wise holds a press conference and subsequently Jewish leaders finally obtain a meeting with President Roosevelt; they present him a summary of what is known of the Holocaust to date. Bills introduced in Congress to allow refugees temporary asylum in the United States make no headway. Apart from issuing condemnatory statements, the United States takes no concrete measures in response.

Representatives of the world Zionist movement from the United States, Canada, Europe, and Palestine gather to issue the "Biltmore Platform" advocating the formation of a Jewish Commonwealth in Palestine to replace the British Mandate. The event is significant in placing virtually the entire organizational structure of American Jewry behind the Zionist enterprise.

1943   Warsaw ghetto uprising takes place; there are also uprisings in Treblinka and Sobibor, and the Jewish partisans of Vilna are formed.

Jan Karski, a courier of the Polish resistance who was smuggled into the Warsaw Ghetto, meets with FDR, providing an eyewitness account of the Holocaust

In "Operation Harvest Festival" tens of thousands of Jews are machine-gunned at the Majdanek death camp.

First transports of Jews from Salonika arrive at Auschwitz, and the Jews of Thrace are transported to Treblinka.

The mass deportation from the Warsaw ghetto to Treblinka begins.

1944   Secretary of the Treasury Henry Morgenthau Jr. receives "Report to the Secretary on the Acquiescence of This Government in the Murder of the Jews," detailing history of U.S. indifference to the mass murder of Jews.

Largely in response to the potential embarrassment of Morgenthau's staff's report, the War Refugee Board is established, the first official U.S. effort to aid the victims of the Holocaust.

Beginning of the mass deportation of Hungarian Jews to Auschwitz-Birkenau death camps.

Two prisoners escape from Auschwitz and provide the Jewish underground in Slovakia with a full description of the death camp. Appeals from the Jewish underground and Zionist leaders to bomb the railway links to Auschwitz are rejected by the U.S. War Department and the British Foreign Office, although heavy bombing missions involving over 170 bombers are carried out within less than five miles of the gas chambers

Lodz ghetto is liquidated and 74,000 Jews are deported to Auschwitz

The Jewish uprising takes place at Auschwitz

1945 Death marches of concentration camp inmates into the interior of Germany begin, taking 250,000 Jewish lives.

Soviet forces liberate Warsaw, Lodz, and Auschwitz; Americans liberate Buchenwald; and British forces liberate Bergen-Belsen.

Soviet forces liberate Budapest, saving its remaining 120,000 Jews.

Germany surrenders unconditionally to the Allies and the Nuremberg War Crimes Trial commences. The war ends with the virtual destruction of the Jewish communities of Europe, comprising one third of world Jewry. Participating in the destruction of Europe's Jews are the Germans and their collaborators. Among the collaborators in the Final Solution are the governments of puppet regimes, the leaders of fascist states and Germany's cobelligerents, as well as hundreds of thousands of organized and unorganized anti-Semites in German-occupied countries and in countries allied with Germany. The destruction of European Jewry takes place largely amid an atmosphere of indifference on the part of the Western democracies, the relative silence of the Christian churches, and with the passive, if not active, complicity of large proportions of the population throughout occupied Europe.

1945-1947 Survivors assemble in refugee and displaced persons camps. Their Christian countrymen, especially in parts of Eastern Europe, kill many Jewish survivors who attempt to return to their homes to look for surviving family members. Anti-Jewish riots break out in Krakow and other areas of Poland, and hundreds are killed. Many Jews are killed in the notorious Kielce pogrom, started by a rumor, harking back to medieval times, that Jews have ritually murdered a Christian child. Pressure mounts to bring the Jewish refugees to Palestine.

Anti-Zionist riots break out in Egypt and Libya, Jewish riots in Tel Aviv break out in response to British unwillingness to increase immigration.

1946 Violence between the British and the Jewish underground in Palestine increases. British commissions seek a solution but fail.

Great Britain separates Transjordan from the Mandate and grants it independence.

UN Special Commission for Palestine is established.

1947   In November, after much discussion and back-room politicking, the United Nations General Assembly votes in favor of partition of Palestine into independent Jewish and Arab states with Jerusalem internationalized. The Zionists express their reluctant support for the plan but the Arabs reject it out of hand. Jews and Arabs in Palestine begin jockeying for advantage in what will clearly be a military conflict.

1948   War breaks out, troops from Lebanon, Transjordan (to be renamed Jordan the following year), Iraq, Syria, and Egypt enter Palestine to engage the Jewish forces. Fighting occurs on all fronts and throughout Palestine.

1949   Armistice agreements are concluded with Egypt, Lebanon, Jordan, and Syria, thereby ending the military phase of the war. Known as the "War of Independence" to Jews, it is called the *Nakba* or "disaster" by the Palestinians. The war produces a large Palestinian refugee population. The areas designated to be the independent Arab state by the UN are either taken by the Israelis in battle or annexed by neighboring Arab countries. Arab Palestine does not exist, and Palestinian refugees live mainly in squalid camps within areas annexed by neighboring Arab states, i.e. Egypt (Gaza) or Jordan (West Bank). The Arab states place an economic boycott on Israel, and Arab reactions throughout the Middle East to the success of the Jewish state endanger the lives and property of local Jews. The new state of Israel begins to transport them en-masse to Israel along with the hundreds of thousands of Holocaust survivors waiting in transit camps in Europe.

1949-1950s Situation of Jewish communities in Iraq, Syria, Lebanon, and Egypt drastically deteriorates. Jews are tried for espionage and are otherwise harassed by governments and are attacked by rioting mobs. Most Jews, numbering in the hundreds of thousands, emigrate, and many of them go to Israel. Cross-border attacks by government-supported fedayeen (guerrillas) from Arab countries cause loss of life and property in Israel. Israel engages in reprisal attacks in neighboring Arab countries. A "warm" state of war continues throughout the period. The Arab residents of Israel are considered a security threat and their civil rights are curtailed.

1950 Egypt closes the Suez Canal to Israeli shipping. It will prevent other countries' ships from passing through the waters at its borders to trade with Israel.

1952 Most Jews of Algeria are completely emancipated.

1955 The Conference of Presidents of Major American Jewish Organizations is founded. Formed to promote unified action to strengthen peace in the Middle East, the Conference emerges as a powerful voice for the leadership of the organized American Jewish community regarding issues of concern both internationally and nationally. Its creation suggests the degree to which American Jewry has become largely unified and is able to coalesce around issues and advocacy.

1956 Egypt nationalizes the Suez Canal in retaliation for the United States pulling out of the Aswan Dam project. Britain and France consider this a threat to world peace and begin planning military action. Israel joins in the plans, and in October Israel invades the Sinai Peninsula with British and French air support. Egypt withdraws from Sinai. The Soviet Union threatens use of atomic weapons against Britain and France. The United States pressures the parties to withdraw, and the UN adopts a resolution for withdrawal.

1957 Israel withdraws from Sinai with assurances that its shipping and trade would no longer be impeded by Egypt. Egyptian repercussions against local Jews occur in response to the war with Israel, and 20,000 Jews flee.

1957-1967 Continuing border incursions from Jordan, Syria and Lebanon cause more deaths and disruption in Israel. Israel's Arab citizens remain subject to security regulations that limit their civil rights.

1960 Adolf Eichmann, chief of the Gestapo's Jewish section, responsible for overseeing the deportation and murder of millions of Jews during the Holocaust, is captured by Israeli agents in Argentina, brought to Israel, and is tried and hanged. The landmark trial, televised around the world, is a key factor in stimulating the beginning of serious engagement with historical, philosophical, moral, and legal engagement issues associated with the Holocaust. Largely ignored for a complex series of reasons ranging from survivor guilt to fears of national political embarrassment to attempts to avoid payment in the billions for financial compensation to victims and State of Israel's urgent needs, the trial thrusts the Holocaust onto center stage. There is an explosion of Holocaust related studies, literature, art (including within popular culture) and commemoration that continues to the present. The Holocaust also becomes a central aspect of Jewish identity and the focus of Jewish thought, including religious and philosophical thought.

1966 The Arab citizens of Israel are released from the previous security arrangements and granted broadly increased civil rights.

1967   Egypt's President Gamal Abdel Nasser (1918–70) demands and obtains the removal of United Nations emergency force (UNEF) from Egyptian territory in May and Egyptian troops take up positions in the Sinai. He then orders a blockade of the Strait of Tiran, closing the Israeli port of Eilat on the Gulf of Aqaba. Egyptian and Syrian forces mobilize along their borders, as does Israel's. The USSR warns Egypt of an impending Israeli attack on Syria. Egypt intelligence reports no Israeli troop concentrations but notes Syria's low state of military readiness. Israel begins a general mobilization. Nasser reinforces troops in Sinai. Israel orders a full mobilization. President Nasser, in an address to the Egyptian National Assembly, threatens "to totally exterminate the State of Israel." Jordan mobilizes and invites Iraqi troops to take positions along the Israeli border. Saudi Arabia, Algeria, and Kuwait announce they are putting troops at Egypt's disposal. The USSR informs the United States that they have information Israel is planning an attack and, if so, they will assist the attacked state. Iraq's president Abd al-Rahman Aref addresses his air force saying, "We shall, God willing, meet in Tel Aviv and Haifa." Israel begins a preemptive air attack on June 5, destroying the air forces of Egypt, Jordan, and Syria. Egyptian, Jordanian, Syrian and Iraqi ground forces join against Israel, which succeeds in capturing the West Bank, Gaza Strip, Golan Heights, and Sinai, with the war ending on June 10.

1967-1970 Sometimes referred to as the "War of Attrition," continuing artillery exchanges, skirmishes and incursions occur on both sides of the new borders, especially between Israel and Egypt, resulting in many casualties. Terrorist bombings within the borders of Israel in civilian areas result in Israeli reprisals, some against government or military targets and some against civilian targets in Arab countries. The first bombing of a jetliner occurs in Athens, where an Israeli commercial plane is held by terrorists.

1969 Yasir Arafat, leader of al-Fatah, becomes head of the PLO.

1970 Four airliners are attacked by the Popular Front for the Liberation of Palestine. King Hussein moves against Palestinians threatening his regime, Syria moves tanks into Jordan on behalf of the Palestinians but does not engage the

Jordanians. Israel warms Syria that it will intervene against them if they move against the Jordanians. The Palestinians suffer large numbers of casualties in battles against the forces of King Hussein that Palestinians later memorialize as "Black September." Israel begins building a few settlements in the capture West Bank.

1970-1980 Unprecedented number of Soviet Jews is released and allowed to emigrate to Israel, increasing the Israeli population by hundreds of thousands.

1972 Terrorists of the "Black September" organization kill two and hold nine Israeli Olympic athletes hostage at the Olympic Village in Munich. In a shoot-out with West German police attempting to free them, all the hostages and terrorists are killed. International terrorism against Israelis and Jews increases. Israel reacts with retaliatory assassinations of Palestinian terrorists and leaders.

1973 In October, on the Jewish High Holy Day of Yom Kippur, Egypt and Syria launch massive coordinated attacks that take Israel completely by surprise. Syria and Egypt initially succeed in significantly penetrating Israeli territory, but lose ground when the Israeli forces are fully mobilized. The USSR supports and resupplies Egypt and Syria, while the United States resupplies Israel. The Arab oil-exporting countries begin an oil embargo of the West. The war remains contested, with both Egypt and Israel claiming ultimate victory.

The war is called the "Yom Kippur War" by Israel and the "October War" by the Arab countries.

1974 The ultranationalist Jewish settler organization Gush Emunim is founded and becomes extremely successful in building settlements on the West Bank and Gaza territories, and in lobbying the government and the Israeli populace to retain permanent Jewish control over all territories captured in Israel's wars. Palestinian terrorist attacks increase from the Lebanese border as the Palestinian community there organize what they call their own Palestinian "ministate." This invites numerous Israeli reprisals and incursions into Lebanon and largely destabilizes the delicate and problematic political balance there.

1975 Disengagement agreements are signed by Israel, Egypt, and Syria. The first Israel-bound freighter to pass through the Suez Canal in 15 years is allowed through. UN resolution 3379 "determines that Zionism is a form of racism and racial discrimination." This resolution will be revoked by a vote of the UN in 1991. Civil war breaks out in Lebanon.

1977 Egyptian President Anwar Sadat startles the world and comes to Jerusalem and addresses the Israeli Knesset, offering a new future based on peaceful relations. Intensive negotiations follow between Sadat and Israeli Prime Minister Menahem Begin under the auspices of U.S. president Jimmy Carter that will return the Sinai Peninsula to Egypt. The

The United States supports the agreement with massive economic support for both countries.

1978 After repeated terrorist incursions from Lebanon, Israel invades Lebanon and exercises control over a large area in the south of the country. When it withdraws, it will leave part of the area under the military control of a Lebanese Christian militia aligned with Israel in order to try to prevent further border incursions.

1980 Egypt and Israel exchange ambassadors. Palestinian terrorists kill and injure Jews in a number of attacks. For the first time since the establishment of Israel, a Jewish civilian underground begins to engage in acts of terrorism against Palestinians, killing and maiming a number of innocent people. Israel tries to support the Christian Lebanese militias in their warring against Muslim, Druze, and Palestinian militias. Palestinian fighters continue to cross the border into Israel from Lebanon.

1982 After increased Palestinian terrorist incursions, Israel invades Lebanon. Initially instructed to push the Palestinians back 40 kilometers from the Israeli border, the army eventually surrounds Beirut, with great loss of civilian life and high and unexpected Israeli casualties. Hoping to control internal Lebanese politics, Israel becomes bogged down and finds it impossible to pull itself entirely out of Lebanon until 2000. During the height of the invasion, in an area of Beirut under Israeli control, Christian Phalangist allies of Israel massacre some 800 Palestinians at the Sabra and Shatila refugee camps. Israel's defense minister, Ariel Sharon, is forced to resign after being found indirectly responsible by an official Israeli commission of inquiry. Many Israelis are horrified at the Israeli invasion and its consequences, the first large-scale operation committed not entirely for purposes of defense. A hundred thousand Israelis protest in a rally in Tel Aviv shortly after the invasion.

1980s Palestinian terrorist attacks continue, with bus hijackings and car bombs and other acts occurring within Israel proper. Israel engages in counterattacks, including assassinations through its secret service, some of which result in mistaken deaths. Large numbers of Israeli settlements are built on the West Bank, with the Jewish population growing to more than 100,000 residents.

1987 The intifada or "great tremor" begins, a grassroots mass protest by Palestinians throughout the West Bank and Gaza that, over a number of years, clearly demonstrates Palestinian unwillingness to live under Israeli occupation. New Jewish settlements continue to be built in the West Bank.

1989 A vote of Jordanian parliament formalizes Jordan's decision to separate from the West Bank, relieving great pressure on the Palestinians to push for independence.

1990 Iraq invades and seizes Kuwait. This will eventuate in a coordinate attack on Iraq by U.S.-led forces. Israel remains outside of the action but suffers from a small series of missile attacks from Iraq that, it was feared, contained chemical weapons. Twenty-one Palestinians are killed and over 100 wounded as Israeli police open fire on rioting Palestinians after they hurled stones from the Temple Mount in Jerusalem onto thousands of Jews gathered below at the Western Wall to celebrate the festival of Sukkot.

1990s The continuing intifada places great social, military, and economic pressure on Israel. It is countered with intense lobbying and settling under the auspices of the ultranationalist Gush Emunim and its sister organizations. With the fall of the USSR, hundreds of thousands of former Soviet Jews and their families immigrate to Israel. Many of the immigrants from the FSU claiming to be Jewish are not.

1993 Yitzhaq Rabin and Yasir Arafat meet in Washington and sign a series of agreements that begin the process of transferring limited government and services to the Palestinian Authority. The accords are vague and open to varied interpretations, thereby allowing for a formal agreement but destined to be interpreted so differently by the two parties that they can never be fully implemented.

1994 Barukh Goldstein, an ultranationalist religious Jew, guns down 30 Muslims at prayer in the mosque at the Machpelah cave on the holiday of Purim.

The building housing the Argentine Israelite Mutual Aid Association (AMIA) and also the Jewish School System headquarters, a Yiddish theater, a library, and the DAIA (umbrella organization of Jewish institutions in Argentina) and other Jewish agencies is destroyed in a terrorist bombing that results in 86 deaths and hundreds injured. Among the suspects in an ongoing and much-criticized investigation led by Judge Juan José Galeano (attacked principally for ignoring the possibility of local co-conspirators) are Iranian agents as well as operative of the terrorist group Islamic Jihad.

1995 Culminating a "back channel" diplomatic process, representatives of Israel and the Palestinians sign the "Declaration of Principles" (DOP), also known as the Oslo Agreement, beginning the so-called Oslo Peace Process. The DOP commits the Israelis and Palestinians to "put an end to decades of confrontation and conflict, recognize their mutual legitimate and political rights . . . and achieve a just, lasting and comprehensive peace settlement and historic reconciliation." The Oslo Agreement leads to the famous handshake between Yitzhaq Rabin and Yasir Arafat on the White House lawn on September 13. The DOP raises hopes of an inevitable, even imminent breakthrough in Israeli-Palestinian relations (later to be dashed), and intensifies Clinton administration diplomatic activism in the "Peace Process."

Yitzhaq Rabin is assassinated by a radical Jewish Israeli religious nationalist who opposes the return of territories to the Palestinians.

1995-2000 The new Palestinian Authority is run by Palestinian officials who are blatantly taking communal funds for their personal use, increasing the anger of the local population. The Peace Process is slowed by the assassination of Rabin and eventually stopped. Jewish settlements expand and new ones are built, doubling the Jewish population of the West Bank to some 200,000. The worsening economic and political situation causes Palestinians deep frustration, as does the entrance of Palestinian leadership from outside the Palestinian territories to positions of power and authority over local Palestinians.

2000 In a landmark legal case dealing with the denial of the Holocaust, a mainstay of anti-Semites, American scholar Deborah Lipstadt prevails in a London court in a libel suit brought against her and her publisher, Penguin Books Ltd, by David Irving, a well-known British writer on the Second World War whom she describes as a Holocaust denier in her work *Denying the Holocaust*. Hitherto regarded by many as a respectable scholar, Irving is found to have deliberately falsified and misrepresented historical evidence in claiming, among other things, that there were no gas chambers in Auschwitz. Irving is also described as an anti-Semite and a racist who is closely associated with extreme right-wing groups. By prevailing against the icon of "revisionist" historians, the trial's verdict shatters any appearance of academic respectability for Holocaust denial.

The lack of progress in the Peace Process and transfer of authority builds to a point of explosion that occurs in October with a new intifada. It is called the *Intifadat al-Aqsa*, "The El-Aqsa Intifada," because it began at the al-Aqsa mosque in

Jerusalem following a visit there by Likud Party leader Ariel Sharon. This intifada includes far more shooting of weapons on the part of Palestinians, including members of the official Palestinian security services. This is countered by a large increase in violence by Israeli forces, resulting in the shooting deaths of hundreds of Palestinian and the wounding of thousands, and the killing of dozens of Israelis.

Senator Joseph Lieberman of Connecticut, an Orthodox Jew, runs on the Democratic Party ticket as its vice presidential candidate. It is the first time a Jew runs on the national ticket of one of America's two leading political parties. Lieberman's selection by the Democratic Party, as well as the essentially universal praise for its choice, symbolizes the high water mark of acceptance of Jews in the United States.

2001 The election of Ariel Sharon as prime minister of Israel signals the collapse of the Oslo Peace Process.

Glossary

Words set in SMALL CAPS are defined elsewhere in the Glossary.

adonai A word that replaces the unutterable name of God; usually translated as "Lord."

aggadah Nonlegal material (homilies, legends, parables, ethics, etc.) found in Jewish traditional texts.

aliyah Literally, "going up": (1) being called up in SYNAGOGUE to read from the TORAH scroll; (2) the act of traveling to the Land of Israel or moving there.

amidah Literally, "standing [prayer]." The central prayer of every daily, SABBATH, and festival prayer service. Also known as the *Shemoneh Esreh*, or "Eighteen Benedictions."

Aramaic A Semitic language, closely related to HEBREW and Arabic, that was the spoken vernacular of Jews in Palestine, BABYLON, and other parts of the Near East for the first several centuries of the common era. The Gemara portion of the TALMUD is written in Aramaic, as are a few small parts of the HEBREW BIBLE and some liturgical works.

Ashkenazim Jews who trace their immediate ancestry to Europe. *See also* Sepharadim.

Babylon The ancient name for Mesopotamia (modern-day Iraq). A great Jewish community grew up in this region starting with the Babylonian Exile in the sixth century B.C.E. For many centuries after the end of the Babylonian Empire, the Jews of the region continued to refer to themselves as Babylonians.

bar/bat mitzvah The age of majority in Judaism (twelve for girls, thirteen for boys), after which one is responsible for observing Jewish law and tradition.

B.C.E. "Before the common era"; designates dates preceding the Christian era. *See also* C.E.

berit Literally, "covenant." Also, the ceremony in which boys are circumcised at the age of eight days.

berit milah The ceremonial circumcision marking the covenant of circumcision.

Bible *See* Hebrew Bible.

C.E. "Common era"; designates dates on the Christian calendar. *See also* B.C.E.

chazan Cantor; musically trained singer and leader of worship services in SYNAGOGUE.

Days of Awe The ten-day period from ROSH HASHANAH to YOM KIPPUR; a time of solemn reflection and self-examination.

Diaspora Literally, "Dispersion." The many communities of Jews living outside the Land of Israel. *See also* Galut.

exilarch The head of the Jewish community of BABYLON during its golden age in the medieval period.

galut Literally, "Exile." A negative designation for Jewish life outside the Land of Israel. *See also* Diaspora.

gaon (plural: geonim) Literally, "Excellency." The title of the heads of the two great Jewish academies in BABYLON.

Gemara *See* Talmud.

ghetto Restricted area in European cities in which Jews were compelled to reside in certain periods after the fifteenth century.

Haggadah Liturgical text used at the SEDER.

halakhah Literally, "the way in which one goes." Jewish law and the legal decisions of the developers of Jewish law.

hallah Special braided bread eaten on the SABBATH and festivals.

hallel Psalms 113–118, recited in the SYNAGOGUE as part of the worship service on certain holidays, and in the home at the PESACH SEDER, as an expression of thanksgiving.

Hanukkah Literally, "dedication." Eight-day midwinter holiday commemorating the liberation of Judea from Syrian-Greek tyranny and the rededication of the Jerusalem TEMPLE to the worship of God. Its central home observance is the kindling of candles in a MENORAH.

Hasidism A mystical movement of traditional Judaism that evolved in Poland in the eighteenth century.

Hebrew The language of the HEBREW BIBLE and of ancient Israel, used throughout the ages by Jews for liturgical and other purposes, and revived in modern times as the language of the State of Israel. As a member of the Semitic group of languages, it is closely related to Arabic. *See also* Aramaic.

Hebrew Bible The Holy Scriptures of Judaism, comprising the biblical texts known as the OLD TESTAMENT but not including the NEW TESTAMENT. Often referred to as the TANAKH in Jewish usage.

huppah Canopy under which the bride and groom stand during the marriage ceremony, symbolically beginning their life under a common roof.

Kabbalah A form of Jewish mysticism that developed in the latter part of the Middle Ages in Spain, partially under the influence of Sufism.

matzah Unleavened bread eaten during PESACH in place of leavened bread.

menorah Seven-branched candelabrum used in the ancient TEMPLE; now a symbol of Judaism and of the modern State of Israel. An eight-branched menorah is kindled in the home on each day of HANUKKAH.

mezuzah A small parchment scroll containing selections from the TORAH, including the SHEMA. It is placed in a decorative container and attached to the doorposts of Jewish homes.

Midrash A collection of early traditions that provide commentary on the HEBREW BIBLE. Most of the classical midrashim were collected into books from about the fourth to the twelfth century.

mikveh Ritual bath in which one may completely immerse oneself for ritual ablution; also used for immersion of converts to Judaism.

minhag Custom or practice.

minyan Quorum of ten, the minimum required for reciting the full prayer service during public worship.

Mishnah *See* Talmud.

mitzvah (plural: mitzvot) "Commandment," usually referring to a divine command related to ritual or ethical conduct.

New Testament A collection of scriptural writings {the Gospels, Pauline Letters, Acts, etc.) accepted as sacred by Christians but not by Jews.

Old Testament The Christian term for the HEBREW BIBLE.

Oral Torah (or Oral Law) The classical Jewish traditional texts of the TALMUD and MIDRASH. According to tradition, they were revealed along with the TORAH at Mount Sinai but were not set down in writing.

Pentateuch The first division of the HEBREW BIBLE, often referred to in Hebrew as the TORAH or the Ḥumash. Also known as the Five Books of Moses.

Pesach Eight-day spring festival, also known as Passover, commemorating the Exodus from Egypt.

Pharisees An expression of ancient Judaism during the last century or two before the destruction of the Second TEMPLE in 70 C.E. Its adherents believed in the immortality of the soul, freedom of the will, divine providence, the existence of angels, and the resurrection of the dead.

pilgrimage festivals Three annual festivals of biblical origin (PESACH, SHAVUOT, and SUKKOT) on which the ancient Israelites went up to Jerusalem to worship in the TEMPLE.

priest (Hebrew: *kohen;* plural: *kohanim*) A member of the hereditary caste or guild that ministered in the Jerusalem TEMPLE. There has been no functioning priesthood since the destruction of the Temple, but the special status of Jews descended from the kohanim is still recognized in the worship service.

Purim A carnival-like spring festival occurring exactly one month before PESACH. It commemorates the liberation of the Jews from extermination at the hand of Haman, the grand vizier of the Persian king, as related in the biblical Book of Esther.

rabbi Scholar-teacher. In traditional Judaism, a rabbi is empowered to hand down authoritative decisions on religious law. In modern Judaism, whether traditional or liberal, the rabbi is the spiritual leader of a congregation, although many people who have received rabbinic training work in other professions.

Rosh Hashanah New Year's Day. Fall festival that begins a ten-day period of intense personal introspection and penitence known as the DAYS OF AWE.

Sabbath. The weekly day of rest, occurring each Saturday. There are special services in the SYNAGOGUE as well as a number of home rituals.

seder "Order." The family home service on the first two evenings of the festival of PESACH.

Sephardim Jews who trace their ancestry to Spain or to North Africa and the Middle East. *See also* Ashkenazim.

Shavuot The Feast of Weeks, also known as Pentecost. An early summer harvest festival that commemorates the giving of the TORAH to the Israelites at Mount Sinai.

shema˘ yisrael The first two words of the biblical statement of Jewish faith (Deuteronomy 6:4–9, 11:13–21 and Numbers 15:37–41). The core statement is "Hear [or "listen"], O Israel, Adonai our God is One [or, is a Unity]"

shofar Ram's horn blown on ROSH HASHANAH.

siddur The Jewish prayer book.

Simhat Torah Literally "Rejoicing in Torah." The final day of the fall festival cycle when the annual cycle of TORAH reading is completed and the new one begun; celebrated with joyful processions and dancing with the Torah scrolls.

sukkah A small temporary hut or booth covered with branches and leaves in which families eat their meals during the festival of SUKKOT.

Sukkot Seven-day festival that offers thanks for the fall harvest and commemorates the wanderings of Israel in the desert after the Exodus from Egypt. Also known as Tabernacles.

synagogue House of worship and assembly for Jews since the destruction of the TEMPLE in 70 C.E.

tallit A four-cornered garment with tassels or fringes (*tzitzit*) tied onto its corners, worn to serve as a reminder of the presence of God. The small tallit is sometimes worn by men at all times under their clothes. The large tallit is traditionally worn by men during morning worship and by the prayer leader at all services; sometimes called a "prayer shawl."

Talmud A huge repository of Jewish tradition collected over nearly a thousand years and redacted around the sixth century C.E. It is made up of two distinct parts, the Mishnah (written in HEBREW) and the Gemara (written in ARAMAIC). The Babylonian Talmud, completed about 500 C.E., is, along with the HEBREW BIBLE, the basic source from which Jewish law and codes are derived.

Tanakh The HEBREW BIBLE. The term is an acronym made up of the first letters of the names of the Bible's three divisions: *T* = TORAH, *N* = *Nevi'im* (Prophets), and K = *Ketuvim* (Writings).

tefillin   Small black leather boxes containing parchment scrolls with four scriptural passages (Exodus 13:1, 11; Deuteronomy 6:4–9, 11:13–21). Secured onto the forehead and arm by means of leather bands, they are traditionally worn by men during the morning prayers.

Temple   (1) The complex of buildings and courtyards in Jerusalem where the ancient sacrifices and other official religious rituals on behalf of the nation of Israel were conducted. The First Temple functioned from about 954 to 586 B.C.E., and the Second Temple from about 520 B.C.E. to 70 C.E.   (2) In modern times, an alternative name for the SYNAGOGUE; in this usage the word *temple* begins with a lower-case *t*.

teshuvah   Literally "return" to God. Repentance.

teshuvot   The responsa literature: answers by learned sages to questions on Jewish law.

Torah   (1)   The first of the three divisions of the HEBREW BIBLE, consisting of Genesis, Exodus, Leviticus, Numbers, and Deuteronomy, collectively known as the Five Books of Moses and also, in Hebrew, as the Ḥumash.   (2) The totality of Jewish religious literature and teachings. Weekly readings from the Torah are chanted aloud from a parchment scroll at worship services on the SABBATH and festivals.

tzaddik   A righteous person.

Written Torah (or Written Law) The Scripture of the Jews.

Yom Kippur The Day of Atonement, occurring ten days after ROSH HASHANAH.

Zion A hill in Jerusalem; the name has come to refer to Jerusalem as a whole or even to the entire Land of Israel.

Zionism The modern political and religious movement to establish a Jewish state and center of Jewish life in the ancient Land of Israel.

Recommended Reading

Abramson, Glenda, ed. *The Blackwell Companion to Jewish Culture: From the Eighteenth Century to the Present*. Oxford: Basil Blackwell, 1989.

Antler, Joyce. *The Journey Home*. New York: Schocken Books, 1998.

Ben-Sasson, H. H. ed. *A History of the Jewish People*. Cambridge: Harvard University Press, 1976.

Cohen, Mark. *Under Crescent and Cross*. Princeton: Princeton University Press, 1994.

Cohen, Norman. *The Way into Torah*. New York: Jewish Lights, 2000.

Dawidowicz, Lucy S. *The War Against the Jews 1933-1945*. New York: Holt, Rinehart & Winston, 1975.

Gilbert, Martin. *The Holocaust*. New York: Holt, Rinehart & Winston, 1985.

Glick, Leonard B. *Abraham's Heirs*. Syracuse: Syracuse University Press, 1999.

Goitein, S. D. *Jews and Arabs*. New York: Schocken Books, 1974.

Goodman, Lenn E. *Judaism, Human Rights and Human Values*. New York: Oxford University Press, 1998.

Greenberg, Irving. *The Jewish Way*. New York: Touchstone Books, 1993.

Heschel, A. J. *The Sabbath*. New York: Noonday Press, 1996.

Holtz, Barry. *Back to the Sources*. New York: Summit Books, 1998.

Gerber, Jane. *The Jews of Spain*. New York: Macmillan, 1992.

Jewish Timeline Encyclopedia, rev. ed. Northvale, N.J.: Aronson, 1997.

Kertzer, Morris, rev. by Rabbi Lawrence Hoffman. *What Is a Jew?* New York: Collier Books, 1997.

Kushner, Lawrence. *Honey from the Rock*, 3rd ed. New York: Jewish Lights, 2000.

Lewis, Bernard. *The Jews of Islam*. Princeton: Princeton University Press, 1984.

Marrus, Michael P. *The Holocaust in History*. Boston: University Press of New England, 1984.

Newby, Gordon. *A History of the Jews of Arabia*. Columbia: University of South Carolina Press, 1989.

Sachar, Howard M. *A History of Israel from the Rise of Zionism to Our Time*, 2nd ed. New York: Knopf, 1996.

Scheindlin, Raymond. *A Short History of the Jewish People*. New York: Macmillan, 1998.

Steinberg, Milton. *As a Driven Leaf*. New York: Behrman House, 1996.

Stillman, Norman. *The Jews of Arab Lands, 1. Modern Times*. Philadelphia: Jewish Publication Society, 1991.

Strassfeld, Michael. *Jewish Holidays*. New York: HarperCollins, 1985.

Telushkin, Joseph. *Jewish Literacy*. New York: William Morrow, 1991.

Telushkin, Joseph. *The Book of Jewish Values*. New York: Bell Tower, 2000.

The Way into Jewish Prayer. New York: Jewish Lights, 2000.

Trepp, Leo. *History of the Jewish Experience*. New York: Behrman House, 1996.

Trepp, Leo. *The Complete Book of Jewish Observance*, 4th ed. New York: Behrman House, 1980.

Visotzky, Burton, and David Fishman, eds. *From Mesopotamia to Modernity* (Boulder: Westview Press, 1999).

Wiesel, Elie. *Night*. New York: Bantam Books, 1982.

Index